D1282250

C++ SCIENTIFIC
PROGRAMMING

C++ SCIENTIFIC PROGRAMMING

Computational Recipes at a Higher Level

John R. Berryhill

A WILEY-INTERSCIENCE PUBLICATION

JOHN WILEY & SONS, INC.

New York · Chichester · Weinheim · Brisbane · Singapore · Toronto

Copyright © 2001 by John Wiley & Sons, Inc. All rights reserved.

Published simultaneously in Canada.

For ordering and customer service, call 1-800-CALL-WILEY.

Library of Congress Cataloging-in-Publication Data:

Berryhill, John R.
    C++ scientific programming: Computational recipes at a higher level / John R. Berryhill.
      p. cm.
    ISBN 0-471-41210-4 (cloth: alk. paper)
    1. C++ (Computer program language)   2. FORTRAN (Computer program language)
   I. Title.
    QA76.73.C153 B49   2001
    005.13′3—dc21   2001024229

Printed in the United States of America.

10 9 8 7 6 5 4 3 2 1

To Millie and Ralph

CONTENTS

PREFACE

The reader will benefit most who follows along with a C++ compiler, executing the examples and, preferably, stepping through the executions with a debugger. The source code is available without further cost from the publisher's `ftp` site. It is not necessary to type in the code manually.

I have attempted to maintain a consistent use of typefaces in this book to distinguish things that are different:

Source code: `x y z alfa beta gama operator+`

Scalars and subscripts: $x\ y\ z\ \alpha\ \beta\ \gamma\ i\ j\ k$

Vectors: $\mathbf{x}\ \mathbf{y}\ \mathbf{z}\ \mathbf{a}^{\mathrm{T}}\ \mathbf{b}^{\mathrm{H}}$

Matrices: $\mathbf{A}\ \mathbf{A}^{\mathrm{T}}\ \mathbf{C}\ \mathbf{C}^{\mathrm{H}}$

The occasional Greek capital letter scalar (Φ) is not italicized. The problem addressed most often is $\mathbf{A}\mathbf{x} = \mathbf{b}$.

My language reference of choice is Kernighan and Ritchie's *The C Programming Language,* ANSI edition [18]. I recommend no particular C++ reference. I own Buzzi-Ferraris' book [7], but I disagree with its conclusions. The single most illuminating reference that I have read is a brief article by Bruce Eckel [10].

In the first three chapters, I disclose what I think is needed to take scientific programming to a higher level. In the next eleven chapters, I demonstrate that it actually works. Two sources were particularly helpful in this respect. Both contain up-to-date algorithms expressed in the form of pseudocode that made translating them to C++ straightforward. Golub and Van Loan's classic *Matrix Computations* [14] is my primary source for Chapters 4 and 6. Vanderbei's recent *Linear Programming* [28] is my principal source for Chapters 10 and 11. Readers who feel I have slighted the theory will find satisfaction in consulting these original sources.

The reader I have in mind is primarily an individual problem solver. My message is not directed toward corporate computing on an industrial scale. The advantages of my approach to coding may not be apparent to those who specialize in particular computational methods, but the point is to expand the range of methods accessible to nonspecialists.

I come to praise FORTRAN, not to bury it. I made a nice living writing FORTRAN. I am aware that additional features continue to accrete to it [11]. However, I fear that FORTRAN's success a generation ago means that it now cannot make the break required to go in the direction I think desirable, which I outline in this book.

The source code files can be obtained from `ftp://ftp.wiley.com/public/sci_tech_med/scientific_program/`. The names of the files are:

SPARSE.H	SPARSE.CPP
VECTOR.H	VECTOR.CPP
MATRIX.H	MATRIX.CPP
METHOD.H	METHOD.CPP
CPLXFY.H	CPLXFY.CPP
QUATERN.H	QUATERN.CPP
AUTDERIV.CPP	
EXAMPLES.TXT	
LICENSE.TXT	

The total size is about 144k bytes. Please read the License and Disclaimer in LICENSE.TXT. In the book, a few long lines of code have been wrapped around to fit into the format, and the online code files differ from the printed text in that respect.

The source code was developed using a succession of Borland C++ compilers, most recently Borland C++ 5.0 [6]. I am especially fond of the Turbo Debugger, which still works in the 32-bit environment. I regret the fact (and the reason) that these products are no longer commercially prominent.

Jarrell Burton suggested numerous improvements in the manuscript. Brian Morgan prepared the illustrations.

JOHN R. BERRYHILL

1 Overview

This is the book I wish I had found when I first heard of C++. For decades I had written FORTRAN programs for scientific applications on machines ranging from the IBM 1410 to the Cray Y-MP to the Sun Sparcstation. I had become familiar with C, and was unimpressed. Then C++ came along and seemed to promise very important new capabilities.

The great virtue of FORTRAN when it first appeared was to enable a scientist or engineer to write computer instructions in a syntax that mimicked familiar mathematics. No longer did the program writer need to keep account, personally, of the memory location of each variable, and remember to fetch old values and store new ones. The compiler could and did handle these machine-oriented tasks. However, FORTRAN never extended this service to anything beyond scalar arithmetic. To be sure, the notion of a vector, matrix, or multidimensional array underlay FORTRAN's use of subscripts, but the FORTRAN compiler's assistance in handling these structures stopped at accessing their elements as scalar quantities. The limitations of FORTRAN became especially apparent in the heavily machine-oriented ways that were adopted for representing sparse matrices. Not a vestige of mathematical matrix syntax remained to be seen in sparse-matrix FORTRAN code.

C had its shortcomings, too. There was the annoyance that for no apparent reason, subscripts were enclosed in brackets [ ] and ranged from 0 to $n-1$. There was the fact that C, incredibly, provided no built-in complex arithmetic, seeming to imply that we didn't need it. C did, grudgingly, provide a way for us to roll our own complex numbers. The keywords typedef and struct could be combined to permit a user-specified complex-variable type. In this way, complex variables could be declared, defined, passed to subroutines, and returned as function values. However, ordinary complex arithmetic $(+, -, *, /)$ could not be conventionally notated; instead, explicit subroutine calls were required.

When C++ was introduced, it overcame such limitations by greatly extending C's facilities for handling user-specified data structures and variable types. C++ enabled us to create an algebraic syntax customized for any type of data structure whatsoever. C++ allowed the user to specify the functioning of all the familiar operators in relation to each structure: $+, -, *, /, [ ], ( )$, and more. One could imagine defining vector, matrix, and sparse-matrix *variables,* and combining and manipulating these through a syntax that closely resembled linear algebra.

FORTRAN writers familiar with C are aware that C code typically shows an excessive reliance on what are called *pointers*. The reason for this style in numerical applications is to evade a restriction in C that requires passing all function arguments

1

by value. As a second benefit, C++ mitigated the overdependence on pointers that we see in C scientific programming. C++ provided for passing function arguments by *address*, like FORTRAN.

The potential of C++ to improve on both FORTRAN and C was enticing, but would there be a catch? My goal in the research leading to this book was to discover a set of practices that would allow scientific programmers to embrace the attractive features of C++ without incurring undesired side effects and hidden costs. I find that there is a rather narrow path that must be followed to avoid the potential pitfalls.

This book is not so much an explication of C++ as a demonstration of a particular coding style useful in a wide range of scientific numerical applications. The detailed recommendations that I present will include all the do's and don'ts important for implementing applied math as it is currently practiced. This book presents working examples of everything I have discovered to be useful and omits what I have found to be irrelevant.

My purpose is to advance the historical trend that shifts the burden of human–machine communication toward the machine. Not long ago, minimizing machine cost was the only criterion in scientific program design. In those days, an hour of Cray time, for example, cost more than an entire workstation does now. Worse, a job that required as much as an hour might not even be allowed to run. Now, compared to an engineer's own time, central processing unit (CPU) time is a very cheap commodity. Rather than expecting the scientist to make mathematics convenient for the computer, it's high time for the computer to make coding convenient for the scientist.

Two generations of engineers now have been taught to do theory in matrix notation, and then, for lack of an expressive programming language, to abandon that viewpoint when it comes to getting concrete answers. The reader will find that the concise syntax of linear algebra is as powerful and suggestive in programming as it is in theory. When the computer program is written in terms of matrix variables—especially sparse-matrix variables—a wider range of possibilities becomes accessible.

1.1 CLASSES AND OPERATORS

The foundation of scientific programming in C++ comprises the classes `real_ vector`, `matrix`, `sparse`, and the relationships among them. In the practice of C++ that I recommend, each named variable of the structure type that I call

```
class real_vector;
```
                                                object

contains the address and dimension of a block of `double` floating-point memory locations: a pair of 4-byte items. If we allocate a C-style array such as `double data[10000];`, we can construct a `real_vector` from it by coding

```
real_vector d(data, 10000);.
```

Most often, we allocate `real_vector` objects dynamically: for example,

```
real_vector a(mrows), b(ncols), c(ncols);
```

Access to the individual components of a `real_vector` is gained by defining the parentheses operator `()` to work as in FORTRAN:

```
for( i=1; i<=ncols; i++) b(i) = 0.;
```

and the brackets operator `[]` to work as in C:

```
for( i=0; i<ncols; i++) b[i] = 0.;
```

Both the foregoing loops perform the same function: zeroing all the elements of b. Both forms of subscript are useful, depending on the context in which they appear. These access methods both get data and put data, and they can be cascaded:

```
a(j) = b[k] = 1.;   c[ncols-1] = b(ncols) = 2.;
```

I take a similar approach in representing dense matrices. I define a

```
class matrix;
```

and provide for dynamic allocation as, for example,

```
matrix A(mrows, ncols);
```

We can then access elements contained in a `matrix` just as in a FORTRAN array:

```
A(i, j) = 1.;   x = A(i, j);
```

The meaning of brackets `[]` in the `matrix` class models an idiosyncrasy of C and is described later.

Where C++ goes beyond FORTRAN and C is that after we have allocated vectors and matrices as above, we can use them as variables in statements whose meaning is obvious from our knowledge of mathematics. Consider

```
a = A * (b + c);
```

This statement instructs the computer to add vectors **b** and **c**, multiply the vector sum (from the left) by matrix **A**, and overwrite **a** with the vector result of the multiplication. The reader can verify that the dimensions of a, b, c, and A given above conform to mathematical requirements. Beyond that, a C++ compiler is able to translate this statement because the `matrix` and `real_vector` classes have given definitions of

```
operator+ (real_vector&, real_vector&);
operator* (matrix&, real_vector&);
operator= (real_vector&);
```

This C++ syntax means that when a + appears between two `real_vector` variables, or when a * appears between a `matrix` and a `real_vector` (in that order), or when a `real_vector` appears to the right of an equal sign, then a function or subroutine exists that executes the specified action. The term for this in C++ is "overloading" the operators.

C++ is utterly strict regarding what type of variable it is working with, and it readily distinguishes `operator*` `(matrix&, real_vector&)` from `operator*` `(real_vector&, matrix&)`, as well as `operator*` `(double, real_vector&)`. The ampersand & in this context denotes that the function in question receives an argument passed by address. A function used often in this book is `operator*` `(real_vector&, real_vector&)`, defined to be the scalar (dot) product of two vectors, as in `b * c`.

This is not to imply that we are under any compulsion to overload every operator for every class. We should do so only where mathematical requirements and good programming sense coincide. For example, we would *not* define the sum of two `matrix` objects, because we would not wish to waste space storing the result, and `(A + B) * c` can always be obtained as `(A * c) + (B * c)`.

Perhaps the crowning glory of C++ is how it enables us to model sparse matrices. We can define a class and a straightforward means of dynamic allocation:

```
class sparse;
sparse S(mrows, ncols, maxnz);
```

and we can access the elements it contains as if for a `matrix`, by way of subscripts:

```
S(i, j) = 1.;    x = S(i, j);
```

Sparse matrices are special because, although they are nominally gigantic (30,000 by 30,000, say), all but a relatively few elements (1,000,000, say) are zero. For this hypothetical case, one would code

```
sparse S(30000, 30000, 1000000);
```

The basis of sparse-matrix programming is to avoid storing the zero elements of a matrix, but instead, to keep track of exactly where the *nonzero* elements are located.

The overriding concern in sparse-matrix programming is to avoid introducing additional nonzeros, even if extreme measures are required.

The access method S(i,j) both gets and puts data, so it can be treated like a regular variable: for example, S(i,j) += 1. Using S(i,j) in any expression causes the element to be initialized if it does not already exist. So it is also useful to have a read-only method, namely,

```
x = S.getval(i, j);
```

which simply returns 0.0 if S(i,j) is not an existing known nonzero element. Similarly, I recommend

```
S.stash(i, j) = 1.;
```

to store a nonzero element that we are certain does not already exist, to save the cost of checking.

The syntax object.function(arguments) [as in S.stash(i,j)] in C++ identifies what is called a *member function*. Member functions are perhaps the most reliable and dependable feature of the language. Our first choice of how to accomplish *anything* should be a member function whenever possible.

Operators such as operator= and operator[] above are member functions with a special property. The ".operator" and the parentheses embracing the argument are allowed to disappear, and they are replaced by the operator's symbol. However, a C++ compiler would nevertheless recognize an explicit form such as c.operator= (b) and handle it the same as c = b;.

Among the most important candidates for member-function operators are the combined-assignment operators familiar from C: +=, -=, *=, /=, and so on. These overwrite their results onto the left-hand-side object. The statement b += c; is equivalent to the statement b = b + c; but is more efficient to execute. These operators can be combined into compound statements such as

```
(b += c) *= 2.0;
```

This expression implements b = (b + c) * 2.0;.

It is especially sound to design other member functions to behave in the same reflexive way as these operators; that is, the output overwrites the object to which the function is attached. For example,

```
A.plus_outer (a, b);
```

adds to matrix A the outer product (ab^T) of a and b. (The dimensions of A, a, and b chosen in our ongoing example are consonant with the mathematical requirements to do this.)

On such a foundation we can construct some very powerful and concise code. For example, Householder premultiplication of dense matrix **A** by vector **a** is accomplished by

```
A.plus_outer (a, (a*A) *= (-2./(a*a)) );
```

This implements page 197 of Golub and Van Loan, *Matrix Computations* [14]. This expression may appear daunting at first, but we (or a good stepwise debugger) can easily parse it out. The second argument (a*A) is a (temporary) `real_vector` object of dimension `ncols`. It gets multiplied by a scalar ratio whose denominator is the dot product of a with itself. The fully evaluated temporary and a itself are the inputs to `matrix` member function `plus_outer()`, which modifies A as the algorithm dictates.

1.2 MEMORY DYNAMICS

A superior feature of C++ for mathematical programming is that the subroutines we create need never require the caller to supply a work array. Instead, we can empower the compiler to allocate temporary vectors when they are needed and to deallocate them automatically when they are no longer needed. This also helps to avoid undue restrictions when formulating compound expressions.

The policy that is followed in this book in regard to temporary vectors has four main points:

- Only the programmer can allocate and deallocate a `real_vector`.
- Only the compiler can allocate and deallocate a `temp_real_vector`.
- A `temp_real_vector` *is* a `real_vector` in every other respect.
- The assignment operator (=) *copies* the data from the right-hand-side vector to the left-hand-side vector.

These four principles work together harmoniously to encourage coding that is elegant and efficient and free of pitfalls.

The usual arithmetic operators (+, -, *, /) in C are termed *binary* because their operands number two, although there is always a third object involved: the hidden temporary that stores the result of the operation. In C++, when we overload these binary operators, we make this fact explicit. For example, the statements

```
temp_real_vector operator+ (real_vector&, real_vector&);
temp_real_vector operator- (real_vector&, real_vector&);
```

declare that the sum or difference of two `real_vector` objects is an object of type `temp_real_vector`. The `temp_real_vector` type also receives results from binary operators involving other classes:

```
temp_real_vector operator* (sparse&, real_vector&);
temp_real_vector operator* (real_vector&, matrix&);
temp_real_vector operator* (real_vector&, double);
```

and it may return the results from a more general function:

```
temp_real_vector Householder (matrix&, unsigned);
```

In translating a statement such as b = (b + c) * 2.0;, the stated principles work to allocate temporary storage for the result (b+c), then the result (b+c)
*2.0, and then to copy that final result safely to permanent storage in b. More-
over, the compiler deletes each temporary vector automatically, as soon as it is no
longer needed.

The class temp_real_vector is said in C++ parlance to be "derived" from
the real_vector class. This concept has been elaborately embellished in C++.
Its simplest form is useful in scientific programming when we need to access an existing data structure in an alternative way, without recopying the data. An example
of how this works is the derived class submatrix;, which is intended to be
used as in

```
submatrix Aprime( A, I, J);
```

This statement establishes a view of the content of matrix A as a matrix
Aprime, of reduced dimension, whose leading element is the element A(I,J).

For the most part, the real_vector implementation does not emulate the distinction between row vectors and column vectors that is observed in mathematics.
In the few cases where we need to model this distinction, coding

```
submatrix (a, 2);
```

for example, enables the content of a real_vector such as a to be viewed as
the elements of a one-column matrix, whose initial element is a(2).

The source code that defines and implements the real_vector and matrix
classes is described in detail in Chapter 2. The real_vector class is the more highly
elaborated, because it is involved with the other classes both as operand and resultant,
and because it provides vector temporary variables through temp_real_vector,
a class derived from real_vector. The matrix class may surprise FORTRAN
writers unfamiliar with C, because it is more complicated than a FORTRAN array of
rank two. The additional structure parallels C practice and, more important, provides
that each row of a matrix is itself a real_vector.

Chapter 3 presents the source code that defines and implements the sparse
class. Each nonzero element of a sparse matrix is included in two linked lists:
one for the row and one for the column. The internal structure of the sparse

implementation is designed to facilitate the coding of linear algebra algorithms, but the external appearance of a `sparse` is quite like that of a `matrix`.

1.3   APPLICATIONS

Chapters 4 through 12 (leaving aside Chapter 9) lay out one application after another that can be implemented based on the fundamental classes described in Chapters 1 through 3. My original motivation for writing these applications was to demonstrate that my vector and matrix syntax was both necessary and sufficient for coding important contemporary numerical methods. Of course, in working this out, I revised and extended the fundamental classes many times.

Chapter 4 shows how much can be accomplished with nothing more than the ability to compute dot products $(\mathbf{x}^T\mathbf{y})$ and matrix $\times$ vector products $(\mathbf{Ax}$ and $\mathbf{x}^T\mathbf{A})$. A Gram–Schmidt algorithm is encoded to orthonormalize the rows of a `matrix`. The simplicity (and shortcoming) of the steepest-descent method is demonstrated as a prelude to conjugate-gradient (CG) methods proper. Three variants of CG are encoded, of increasing complexity. Since we now have a satisfactory representation of sparse matrices, it is appealingly straightforward to obtain solutions of least-squares linear regression problems by the conjugate-gradient method.

Chapter 5 presents the first applications that depend on the internal details of the `sparse` class. Triangular systems of equations yield to recursive methods of solution. To encode these, we must become adept at traversing the internal linked lists of the `sparse` class, both by column and by row. Subroutines such as `Lsolve(sparse&)` and `Usolve(sparse&)` are encoded for use after matrix factorization. The textbook solution for fitting cubic splines is then factored algebraically, so that spline fitting can serve to demonstrate general forward and backward recursive solutions. The matrix factorization methods described in later chapters generally use row and column permutations, so my `pivot` class and its use are introduced here.

Chapter 6 is devoted to factorizations of dense matrices, the chief of which is QR factorization. This is based on the Householder transformation, which is a specific outer-product update of the matrix in question. The internal structure of the `matrix` class, together with the convenience of the derived `submatrix` class, leads to a very compact expression of this algorithm. Recursive solvers `Qsolve()` and `Usolve(matrix&)` are provided to complete the solution. If the system $\mathbf{Ax} = \mathbf{b}$ is overdetermined, QR produces the least-squares solution. Linear regression provides a concrete example of this. The Householder transformation can also be employed to make symmetric matrices tridiagonal. Tridiagonal matrices can, in turn, be diagonalized by iterative application of Givens transformations, thereby determining the eigenvalues of the original matrix.

Singular value decomposition (SVD; Chapter 7) embodies a generalization of the eigenvalue concept that is applicable even to unsymmetric and rectangular matrices. The SVD method encoded for dense matrices employs Jacobi transformations iteratively to orthogonalize the rows of the input `matrix`. The system $\mathbf{Ax} = \mathbf{b}$ has a convenient pseudoinverse solution following `SVD()` of $\mathbf{A}$ or $\mathbf{A}^T$. By the same token, **A** can be expressed or approximated as a sum of eigenmatrices. The SVD of a rectangular matrix **A** is equivalent to diagonalizing the partitioned matrix

$$\left[\begin{array}{c|c} \mathbf{0} & \mathbf{A} \\ \hline \mathbf{A}^{\mathrm{T}} & \mathbf{0} \end{array}\right]$$

which is symmetric by construction. For `sparse` matrices, `LanczosTridiag()` produces a tridiagonal output without modifying the input.

A factorization method important for both dense and sparse symmetric matrices is Cholesky decomposition, $\mathbf{LDL}^{\mathrm{T}}$ (Chapter 8). The method that is derived and encoded, known as the Doolittle algorithm, demonstrates additional internal details of the `sparse` class. If sparse matrix **A** is positive definite as well as symmetric, its rows and columns may be rearranged by `Sym_Pivot()` for the sole purpose of minimizing the introduction of additional nonzeros during the factorization. The solution of **Ax** = **b** by the Cholesky approach requires only one additional solver, `Dsolve()`. Matrices of the form

$$\left[\begin{array}{c|c} -\mathbf{E} & \mathbf{A} \\ \hline \mathbf{A}^{\mathrm{T}} & \mathbf{F} \end{array}\right]$$

are termed *quasidefinite,* and special versions of $\mathbf{LDL}^{\mathrm{T}}$ factorization are provided to handle them.

The topic of constrained optimization (Chapter 10) is introduced through linear programming (LP), in which a linear objective function $\mathbf{c}^{\mathrm{T}}\mathbf{x}$ is to be maximized subject to restrictions **Ax** ≤ **b**. The primal and dual forms of the problem are distinguished, and complementarity is defined. A path-following interior-point method is encoded that essentially treats optimization as just another linear algebra problem. The core of this method is solution of the Karush–Kuhn–Tucker system using the quasidefinite Cholesky decomposition `LDLt_QD()`. How to set up LP problems using slack variables is described, and examples are worked in which the constraints have a geometrical interpretation. Subroutine `INT_PT()` is seen to be a versatile tool, not merely a specialist method.

In Chapter 11 I suggest further applications of the interior-point approach. Linear regression using an L^{1} or L^{∞} criterion (rather than L^{2}, least-squares) is a suitable `INT_PT()` application. Quadratic programming (QP) denotes a form of optimization having linear constraints but a quadratic objective function $\mathbf{c}^{\mathrm{T}}\mathbf{x} + \frac{1}{2}\mathbf{x}^{\mathrm{T}}\mathbf{Qx}$. Matrix **Q** must be diagonal and positive semidefinite. The KKT system is modified but still solvable using a quasidefinite Cholesky decomposition `LDLt_QDt()`. A further extension of the interior-point method is successive quadratic programming (SQP). In this variation, the quadratic objective function is viewed as only an approximation of a general nonlinear objective function, defined in terms of its gradient and Hessian. QP and SQP are demonstrated by examples interpretable in terms of three-dimensional ray tracing.

Chapters 10 and 11 make extensive use of `real_vector`, `sparse`, and `matrix` variables but are quite oblivious to the internal details of these classes. In Chapter 12 we must again become cognizant of how the `matrix` and `sparse` classes really work. LU factorization is applicable to matrices lacking the desirable properties that guarantee the satisfactory performance of other methods. One version of LU, the Crout algorithm, is suitable for application to dense matrices in conjunction with partial pivoting (row exchanges). Another version, the Gauss algorithm, is suitable for application to sparse matrices in conjunction with threshold pivoting to reduce fill-in. Selecting pivots is expedited by a feature of `sparse` that maintains a count of the number of nonzeros in each row and column.

Chapter 13 takes a nontraditional view of its subject. Every C++ compiler now comes with one or more versions of complex arithmetic built in, complete with overloaded operators and standard math functions. When I first encoded Fourier transforms in C++, I naturally developed a class `complex_vector` analogous to `real_vector`. Then I saw that I would also need complex equivalents of `matrix` and `sparse` classes, and so on. The prospect of supporting a complex counterpart of every real class seemed tedious and inelegant. The point of C++ is to reuse proven code, not just to duplicate it and change `"double"` to `"complex."`

Banal duplication can be avoided. The alternative to arrays of complex numbers is to structure complex vectors or matrices as ordered pairs of `real_vector` or `matrix` variables, which we accordingly label "real" and "imaginary." The operators and functions required for complex arrays then simply call the operators and functions already defined for the real array classes.

C++ has a feature that implements this design very compactly. The statement

```
template<class T> struct cplxfy {T* re, T* im;};
```

declares that a structure named `cplxfy<T>` contains objects of type T named `re` and `im` (technically, C pointers thereto). The meaning of `"template"` is that for T we can insert `real_vector`, `matrix`, `double`, or whatever. This is the starting point for an implementation of complex vectors and matrices that makes maximum use of the `real_vector` and `matrix` methods already defined.

Chapter 14 makes use of the complex methods created in Chapter 13. The discrete Fourier transform (DFT) is shown to be multiplication of a complex vector by a complex matrix. The fast Fourier transform (FFT) is shown to gain its speed from a particular factorization of the DFT matrix. FFT subroutines are encoded and demonstrated that can be combined to perform two-dimensional real-to-complex DFTs. Frequency-domain operations demonstrated include phase-shift and bandpass filtering. An example of two-dimensional wave propagation is presented.

Finally, but not least, Chapter 9 stands apart from the main stream of vector and matrix development. It demonstrates some features of C++ that have no counterparts in FORTRAN, and it combines these to produce exact derivative values automatically through run-time application of the chain rule.

C++ has a concept of "pointers to functions" that is easy to define and accept. Instead of hard-coding a function *name,* we let which function to call be a *variable.* Such a variable must by nature translate to an *address.* However, the notation for this is rather abstruse:

```
typedef double (*differentiable) (double);
```

This says that a variable of type `differentiable` is a pointer to some function whose argument is type `double` which returns type `double`. Together with another C++ concept, the "abstract base class," function pointers provide the basis of a method that automatically obtains the derivative values of algebraic combinations of functions. The class structure worked out is only one-dimensional, but it is applicable to multidimensional line searches.

1.4 SUMMARY AND CONCLUSIONS

If $\mathbf{A}$ is a sparse or dense matrix, $\mathbf{x}$ and $\mathbf{y}$ are vectors, and c is a scalar, in C++ we shall represent:

Components

Element a_{ij} of $\mathbf{A}$ as `A(i,j)`
Component x_i of $\mathbf{x}$ as `x(i)` or `x[i-1]`

Arithmetic

$\mathbf{x} + \mathbf{y}$ as `x + y` and $\mathbf{x} - \mathbf{y}$ as `x - y`
$\mathbf{x}c$ or $c\mathbf{x}$ as `x * c` or `c * x`
$\mathbf{x}^T\mathbf{y}$ or $\mathbf{y}^T\mathbf{x}$ as `x * y` or `y * x` (scalar product)
$\mathbf{x} \leftarrow \mathbf{x}c$ or $\mathbf{x} \leftarrow c\mathbf{x}$ as `x *= c;`
$x_i \leftarrow (x_i + c)$, for all i, as `x += c;`
$\mathbf{x} \leftarrow (\mathbf{x} + \mathbf{y})$ as `x += y;`
$\mathbf{x} \leftarrow (\mathbf{x} - \mathbf{y})$ as `x -= y;`
$\mathbf{x} \leftarrow (-\mathbf{x})$ as `-x;`
$\mathbf{A}\mathbf{x}$ as `A * x`
$\mathbf{x}^T\mathbf{A}$ as `x * A`

Loops

```
for (i=0; i<n;  i++) x[i] = 1.0; and
for (i=1; i<=n; i++) x(i) = 1.0;
```
are both equivalent to the FORTRAN loop:
DO I=1,N
X(I) = 1.0
END DO

2 Vector and Matrix Basics

In this chapter I present in detail how my classes for floating-point vectors and dense matrices are implemented. There are many intimate connections between these two types of structures. The fundamental class in this scheme is the double-precision floating-point vector:

2.1 VECTOR CLASS

```
class real_vector { double* ptr;  unsigned n; };
```

Viewed as a data structure, `real_vector` contains just two items: `ptr` and `n`. Whatever your C reference says about pointers applies to `ptr`. It is the address of the initial element of a one-dimensional floating-point array of type `double`. The expressions `ptr[i]` and `*(ptr+i)` indicate the same thing: namely, the ith element of the array—the actual value, not just its address.

The length of the array whose origin is `ptr` is given by `n`, an `unsigned` integer. It is informative to use `unsigned` for integers that should never be negative. The compiler can detect certain obvious errors. Decrementing below 0 yields an anomalous positive value. Anything else we include inside the braces `{}`; of the `class` declaration is considered a member of that class, in some sense. Members have privileges that set them apart from nonmembers. In the case of `real_vector`, members are allowed direct access to `ptr` and `n`, and nonmembers are not.

2.1.1 Access to Innards

```
class real_vector
{
   double* ptr;  unsigned n;
   double& operator[] (unsigned i) const { return
      ptr[i]; }
   double& operator() (unsigned i) const { return
      ptr[i-1]; }
   unsigned N() const { return n; }
};
```

These member functions exist to provide an intuitive way to access data represented by a `real_vector` variable, say `x`. We may code `x[i]` to emulate C notation or x(i) to mimic FORTRAN subscripts. We may use x.N() for the length of x.

These definitions occur inside the class braces proper. They are implemented *inline,* as if by a precompiler, and not as actual subroutine calls and returns. In a real sense, x(i) is just an *alias* for x.ptr[i-1]. The subscript operators [] and () yield type double *by address* and therefore can be used to get or set a value. In contrast, x.N() is a read-only function. The qualifier const indicates that these member functions do not themselves modify the member to which they are attached. Consider this example:

```
for(unsigned i=1; i<x.N(); i++) x(i) = x[i];
```

This loop moves each of the last x.n−1 entries of x.ptr[] one index earlier.

2.1.2 Allocation and Deallocation

```
class real_vector
{
   double* ptr;  unsigned n;
   real_vector() { ptr = NULL;  n = 0; }
   real_vector (double* data, unsigned len) { ptr = data;
      n = len;}
   real_vector (unsigned length) {n = length;
      ptr = new double [n];}
   double* zap() { delete ptr; return ptr; }
   real_vector& init (unsigned = 0, double* = NULL);
};
```

A function whose name is the same as the name of its class is called a *constructor.* Its purpose is to incarnate an actual exemplar, or instance, of the class: in other words, a specific named variable. A class can have different constructors taking different arguments.

The default constructor real_vector() is invoked when we code, for example, real_vector z;. This z then contains a null pointer and a zero length. Therefore, z should not be used before it acquires some actual content.

If we have a suitable array double stuff [512];, say, we can invoke the two-argument constructor as real_vector y (stuff, 512);. Then y(j) is equivalent to stuff[j-1]. This constructor effectively converts a C-style double array to a real_vector. I use this often in setting up small examples.

The one-argument constructor is the most useful, and it is intended for use as in real_vector a(mrows), b(ncols);, for dynamic allocation. This constructor allocates storage using new[], a C++ memory-allocation utility. The caller therein acquires an obligation to call a.zap() and b.zap() to release this space when it is no longer needed. Function zap() calls delete, the converse of new. This constructor does not initialize the storage it acquires. The caller can invoke a.init() and b.init() to set it all to zero.

The syntax init(unsigned=0,double*=NULL) indicates that function init() takes two arguments, both of which assume default values if omitted. The behavior of the function therefore depends on how many arguments the caller specifies.

```
real_vector& real_vector::init (unsigned len, double* buf)
{
   if (len != 0)
   {
      if (n != len)
      {
         if (ptr != NULL) exit(1);
         n = len; ptr = buf;
         if (buf != NULL) return *this;
         ptr = new double [n];   checkptr(ptr);
      }
   }
   if (n > 0) memset(ptr, 0, n*sizeof(double));
   return *this;
}
```

The symbol real_vector:: indicates that what follows is a member of the real_vector class, despite its being implemented outside the class{};. As a consequence of this membership, ptr and n exist implicitly in this function and must be used as defined previously. If both arguments are omitted, init simply zeros all entries of ptr[]. If len is nonzero and buf is omitted, init allocates memory and sets it to zero. If both len and buf are specified, n and ptr are initialized with len and buf, respectively.

Function sizeof() is a C++ utility that tells how many bytes double requires. Function checkptr() aborts execution in event of an allocation failure. The expression exit(1); is a minimal way of responding to an unacceptable conflict of parameters. The statement return *this; is a formal requirement.

2.1.3 Example

```
double d[8] = {0.,1.,2.,3.,4.,5.,6.,7.};
real_vector x(5), y, z;
x.init();
y.init(6);
z.init(7,d+1);
```

The result is that x is initialized to all (five) zeros, y is assigned new storage containing six zeros, and z is given the last seven elements of array d.

2.1.4 Assignment Operators

```
class real_vector
{
    double* ptr;   unsigned n;
    real_vector& operator= (const real_vector&);
    real_vector& operator*= (const double);
    real_vector& operator+= (const double);
    real_vector& operator+= (const real_vector&);
    real_vector& operator-= (const real_vector&);
};
```

The assignment operators are member functions slightly too complicated to define inline. The most important of these is, of course,

```
real_vector& real_vector::operator= (const
    real_vector& rhs)
{
    if (ptr == NULL) {n = rhs.n; ptr = new double [n];}
    memcpy(ptr, rhs.ptr, n*sizeof(double));
    return *this;
}
```

Suppose that we code x=rhs; . The compiler interprets this as x.operator= (rhs); . The ptr and n referred to in the operator implementation then are those belonging to x. If ptr is NULL (as coding just real_vector x; would produce) the function first dynamically allocates the correct size array to receive the data from rhs. In any case, the data are copied by memcpy from rhs.ptr to ptr. The const asserts that the operator does not change rhs.

```
real_vector& real_vector::operator+= (const double c)
{
    for(unsigned i=0;  i<n;  i++)  *(ptr+i)  += c;
    return *this;
}
```

This operator is invoked when we code x+= any scalar value. The function is a simple loop that adds c to each element of the data using the ordinary += operator for type double. The other assignment operators declared above implement x*= c; , x+=z; and x-=z; , where z has the same dimension as x. The details are similar to x+=c. For example:

```
real_vector& real_vector::operator-= (const
    real_vector& v1)
```

```
{
    for(unsigned i=0; i<n; i++) *(ptr+i) -= *(v1.ptr+i);
    return *this;
}
```

2.1.5   Reflexive Member Functions

```
class real_vector
{
    double* ptr;  unsigned n;
    real_vector& operator- ();
    real_vector& sum (const real_vector&, const
        real_vector&);
    real_vector& dif (const real_vector&, const
        real_vector&);
    real_vector& byc (const real_vector&, const double);
};
```

These functions have the important property that they update a `real_vector` that already exists and do not require additional storage to be allocated. Consider

```
real_vector& real_vector::operator- ()
{
    for(unsigned i=0; i<n; i++) ptr[i] = -ptr[i];
    return *this;
}
```

This operator is invoked as in $-x$; . This innocuous expression executes a loop that negates each element of the data, in place. A little more complicated is

```
real_vector&
real_vector::sum (const real_vector& v1, const
    real_vector& v2)
{
    if (n != v1.n || n != v2.n) exit(1);
    for(unsigned i=0; i<n; i++) *(ptr+i) = *(v1.ptr+i) +
        *(v2.ptr+i);
    return *this;
}
```

This member function takes two `real_vector` arguments. It is invoked as in `v3.sum(v1,v2);`. It requires that all three vectors be of the same length, in which case it executes a loop that performs element-by-element addition.

2.1.6 Review Question

What does this do?

```
double d[5] = {0.,0.,0.,0.,0.};
real_vector z;
-( z.init(5,d) +=1.);
```

Answer: Vector variable z is initialized with (or, equivalenced to) array d. Then 1.0 is added to each of its elements. Then that result is negated. Therefore, d finally ends up as {-1.,-1.,-1.,-1.,-1.}. This illustrates how member functions can be cascaded. The output from each is the input to the next, in a seamless expression.

2.1.7 Derived Class

The chief use of sum() is in

```
temp_real_vector
operator+ (const real_vector& v1, const real_vector& v2)
{
    if (v1.n != v2.n) exit(1);
    real_vector s (v1.n);
    s.sum (v1, v2);
    return temp_real_vector(s);
}
```

This nonmember operator (v1+v2) creates a real_vector s of appropriate size and into it sums v1 and v2. The returned type is not real_vector but temp_real_vector, which enables the compiler to delete s.ptr automatically when it is no longer needed. This is accomplished with the help of

```
class temp_real_vector : public real_vector
{
private:
    temp_real_vector (const real_vector& t) { n = t.n;
        ptr = t.ptr; }

public:
    ~temp_real_vector() { delete ptr; }

friend:
    temp_real_vector operator+ (const real_vector&,
        const real_vector&);
```

```
temp_real_vector operator- (const real_vector&,
   const real_vector&);
temp_real_vector operator* (const real_vector&,
   const double);
temp_real_vector operator* (const double c, const
   real_vector& v)
   { return v * c; }
};
```

The :public syntax means that the temp_real_vector class is *derived* from the real_vector class. A derived class is the same as the class from which it is derived but with something added. Each temp_real_vector object has ptr and n, since it *is* a real_vector. The additional features are a new constructor and an explicit destructor (~temp_real_vector()).

The only way to create an actual temp_real_vector is to convert an actual real_vector, as in temp_real_vector T(t);. This constructor is defined inline, and we can see that T is essentially an alias for t. The difference is that ptr, or more precisely, the memory allocated to it, can be freed up automatically by the C++ compiler using the defined destructor ~temp_real_vector(). We see that the destructor is merely a call to delete the ptr previously set by new.

Because the temp_real_vector constructor is declared private, the non-member functions in which it is used must be declared friend. (A friend is something outside the class that is permitted to access the private parts.) The case of operator+() for adding two vectors is typical. A new real_vector s is allocated dynamically to receive the result of the calculation. At the very moment the function returns, s is converted to temp_real_vector.

The exact phrasing return temp_real_vector(s); is critical [10]. It defeats the tendency of C++ to generate extraneous copies of things. Had we instead coded temp_real_vector S(s);, then return S;, as separate statements, C++ would have generated a surreptitious copy of S and returned that after *destroying* S! What's even worse, such a copy would be defective. The C++ default copy constructor does not anticipate that ptr has dynamic storage allocated to it. We're not about to tell it, either (by defining a special copy constructor), because we don't want our code permeated by redundant hidden copies.

I'm not making this up. This is another consequence of the insistence on passing all arguments by value that we encounter in C. The intent is to prevent the inadvertent modification of shared parameters. If most of the data are of simple char and int type, the cost is probably acceptable. Despite its solicitous concerns about inadvertent data corruption, C++ permits the following ambiguity:

```
real_vector c(100000);  c.init();
real_vector a;  a = c;    // Case 1
real_vector b = c;        // Case 2
```

In the first case, as we would expect, C++ invokes `operator=` as we have defined it, and a gets initialized as a separate copy of `c`. In the second case, C++ volunteers its default copy constructor and initializes `b.ptr=c.ptr; b.n=c.n;`. So b becomes merely an alias for `c`.

The nonmember operators for `(v1-v2)` and `(v*c)` are similar to that for `(v1+v2)` and make use of member functions `dif` and `byc`, respectively. The operator for `(c*v)` is inline and says, "Use `(v*c)`." Finally, a very important `friend` of the `real_vector` class is the scalar (or "dot") product of two vectors:

```
double operator* (const real_vector& l, const
   real_vector& r)
{
   double sumprod = 0.0; unsigned i;   if(l.n == r.n)
   for(i=0; i<r.n; i++) sumprod += *(r.ptr+i) *
      *(l.ptr+i);
   return sumprod;
}
```

This function fails and returns a value 0.0 if the two vectors are of unequal length.

2.1.8   Review Question

What is the answer?

```
double d[5] = {1.,2.,3.,4.,5.};
real_vector a, b(5), c(d,5);
b.init() += 5.;    a = c * 2.;
double answer = (a+b)*(b-c);
```

   Answer: 90.

2.2   MATRIX CLASS

The implementation for the dense matrix class builds on the floating-point vector class, and it introduces some additional new topics.

2.2.1   Class Definition

```
class matrix { real_vector* v;   unsigned mrows, ncols,
   size;};
```

My design for a C++ `matrix` class, like a two-index array in C, incorporates more built-in structure than we find in FORTRAN. Each row of a `matrix` is a `real_vector`, of length `ncols`. There are, of course, `mrows` such rows.

In C++, arrays can be declared whose elements are themselves `struct` or `class`. The statement `real_vector* v;` implies that `v[0]` is a `real_vector` *and* the initial item in a list of `real_vectors v[i], 0 <= i < mrows`. By itself, `v` is an address.

2.2.2 Example

Coding `new real_vector X[4];` creates an array of four `real_vector` structures, each of which is initialized by the default constructor. A debugger shows:

```
Inspecting X          @:0065FD20
   [0]                {:00000000,0}
   [1]                {:00000000,0}
   [2]                {:00000000,0}
   [3]                {:00000000,0}
```

The *value* of X, a pointer, is the address `:0065FD20`. This is also the address of `X[0]`, a `real_vector` with a `NULL ptr` (`:00000000`) and a 0 `n`. In more detail:

```
Inspecting X[3]       @:0065FD38
  ptr                  :00000000
  n                       0 (0x0)
```

The address of `X[3]` differs from that of `X[0]` by `0x18` or 24 bytes. Each `real_vector`, or `{ptr,n}`, occupies 8 bytes.

2.2.3 Access to Innards

```
class matrix
{
   real_vector* v;   unsigned mrows, ncols, size;
   real_vector& operator[] (unsigned i) const
      { return v[i]; }
   double& operator() (unsigned i, unsigned j) const
      //Fortran style
      { return v[i-1](j); }
   unsigned M() const { return mrows; }
   unsigned N() const { return ncols; }
};
```

The C-like subscript operator `[i]`, applied to a `matrix`, produces the `real_vector` that constitutes the *i*th row. The FORTRAN-like subscript operator `(i,j)` produces the *ij*th matrix element. The number of rows in `matrix` A is `A.M()`, and the number of columns is `A.N()`.

If d is type double, r is type real_vector, and M is type matrix, all the following are valid syntax:

```
d = M(j,k);   r = M[j];
d = r[k] = M[j][k];
```

One way to code matrix-times-vector multiplication $\mathbf{x} = \mathbf{Ay}$ is this:

```
for(i=0; i<A.M(); i++) x[i] = A[i] * y;
```

The right-hand side is the scalar product of two real_vector objects. This is how operator* (matrix&, real_vector&) is coded below in Section 2.2.5.

There are no assignment operators declared for the matrix class, because the need for them is not common in applications. The presumed large size of matrix objects means that we avoid proliferating them. To copy matrix B into matrix A, when necessary, we can use the real_vector assignment operator in a loop:

```
for(i=0; i<A.M(); i++) A[i] = B[i];
```

2.2.4 Allocation

```
class matrix
{
    real_vector* v;   unsigned mrows, ncols, size;
    matrix() {v = NULL;   mrows = 0;   ncols = 0; size = 0;}
    matrix (unsigned, unsigned);
        //dynamic contiguous
    matrix (double*, unsigned, unsigned);
        //caller contiguous
    matrix (real_vector* rows, unsigned i, unsigned j)
            {v = rows; mrows = i; ncols = j; size = 0; }
};
```

Several constructors are available in the matrix class for different purposes. The default, used as in matrix A;, initializes everything to zeros and allocates no storage. The flagship constructor is the one taking two integer arguments and invoked as in matrix A(mrows, ncols);. It dynamically allocates all required storage and arranges that the data occupy a block of size = mrows*ncols contiguous memory locations:

```
matrix::matrix (unsigned i, unsigned j)
{
    mrows = i;   ncols = j;   size = i*j;
        v = new real_vector [mrows];
```

```
    double* space = new double [size]; // contiguous!
    memset(space, 0, size*sizeof(double));
    for (unsigned k=0; k<mrows; k++)
        v[k].init(ncols, space+k*ncols);
}
```

It is worth reviewing what is going on here. Since this is a member function, integers `mrows`, `ncols`, `size`, and pointer `v` exist without being declared. Function `new[]` dynamically allocates arrays of any specified type and size and returns pointers to the initial elements thereof. Array `space[]` is to hold the data and is cleared to zeros by `memset()`; and `v[]` is like `{{ptr,n},{ptr,n},...}`. The final loop sets each n to `ncols` and each `ptr` to the correct address in `space[]`, by calling `real_vector::init()` with two arguments.

The third constructor allocates and initializes v in the same way as before to indicate contiguous storage of the data. The difference is that the data array is provided by the calling program:

```
matrix::matrix (double* data, unsigned i, unsigned j)
{
    mrows = i;   ncols = j;   size = 0;  v = new
        real_vector [mrows];
    for (unsigned k=0; k<mrows; k++) v[k]. init(ncols,
        data+k*ncols);
}
```

The fourth constructor, coded inline above, requires a knowledgeable user to set up the `real_vector  rows[]` array, for contiguous storage or otherwise. The constructor converts this array to a `matrix`.

2.2.5 Friends of Another Class

```
temp_real_vector operator* (const matrix&, const
    real_vector&);
temp_real_vector operator* (const real_vector&,
    const matrix&);
```

These two operators must be `friends` of the `temp_real_vector` class because they invoke that class's `private` constructor:

```
temp_real_vector operator* (const matrix& A, const
    real_vector& b)
{
    if (A.N() != b.N()) exit(1);
    real_vector s (A.M());
```

```
    for (unsigned i = 0; i < A.M(); i++) s[i] = A[i] * b;
    return temp_real_vector(s);
}
```

The right-hand side, A[i]*b; , is a dot product. Matrix multiplication does not commute, so the coding of A*b is distinct from the coding of b*A:

```
temp_real_vector operator* (const real_vector& b,
    const matrix& A)
{
    if (A.M() != b.N()) exit(1);
    unsigned i,j;
    real_vector s;  s.init(A.N());
    for (i = 0; i < A.M(); i++)
        for (j = 0; j < A.N(); j++)
            s[j] += b[i] * A[i][j];// s += (A[i]*b[i]);
    return temp_real_vector(s);
}
```

2.2.6 Derived Class

```
class submatrix : public matrix
{   public:
    submatrix (const matrix&, unsigned, unsigned);
    submatrix& operator--();
    ~submatrix() { delete v; }
    submatrix (const real_vector&, unsigned);
};
```

The submatrix class is derived from the matrix class and therefore contains v, mrows, ncols, and size implicitly. The additional features in submatrix are two constructors, an automatic destructor, and an overloaded decrement operator. All these added functions are declared public.

```
submatrix::submatrix (const matrix& A, unsigned i,
    unsigned j)
{
    i--; j--; mrows = A.mrows-i; ncols = A.ncols-j;
        size = 0;
    v = new real_vector [mrows];
    for (unsigned k=0; k<mrows; k++)
        { v[k].ptr = A[k+i].ptr+j;
          v[k].n   = ncols;        }
}
```

In broadest terms, submatrix is an alias, an alternative name for a subset of an existing matrix. This is implemented by allocating and initializing a new v array to describe the rows of the subset desired. The actual data content of the matrix is irrelevant.

If A is a matrix and we code submatrix B (A,2,3);, then B is a matrix with one less row and two fewer columns than A, whose leading element B(1,1) is the same as A(2,3).

```
submatrix& submatrix::operator-- ()
{
    mrows--; ncols--;
    for (unsigned k=0; k<mrows; k++) --v[k];
    return *this;
}
```

This decrement operator is applied to a submatrix such as B in the familiar C manner: --B;. This statement causes the number of rows and the number of columns represented by B each to be reduced by one. The statement --v[k];, in the loop, in turn invokes the real_vector member function

```
real_vector& real_vector::operator-- () {n--; return
    *this;}
```

This operator decrements the indicated length of a real_vector but does not touch the data.

The destructor ~submatrix() generates inline code to delete the v array allocated by the constructor.

```
submatrix::submatrix (const real_vector& x, unsigned j)
{
    j--; mrows = x.n-j; ncols = 1; size = 0;
    v = new real_vector [mrows];
    for (unsigned k=0; k<mrows; k++)
        { v[k].ptr = x.ptr+j+k;
          v[k].n   = 1;         }
}
```

This submatrix constructor allows a real_vector to be treated as a one-column matrix. If this seems too elaborate, at least the need arises infrequently, as in transposing one row of a matrix. The second argument, j, is usually 1.

2.2.7 Exercise

If A is a matrix, what can you say about --A;?

Answer: C++ recognizes this as an error. A is a matrix, not a submatrix. The operator-- is a submatrix member function. Every submatrix is a matrix, but not every matrix is a submatrix.

2.2.8 Other Member Functions

In factorizing a dense matrix by the Crout LU algorithm (Chapter 12), numerical stability is assured by identifying suitable pivot elements and exchanging rows accordingly. The exchange of two rows does not require any movement of data within a matrix. Instead, only the pointers to the data are swapped:

```
void matrix::swaprows (const unsigned i, const unsigned j)
{
    unsigned l; double* dat;
        //in lieu of real_vector* tmp;
            dat = v[i-1].ptr;              l = v[i-1].n;
    v[i-1].ptr = v[j-1].ptr;    v[i-1].n = v[j-1].n;
    v[j-1].ptr = dat;              v[j-1].n = l;
}
```

I first tried to encode this along the lines of

```
{
    real_vector *tmp;    tmp = v[i-1];   v[i-1]
        = v[j-1]; v[j-1] = tmp;
}
```

This approach failed, because with my compiler, the declaration real_vector *tmp; does not actually create the desired temporary pointer. It is necessary to add tmp = new real_vector; and then delete tmp; . In my view, this mitigates the value of this approach. Fortunately, the entire matrix class is declared a friend of the real_vector class in the header file vector.h. Therefore, matrix member functions such as this are allowed direct access to n and ptr.

The inner product ($\mathbf{a}^T\mathbf{b}$) of two vectors (or dot product) is a scalar value. The outer product ($\mathbf{ab}^T$) is a new matrix. In FORTRAN terms, the new matrix P is defined by P(i,j) = a(i) * b(j). In matrix applications, the outer product usually occurs as an update to an existing matrix. So it is implemented as a member function:

```
matrix&
matrix::plus_outer (const real_vector& l, const
    real_vector& r)
{
    unsigned i,j;
    if (mrows != l.n || ncols != r.n) exit(1);
    for (i=0; i<mrows; i++)
        for (j=0; j<ncols; j++) v[i][j] += l[i] * r[j];
    return *this;
}
```

In this context, C-like subscripting is informative. Member $v[i]$ is a row of the existing `matrix` as well as a `real_vector`. The outer loop goes row by row.

My choices of what to implement or not implement, and how to do it, are motivated by what is required for less tedious coding of modern numerical methods. For example, an important algorithm for QR factorization of a dense matrix can be written as (see Chapter 6)

```
matrix& matrix::HouseholderQR()
{
// Golub & Van Loan p.212; algorithm 5.2.1
   for (unsigned i=1; i<=ncols; i++){
      submatrix C(*this, i, i);
      C.row_house( house(C, 1) );    }
   return *this;
}
```

The called functions `house` and `row_house` are comparably compact.

2.2.9   Review Question

Design a destructor `~matrix()` for the `matrix` class. (*Hint:* Look at `size`.)

2.3   MISCELLANEOUS OBSERVATIONS

In this section I have collected some observations concerning C++ coding that are not specific to vectors or matrices, but don't fit elsewhere, either.

When a loop index is essentially a dummy index not referenced outside the loop, I prefer to make that clear by writing, for example,

```
for(unsigned i=0; i<n; i++) x[i] = y[i];
```

In newer C++ compilers, `i` remains undefined outside the scope of the loop. In C and in older C++ compilers, `i` is considered defined from this point forward, and a second declaration `unsigned i;` is an error.

The use of `unsigned` integers has one huge potential pitfall:

```
for(unsigned i=n; i>=0; --i) x[i] = y[i];
```

This loop never terminates, because `i` never becomes less than zero. Decrementing an `unsigned` whose value is 0 yields a large positive number.

I prefer the specificity provided by setting a value and testing it all in the same statement. A simplified example might be

```
unsigned k, j=1;
if( (k = j) == 0){ /*etc.*/}
```

This has the same effect as

```
k = j;   if( k == 0){ /*etc.*/}
```

A pitfall lurks if we confuse == (logical equality test) and = (assignment operator). The ambiguous statement if(k = j) is syntactically acceptable and evaluates logically as "true"—in this case because k is 1. It is like coding if(1).

C++ contains a unique operator "?:" that takes three arguments and is useful in coding conditional expressions succinctly. For example,

```
s = (1 > 0. ? 1. : -1.);   //(from Power_Method())
```

has the same effect as

```
if( 1 > 0. ) s = 1.;   else s = -1.;
```

By using this operator in a #define statement, we can induce the preprocessor to generate inline code for us:

```
#define max(a,b)   (((a) > (b)) ? (a) : (b))
#define min(a,b)   (((a) < (b)) ? (a) : (b))
```

The C preprocessor is conceptually a text editor that replaces one string of characters with another before the real compiler sees the code. So if our source code contains the statement

```
x = max( x1, x2);
```

the preprocessor rewrites the statement as

```
x = ((x1 > x2) ? x1 : x2);
```

This is inline code, not a function call, and it works on any variable type for which the comparisons ($>$, $<$) are defined.

2.4 SUMMARY AND CONCLUSIONS

The syntax we will find useful includes:

Vectors

```
real_vector a;
```
declares a vector **a** with zero length.

```
real_vector b(n);
```
dynamically allocates a vector **b** of n components.

```
real_vector c(s,100);
```
converts array double s[100]; to vector **c**.

```
x.init();
```
sets **x** to all zeros.

y.init(n); allocates dynamic storage containing *n* zeros to **y**.

z.init(10,s+90); allocates s[90] through s[99] to **z**.

x = y; copies the content of **y** to **x**. Requires x.n to equal y.n or 0.

b.zap(); releases the dynamic storage allocated to **b**.

Matrices

matrix A(m,n); dynamically allocates a matrix **A** of *m* rows by *n* columns.

matrix B(s,5,20); converts array double s[100]; to a 5 by 20 matrix **B**.

submatrix C(A,i,j); creates matrix **C**, whose leading element is A(i,j).

submatrix X(x,1); converts vector **x** to a one-column matrix **X**.

A[i] is a row of matrix **A** *and* a real_vector.

A[i][j] and A[i](j+1) both indicate element A(i+1,j+1).

A.plus_outer(u,v); performs the rank-one update $\mathbf{A} \leftarrow \mathbf{A} + \mathbf{u}\mathbf{v}^\mathrm{T}$.

3 Sparse Matrix Basics

Sparse matrices in my C++ design are as convenient from the user's viewpoint as ordinary matrices. They constitute a recognized variable type, declared as in `sparse S;`, and the elements of the matrix are accessed via subscripts: `S(i,j)`. They can be employed in applications without consideration of their special nature being foremost in the programmer's mind. In this chapter I describe in detail how my C++ class for sparse matrices is implemented.

In the FORTRAN world, sparse-matrix computation is a specialty all to itself, largely because FORTRAN lacks a comparably convenient representation of sparse matrices. FORTRAN employs several different and incompatible sparse storage schemes, and none provides straightforward access to individual nonzero elements. In one FORTRAN approach, a sparse matrix is described by three linear arrays: `E`, `I`, and `L`, say. The nonzero elements are stored in `E`, in column-by-column groups. Integer `I(K)` stores the number of the row to which value `E(K)` belongs. Integer `L(J)` stores the initial value of `K` that pertains to column `J`. Consequently, if `L(J+1).EQ.L(J)`, column `J` is empty. For row-by-row access to the data, it is necessary to sort the arrays into a different order. This was all designed in decades past when memory was expensive and limited.

In my design for a `sparse` class, the convenience of the programmer is the primary criterion. My implementation of the `sparse` class has its subtleties and complications, but most of them are hidden from view in most applications. Neverthess, I disclose them all here.

In outline, the basis of sparse-matrix programming is to avoid storing the zero elements of a matrix, to keep track instead of exactly where the *nonzero* elements are located, and then to avoid introducing *additional* nonzeros. My design begins with a special structure to hold all the parameters of each nonzero element.

3.1 STRUCTURE DEFINITION

```
struct element
{
    unsigned row, col;
    double value;
    unsigned next, mext;
};
```

The name of this type of structure is `element`. A separate `element` is dedicated to each nonzero element of a sparse matrix. Within each `element` is recorded the `row` and `col` (column) to which it belongs, its (nonzero) `value`, and the location of another (`next`) nonzero in the same row and another (`mext`) nonzero in the same column.

All the `elements` belonging to one sparse matrix are stored in a single linear array, consecutively, but in no prescribed order. To begin, `element e [1000];`, for example, declares a linear array e of 1000 `elements`.

3.1.1 Example

Suppose that we print the content of any single `element` in the following format:

```
[(row# , col#): value -> next_in_row next_in_col]
```

Then the `element` lists for row 5 and column 5 of a particular `sparse A` might be, for example:

```
Row 5:                            Column 5:
e[115]:[(5,14): 1 -> 113 114]     e[91]:[(7,5): 1 -> 0 90]
e[113]:[(5,13): 1 -> 101 112]     e[90]:[(6,5): -1.06 -> 0 89]
e[101]:[(5,8): -1 -> 97 100]      e[89]:[(5,5): -1 -> 0 88]
 e[97]:[(5,7): -1 -> 93 96]       e[88]:[(25,5): 0.301 -> 0 0]
 e[93]:[(5,6): -1 -> 89 92]
 e[89]:[(5,5): -1 -> 0 88]
```

In row 5, entry 115 of e (i.e., `e[115]`) corresponds to A(5,14) and points to `e[113]`, which corresponds to A(5,13) and points to `e[101]`, which corresponds to A(5,8) and points to `e[97]`, which corresponds to A(5,7) and points to `e[93]`, which corresponds to A(5,6) and points to `e[89]`, which corresponds to A(5,5) and is the last in the row, since it points to 0.

In column 5, `e[91]` corresponds to A(7,5) and points to `e[90]`, which corresponds to A(6,5) and points to `e[89]`, which corresponds to A(5,5) and points to `e[88]`, which corresponds to A(25,5) and is the end of the column, since it points to 0. Entry `e[89]` appears in both lists because it holds the parameters for the diagonal element A(5,5).

3.2 CLASS DEFINITION

```
class sparse
{
    element* e;
    unsigned mrows, ncols, size, kount;
    element** row;  element** col;
};
```

My `sparse` matrix design is based on what's called a *linked list*. A large *linear* array e of `element` structures is allocated to store the nonzero data. The maximum number of elements that can be stored is `size`, and the number of elements that have been stored up to any time is `kount`. The dimensions of the matrix are `mrows` rows by `ncols` columns.

The syntax `element** row;` means that `row` is a linear array of *pointers* to `element` objects. Specifically, `row[i]` is the *address* of the header `element` for the linked list of `elements` that makes up row `i+1` of the matrix. The syntax `element** col;` means that `col` is a linear array of pointers to `element` objects. Specifically, `col[j]` is the address of the header `element` for the linked list of `elements` that makes up column `j+1` of the matrix.

The first `mrows+ncols` `elements` of e are reserved as header `elements` for the rows and columns, respectively. By "header" I mean that these are not part of the matrix data per se. A row header contains `next=0` if that row is empty; otherwise, `e[next]` is the initial `element` in the linked list for that row. A column header contains `mext=0` if that column is empty; otherwise, `e[mext]` is the initial `element` in the linked list for that column.

The `row` and `col` pointer arrays are very useful in algorithms that require rearranging the order of rows and columns. C++ readily distinguishes these from the `row` and `col` integers that appear *inside* the `element` structure, and I hope the reader will, too.

3.2.1 Updating the Linked Lists

In C++, if `q` is an `element` structure, the `value` it contains is denoted by `q.value`, using a dot (period). If `p` is a *pointer* to an `element` (so that `*p` is an `element`), the `value` it refers to is denoted by `p->value`, using an arrow (so called). Within `sparse`, `e[99].row` is the row to which `e[99]` belongs, for example, and `(e+99)->col` is a pointer-oriented way of indicating the column to which `e[99]` belongs.

The fundamental operation of updating both linked lists to accommodate one additional nonzero is illustrated in the following code from member function `stash()`. `S.stash(i,j)` sets up storage for an element in row `i` and column `j` of `sparse` `S`.

```
double& sparse::stash (const unsigned i, const unsigned j)
{
    element* elem = row[i-1];   unsigned k = kount;
    if(kount >= size) exit(1); // insufficient size!
    e[k].row = i; e[k].col = j;
    e[k].next = elem->next; elem->next = k;
    (more...)
```

Since this is a member function, `e`, `row`, `col`, `size`, and `kount` are already set up. Therefore, `elem` is a pointer to the header `element` for row `i`. Since `kount` is the number of `elements` that have been stored up to now, `e[k]` is the next available. Entries e[k].row and e[k].col are set to i and j, respectively. Entry e[k].next is set to indicate whatever the header elem->next *was* indicating, and elem->next is reset to the location of e[k]. In a sense, the new element is inserted at the head of the list. Continuing,

```
elem = col[j-1];
e[k].mext = elem->mext; elem->mext = k;
(more. . .)
```

Now elem is a pointer to the header element for column j. Entry e[k].mext is set to indicate whatever header elem->mext was indicating, and elem->mext is reset to the location of e[k]. The new element is again inserted at the head of the list. Finally,

```
kount++;
return e[k].value;
}
```

The kount gets incremented by 1, and the function returns e[k].value. It is returned by reference, so the calling program receives an address into which it can store a double. As an example of usage, the following excerpt initializes sparse C (copying from matrix A) within an application discussed in Chapter 11:

```
for(i=1; i<=m; i++)
    for(j=1; j<=n; j++)
        if(fabs(A(i,j)) > EPS) C.stash(j+m,i) = A(i,j);
```

[Note that if A were sparse, we would test fabs(A.getval(i,j)).]

Keep in mind that the details of implementation are invisible when we use a member function in an application. All the above happens automatically, and so does the following.

3.2.2   Traversing the Linked Lists

A fundamental operation in linked-list programming is traversing or scanning a list. A good example of how to do this is shown in the following code from member function dumprow(). S.dumprow(i) prints out each and every element of row i of sparse S. It is what I used to produce the row list in Section 3.1.1.

```
void sparse::dumprow (const unsigned i) const
{
    element* elem = row[i-1];   unsigned k;
    while ((k = elem->next) != 0){ elem = e+k;
        cout << k << *elem << "\n"; }
}
```

Pointer `elem` initially addresses the header `element` for row `i`. If `k`, which is the `next` entry in that `element`, is not 0, `elem` is changed to `e+k`, that is, the address of `e[next]`. Then the test of `elem->next` is repeated. This cycle of test and update continues until a `next` entry of 0 is finally encountered. Also within this cycle, each `element` structure `*elem` is printed out as it is encountered. The line that begins `"cout"` does the printing.

I provide a comparable member function for printing out the `elements` in a specific column:

```
void sparse::dumpcol (const unsigned j) const
{
    element* elem = col[j-1];   unsigned k;
    while ((k = elem->mext) != 0){ elem = e+k;
        cout << k << *elem << "\n"; }
}
```

The difference is that `elem` initially addresses the header for column `j` and that the loop is based on testing `elem-> mext`.

3.2.3   Allocation and Deallocation

```
class sparse
{
    element* e;
    unsigned mrows, ncols, size, kount;
    element** row;   element** col;
public:
    sparse() {e=0; row=0; col=0; mrows=0; ncols=0;
        size=0; kount=0;}
    sparse (const unsigned, const unsigned,
        const unsigned);
    ~sparse() { delete e;   delete row;   delete col; }
};
```

The default constructor, invoked as in `sparse S;`, simply initializes everything to 0. The principal constructor is invoked by specifying the number of rows, the number of columns, and the maximum number of nonzeros provided for, as in `sparse S(mrows, ncols, maxnz)`:

```
sparse::sparse(const unsigned i, const unsigned j,
    const unsigned max)
{
    mrows = i;   ncols = j;   kount = mrows+ncols;
        size = max+kount;
    row = new element* [mrows];   col = new element*
        [ncols];
```

```
   e = new element[size];
   memset(e, 0, size*sizeof(element));    unsigned k;
   for (k=0; k<mrows; k++) row[k] = e + k;
   for (k=0; k<ncols; k++) col[k] = e + mrows + k;
}
```

The size of array e includes the mrows+ncols header elements, in addition
to max. Array e is initialized to all zeros by memset(). Array row is initialized
with the addresses of the row headers, and array col is initialized with the addresses
of the column headers. (Recall that e + k is pointer arithmetic.)

The destructor ~sparse() is invoked by the compiler in accordance with its
normal rules, and it deletes the three arrays that were allocated using new.

3.2.4 Access to Innards

```
class sparse
{
   element* e;
   unsigned mrows, ncols, size, kount;
   element** row;  element** col;
public:
   unsigned M() const { return mrows; }
   unsigned N() const { return ncols; }
   unsigned NZ() const{ return kount-mrows-ncols; }
   element& nonz (const unsigned k) const { return
      e[mrows+ncols+k]; }
   double& stash (const unsigned, const unsigned);
      //Unconditional
   double& operator() (const unsigned, const unsigned);
      //Fortran style
   double getval (const unsigned, const unsigned) const;
      //read-only
};
```

Functions M() and N(), employed as in S.M() and S.N(), return the values
of mrows and ncols, respectively, to the caller. S.NZ() returns the number of
nonzeros currently stored in e, not counting the row and column headers.

Function nonz() is intended to get or set parameters in any element in e,
not counting the row and column headers. For example,

```
   for(unsigned k=0; k<S.NZ(); k++)
      if( S.nonz(k).value > 1.) S.nonz(k).value = 1.; .
```

Note that the range of k in this example is 0 through S.NZ()-1.

A compelling advantage of this C++ sparse-matrix design is the functionality provided by the FORTRAN-style subscript operator, invoked as in S(i,j):

```
double& sparse::operator() (const unsigned i, const
   unsigned j)
{
   element* elem = row[i-1];  unsigned k;
   while ((k = elem->next) != 0){ elem = e+k;
      // scan row i
        if(elem->col == j) return elem->value; }
          // return if j found
   (more...)
```

This function traverses row i as we saw before in dumprow(), but in this case compares the col in each element to j. If a match is found, the function immediately reports the value corresponding to i and j. The return is by reference [i.e., address (double&)], so that S(i,j) can appear on either side of the assignment operator: S(10,20) = S(20,10);.

If the traversal of row i finds that an element in column j does not exist already, the function proceeds to create one, just as we saw earlier for stash():

```
   if(kount >= size) exit(1); // insufficient size!
   k = kount;  e[k].row = i;  e[k].col = j;
   elem = row[i-1];  e[k].next = elem->next;
      elem->next = k;
   elem = col[j-1];  e[k].mext = elem->mext;
      elem->mext = k;
   kount++;  return e[k].value;
}
```

Just as in stash(), the new element is inserted at the head of the linked lists.

To get just a value for S(i,j) without possibly creating a new element, I provide member function S.getval(i,j);:

```
double sparse::getval (const unsigned i, const
   unsigned j) const
{
   element* elem = row[i-1];  unsigned k;
   while ((k = elem->next) != 0){ elem = e+k;
      if(elem->col == j) return elem->value; }
   elem = col[j-1];
   while ((k = elem->mext) != 0){ elem = e+k;
      if(elem->row == i) return elem->value; }
   return 0.;
}
```

For completeness, I show a traversal of column j seeking `row == i`, as well as a traversal of `row i` seeking `col == j`. Generally, if one of these loops runs its course, so does the other, and the function returns 0.

3.2.5   Row and Column Counts

So far, I have described how the reserved header `elements` store `next` and `mext` entries to initiate row and column traversals, respectively. I also use the headers to maintain a count of the population of each row and column. In each row-header `element`, the `col` entry is reserved to keep a count of the columns occupied in that row, and in each column-header `element`, the `row` entry is reserved to keep a count of the rows occupied in that column. Two `sparse` inline member functions provide rapid access to these numbers:

```
inline unsigned&
sparse::rowcount (const unsigned i) const { return
   row[i-1]->col; }

inline unsigned&
sparse::colcount (const unsigned j) const { return
   col[j-1]->row; }
```

Whenever `stash()` and the subscript `operator()` add a new `element` to the linked lists for row i and column j, they also execute `rowcount(i)++;` and `colcount(j)++;` to increment the respective counts. I omitted showing this before.

3.2.6   Unlinking an Element

Sometimes it is necessary to remove an element from a sparse matrix. For example, some algorithms require removal of any element whose absolute value has decreased below a *drop tolerance*. In my design, this is done by breaking the links that enable the `element` to be found by traversal loops, as the following code from member function `unlink()` illustrates.

```
void sparse::unlink (const unsigned i, const unsigned j)
{
   element* elem = row[i-1];   unsigned k;
   while ((k = elem->next) != 0){
      if(e[k].col == j){
         elem->next = e[k].next;   e[k].next = e[k].col = 0;
         rowcount(i)--;   break; }
      elem = e+k; }
   (more...)
```

The `while()` loop traverses the list of `elements` for row i. If the element indicated by next is in column j, next is reset to point *past* the element in question, whose internal parameters are then summarily zeroed. The count of the row is decremented, and we `break;` from the `while()` loop. Continuing, we have

```
    elem = col[j-1];
    while ((k = elem->mext) != 0){
        if(e[k].row == i){
            elem->mext = e[k].mext;  e[k].mext = e[k].row = 0;
            colcount(j)--;    break;}
        elem = e+k; }
}
```

The `while()` loop traverses the list of `elements` for column `j`. If the element indicated by `mext` is in row `i`, `mext` is reset to point *past* the element in question, and its internal parameters are zeroed. The count of the column is decremented, and we `break;` from the `while()` loop and exit.

Note that the same target `element` is found by both scan loops, and it ends up with `row = col = next = mext = 0`. The reason for executing two traversals is to find the two list items that *lead* to the target `element`. The unlinked `element` is now undetectable in list traversals, but it will still be found by `nonz()`, and `kount` is unaffected. The `unlink()` protocol does not call for zeroing the `value` entry of the unlinked `element`, but it reasonably could.

3.2.7 Example

Unlink the diagonal element `A(5,5)` from the linked lists for row 5 and column 5 of sparse matrix `A`, shown in the example in Section 3.1.1:

```
Row 5:                          Column 5:
e[115]:[(5,14): 1-> 113 114]    e[91]:[(7,5): 1  -> 0 90]
e[113]:[(5,13): 1-> 101 112]    e[90]:[(6,5): -1.06 -> 0 88]
e[101]:[(5,8): -1-> 97 100]     e[89]:[(0,0): -1 -> 0 0]
 e[97]:[(5,7): -1-> 93 96]      e[88]:[(25,5): 0.301 -> 0 0]
 e[93]:[(5,6): -1-> 0 92]
 e[89]:[(0,0): -1-> 0 0]
```

3.2.8 Friends of Another Class

```
temp_real_vector operator* (const sparse&, const
    real_vector&);
temp_real_vector operator* (const real_vector&, const
    sparse&);
```

These are the very important operators that perform `A*b` and `b*A`. Just as in the `matrix` class, these two multiplication operators are `friends` of the `temp_ real_vector` class, because they invoke that class's `private` constructor in order to return the appropriate type of variable. They must be `friends` of the `sparse` class as well, because they need direct access to `private` members in order to traverse the linked lists.

```
temp_real_vector operator* (const sparse& A, const
    real_vector& b)
{
    if (A.N() != b.N()) exit(1);
    real_vector s; s.init(A.M());
    element* elem; unsigned i, k;
    for(i = 0; i < A.M(); i++) { elem = A.row[i];
        while ((k = elem->next) != 0){ elem = A.e+k;
            s[i] += b(elem->col) * elem->value;}
    }
    return temp_real_vector(s);
}
```

The number of columns in A must equal the dimension of b, in which case output vector s is initialized with dimension equal to the number of rows in A. Each entry s(i) of the output is essentially the dot product of b with row i of matrix A. Each traversal of the linked list for a row of A picks up only the `elements` that have been created in that row. The `private` members of operand A are addressed as A.row and A.e.

```
temp_real_vector operator* (const real_vector& b,
    const sparse& A)
{
    if (A.M() != b.N()) exit(1);
    real_vector s; s.init(A.N());
    element* elem; unsigned j,k;
    for  (j = 0; j < A.N(); j++){ elem = A.col[j];
        while ((k = elem->mext) != 0){ elem = A.e+k;
            s[j] += b(elem->row) * elem->value;}
    }
    return temp_real_vector(s);
}
```

The number of rows in A must equal the dimension of b, in which case output vector s is initialized with dimension equal to the number of columns in A. Each entry s(j) of the output is essentially the dot product of b with column j of matrix A. This time, the linked-list traversal picks up the nonzeros for each column, in turn.

3.2.9 Sparse Utility Functions

Another example of how arithmetic is controlled in a linked-list traversal is the member function defined to add one row of a sparse matrix into another:

```
void sparse::plus_row (const unsigned i, const
   unsigned j)
{//add row j into row i  (row i += row j)
   element* elem = row[j-1];  unsigned k;
   while ((k = elem->next) != 0){ elem = e+k;
        (*this)(i, (elem->col)) += (elem->value); }
}
```

This function is invoked as in `S.plus_row(i,j);`, where `S` is a sparse matrix. In the final line of the function, `S` is represented by `(*this)`. Furthermore, `elem -> col` is a column number, which we could call `l`. Therefore, the left-hand side of the final line translates as `S(i,l)`, and this invokes the subscript operator for the `sparse` class. The `while()` loop encapsulates the requisite logic very compactly. Only nonzero values `S(j,l)` come into play. If `S(i,l)` is already nonzero, it is updated; otherwise, a new nonzero is created.

A `sparse` member function that illustrates some further fine points of coding is `swapcols()`. This and its counterpart `swaprows()` are employed in matrix-decomposition algorithms to maneuver selected pivot elements onto the main diagonal.

```
void sparse::swapcols (const unsigned i, const unsigned j)
{
   element* elem = col[i-1];  col[i-1] = col[j-1];
      col[j-1] = elem;
   unsigned k;
   while ((k = elem->mext) != 0){ elem = e+k; elem->
      col = j; }
   elem = col[i-1];
   while ((k = elem->mext) != 0){ elem = e+k; elem->
      col = i; }
}
```

The third line interchanges the pointers to the header `element`s for columns i and j. This makes `col[i-1]` point to what was column j, and vice versa. The first `while()` loop changes the column numbers to j within the `element`s of new column j. The second `while()` loop changes the column numbers to i within the `element`s of what is now column i. The `element`s that belong to the two columns remain where they are in array e. Subroutine `swaprows()` operates similarly:

```
void sparse::swaprows (const unsigned i, const unsigned j)
{
   element* elem = row[i-1];  row[i-1] = row[j-1];
      row[j-1] = elem;
   unsigned k;
```

```
while ((k = elem->next) != 0){ elem = e+k;
    elem->row = j; }
elem = row[i-1];
while ((k = elem->next) != 0){ elem = e+k;
    elem-> row  = i; }
}
```

Standard C++ enables a programmer to output the members of a class to a display device quite conveniently. We write

```
#include <iostream.h>
```

to bring the necessary standard definitions into our code. Then an output format (for `struct element`) is specified by defining the operator

```
inline ostream& operator<< (ostream& s, const element& q)
{
    s << " [(" << q.row << "," << q.col << "): " << q.value
        << " -> "
        << q.next << " " << q.mext << "]"; return s;
}
```

This function is `inline`, but it is not a member of `ostream` or of `element`. It is not even a `friend`. The only requirement is that `q.row`, and so on, be `public`. The format this specifies has been seen in previous `element` examples:

```
[( q.row , q.col): q.value -> q.next q.mext]
```

The operator `"<<"` is employed in `ostream` expressions to indicate the sequence in which objects should be printed out:

```
cout << k << e[k] << "\n";
```

This line prints to the console screen `cout` the index `k` and the kth element of array `e`, followed by a new line `"\n"`.

For use with small `sparse` matrices, the following nonmember function prints a `sparse` including zeros in a conventional matrix grid format:

```
void print_matrix (const sparse& A)
{
    for(unsigned i=1; i<=A.M(); i++){
        for(unsigned j=1; j<=A.N(); j++) cout << '|' <<
            A.getval(i,j);
        cout << "|\n"; }
}
```

For example, if S is the 4 by 4 identity matrix, `print_matrix(S);` produces

```
|1|0|0|0|
|0|1|0|0|
|0|0|1|0|
|0|0|0|1|
```

3.3   SUMMARY AND CONCLUSIONS

The syntax we will find useful includes:

Sparse Matrices

sparse A(m,n,nz); allocates a matrix **A** of m rows, n columns, and nz nonzeros.

A(i,j) is the value of a_{ij}, passed by address for two-way access.

A.getval(i,j) returns the value of a_{ij}, passed by value.

A.stash(i,j) stores a new element a_{ij}.

A.rowcount(i) is the count of nonzeros in row i of **A**.

A.colcount(j) is the count of nonzeros in column j of **A**.

element e; contains:

e.row	row number i within **A**.
e.col	column number j within **A**.
e.value	value of a_{ij}.
e.next	index of another nonzero in this row.
e.mext	index of another nonzero in this column.

A.nonz(k) is the kth element in the linked list, returned by address.

A.NZ() returns the number of nonzeros stored so far.

A.swaprows(i,j); interchanges rows i and j within matrix **A**.

A.swapcols(i,j); interchanges columns i and j within matrix **A**.

4 Conjugate-Gradient Methods

In this chapter I present several methods for solving the matrix equation $\mathbf{Ax} = \mathbf{b}$ by adjusting the components of $\mathbf{x}$ iteratively according to some clever plan. These methods are important in sparse matrix applications because they do not modify $\mathbf{A}$. Implementing these methods only requires computing the product `A*x`, where x is a `real_vector` and A is either a `matrix` or a `sparse`.

4.1 LINEAR INDEPENDENCE AND ORTHOGONALITY

Consider a context where we are dealing with vectors all having n components. The first thing we need is a set of n vectors $\mathbf{e}_i$ that share the property of linear independence; that is, none of the $\mathbf{e}_i$ can be expressed entirely as a weighted sum of the others. (In three dimensions, three vectors are linearly independent if they are not coplanar and no two are parallel.) These n linearly independent vectors are said to *span* an n-dimensional space; any further vector $\mathbf{x}$ *can* be expressed as a weighted sum of the $\mathbf{e}_i$, as in $\mathbf{x} = \Sigma x_i \mathbf{e}_i$. This is not to say that the set $\{\mathbf{e}_i\}$ is the same as a coordinate system. For a coordinate system, we require two additional properties: orthogonality ($\mathbf{e}_i^T \mathbf{e}_j = 0$ if $i \neq j$) and unit length ($\mathbf{e}_i^T \mathbf{e}_i = 1$). We denote both properties at once by saying that the $\{\mathbf{e}_i\}$ are *orthonormal*.

The classic method of converting an arbitrary set of spanning vectors into an orthonormal coordinate system goes by the name *Gram–Schmidt orthogonalization*. Assume that the set $\{\mathbf{e}_i\}$ is represented by the rows of an n by n `matrix`. Then the Gram–Schmidt algorithm is coded as

```
void Gram_Schmidt( matrix& e )
{//Korn&Korn [20] p454
    e[0] *= (1./sqrt(e[0]*e[0]));      //3
    for(unsigned i=1; i<e.M(); i++){   //4
        for(unsigned k=0; k<i; k++) e[i] -= (e[k] *
            (e[i]*e[k]));
        e[i] *= (1./sqrt(e[i]*e[i])); } //6
}
```

Recall that e[i] is a `real_vector` and a row of the `matrix`. The expression e[i]*e[i] is the scalar product of e[i] with itself, so sqrt(e[i]*e[i]) is the length of e[i]. Line 3 divides the top row of the matrix by its own length and thereby makes a unit vector of it. The loop that begins in line 4 is a recursion that subtracts from each row i in turn the sum of its components that are already spanned by the previous rows. Then in line 6, the remainder of row i gets normalized to unit length.

4.1.1 Example

The following code presents an example of the Gram–Schmidt algorithm in action. Line 2 calls a constructor (Section 2.2.4) to convert array y to a 4 by 4 matrix e. The initial content of e is displayed by dumpall(). Gram–Schmidt is applied to e in line 4, and the modified matrix is displayed again.

```
{   double y[16] = {1.,0.,0.,0.,2.,3.,0.,0.,4.,5.,6.,0.,
                    7.,8.,9.,10.};
    matrix e(y,4,4);    //2
    e.dumpall();
    Gram_Schmidt( e ); //4
    e.dumpall(); }
```

Member function dumpall() lists each row number followed by the content of that row. The initial content of e is the content of y:

```
1|1|0|0|0
2|2|3|0|0
3|4|5|6|0
4|7|8|9|10
```

The example is designed so that each row, in order, incorporates one additional vector component. The effect of Gram_Schmidt() on this structure, then, is to convert it into the identity matrix **I**, all ones on the main diagonal, zeros elsewhere:

```
1|1|0|0|0
2|0|1|0|0
3|0|0|1|0
4|0|0|0|1
```

Note that the argument of Gram_Schmidt(matrix&) does not include the keyword const, because the subroutine is specifically intended to modify its input, in place. Moreover, the actual data storage is provided by array y. It is y that is changed into a sequence of ones and zeros.

4.1.2 Conjugate Directions Defined

Two vectors $\mathbf{x}_1$ and $\mathbf{x}_2$ are said to be *orthogonal* if their scalar product $\mathbf{x}_1^T\mathbf{x}_2 = 0$. Two vectors $\mathbf{y}_1$ and $\mathbf{y}_2$ are said to be *conjugate*, with respect to a matrix **G**, if the product $\mathbf{y}_1^T \mathbf{G} \mathbf{y}_2 = 0$. We could say that $\mathbf{y}_1$ and $\mathbf{G} \mathbf{y}_2$ are orthogonal. We could also say that $\mathbf{x}_1$ and $\mathbf{x}_2$ are conjugate with respect to the identity matrix $\mathbf{I}$: $\mathbf{x}_1^T \mathbf{I} \mathbf{x}_2 = 0$.

4.2 STEEPEST DESCENT

To solve the equation $\mathbf{Ax} = \mathbf{b}$ iteratively by adjusting $\mathbf{x}$, an extraordinarily clever scheme is obviously required. In one dimension the problem is quite simple. If $ax = b = a(x_0 + \Delta x)$, where the initial guess for x is x_0, the adjustment Δx required to satisfy the equation is then $(b - ax_0)/a$. In multiple dimensions the challenge is to adjust all the components of $\mathbf{x}$ simultaneously and with coordination. Determining a vector adjustment $\Delta \mathbf{x}$ is, in a sense, picking a direction in which to move.

The quadratic scalar function $f(\mathbf{x}) = \frac{1}{2}\mathbf{x}^T\mathbf{Ax} - \mathbf{x}^T\mathbf{b}$ has a gradient $\nabla f(\mathbf{x}) = \mathbf{Ax} - \mathbf{b}$. The gradient of this function vanishes where the function attains its minimum value. In other words, minimizing $f(\mathbf{x})$ is equivalent to solving $\mathbf{Ax} = \mathbf{b}$. The direction in which $f(\mathbf{x})$ decreases most rapidly is the direction of its (negative) gradient, $-\nabla f(\mathbf{x}) = \mathbf{b} - \mathbf{Ax}$. We also call this vector the *residual*, defining it as $\mathbf{r} = \mathbf{b} - \mathbf{Ax}$.

If the objective is to minimize $f(\mathbf{x})$, the direction $\mathbf{r}$ in which $f(\mathbf{x})$ decreases most rapidly seems a natural direction in which to change $\mathbf{x}$. The question then becomes how large a step to take. The updated value for $\mathbf{x}$ will be $\mathbf{x} + \alpha\mathbf{r}$, and the value of α that, in turn, minimizes $f(\mathbf{x} + \alpha\mathbf{r})$ is $\alpha = \mathbf{r}^T\mathbf{r}/\mathbf{r}^T\mathbf{Ar}$. The practical procedure based on these choices is called the *steepest-descent method*, and it is coded as

```
unsigned steepest_descent(const sparse& A, real_vector& b,
    double tol)
{//G&VL (10.2.1) p517
    unsigned k = 0; double alf, rsq;
    real_vector x(b.N()), r(b.N());  x.init();  r = b;
    while( (rsq = r*r) > tol ){ k++;
        alf = rsq / (r*(A*r));                    //6
        x += (alf * r);
        r = b - A * x;           }
    b = x;  x.zap();  r.zap();
    return k;
}
```

In the mathematical derivation that I have omitted, it is required that $\mathbf{A}^T = \mathbf{A}$ (i.e., $\mathbf{A}$ must be symmetric). Also, the form of the denominator in line 6 of the code necessitates $\mathbf{r}^T\mathbf{Ar} > 0$. All together, this means that $\mathbf{A}$ must be *symmetric positive definite*.

4.2.1 Review Question

Identify all `temp_real_vector` quantities in the `while()` loop above.

Answer: `(A*r)`, `(alf * r)`, `A * x`, and `b - A * x`. Also note that changing one word in the argument list would change this from a `sparse` subroutine to a `matrix` subroutine.

4.3 CONJUGATE GRADIENT

The steepest-descent method leaves room for improvement. In some cases it takes too many too small steps in arriving at the solution, even though it does eventually get there. Suggestions for improving the speed of convergence mainly involve selecting directions less obvious than **r** itself in which to move. If a different direction **u** is chosen, the expression for the step size α must change to `alf = u*r / (u*(A*u))`, replacing line 6 of the code. An obvious restriction is that **u** must not be perpendicular to **r**; else `alf` would be zero and the algorithm would remain forever on the same spot.

In the method of conjugate gradients a particular set $\{\mathbf{p}_k\}$ of direction vectors, mutually conjugate with respect to **A**, is developed in coordination with a sequence $\{\mathbf{r}_k\}$ of mutually orthogonal residual vectors. In essence, two interleaved Gram–Schmidt procedures work together to assure that $\mathbf{r}_i^T\mathbf{r}_j = 0$ and $\mathbf{p}_i^T\mathbf{A}\mathbf{p}_j = 0$, if i and j designate different passes through the iteration loop. One version of the conjugate-gradient method is coded as

```
double CG_Version_One( const sparse& A, real_vector& b)
{//Beckman (in R&W [26]) p70
    double alf, bet, lam;
    real_vector x(b.N()), r(b.N()), p(b.N()), Ap(b.N());
                x.init();   r = b;   p = b;
    for(unsigned k=0; k<b.N(); k++){
        Ap = A * p;   lam = p * Ap;   alf = (r * p) / lam;
        x += alf * p;
        r -= alf * Ap;
        bet = -(r * Ap) / lam;
        p = r + bet * p;
    }
    b = x;   x.zap();   r.zap();   p.zap();   Ap.zap();
    return r*r;
}
```

Compared with `steepest_descent()`, `CG_Version_One()` uses two additional `real_vectors`: p is a new variable, and Ap provides explicit temporary storage for the product $\mathbf{A}\mathbf{p}_k$. The sequence of direction vectors $\mathbf{p}_k$ is specially constructed to span the n-dimensional space, and the solution x is constructed as their weighted sum $\mathbf{x} = \Sigma\alpha_k\mathbf{p}_k$. Therefore, exactly n values of k are required, where b.N() corresponds to n. If all goes well, the return value r*r will reflect only round-off error (squared).

A fully practical version of the conjugate-gradient method must allow for the possibility that an acceptable, if imprecise, solution x may be found in significantly fewer than n iterations. Moreover, for large n, round-off error may lead to a loss of orthogonality among the residuals, so that a full n iterations is not supportable. The following version of the algorithm is adapted to keep account of the magnitudes of the residuals:

```
void Pos_Def_Con_Grad( const sparse& A, real_vector& b)
{//G&VL 10.2.7 p524
   unsigned n = A.N();   if(A.M() != n || b.N() != n)
      exit(1);
   double* space = new double [3*n];
   memset(space, 0, 3*n*sizeof(double));
   real_vector r(space,n), p(space+n,n), Ap(space+n*2,n);
   double alf, bet, rho_1, rho_2, eps = 1.e-10;

   r = b; b.init(); rho_2 = r*r; eps = (eps*eps*rho_2);
   p = r;  Ap = A*p;  alf = rho_2 / (p*Ap);
   b += (p*alf);  r -= (Ap*alf);  rho_1 = r*r;

   for (unsigned k=2; k<=n+3; k++){
      if(rho_1 < eps) break;
      bet = rho_1 / rho_2;  p *= bet;  p += r;
      Ap = A*p;  alf = rho_1 / (p*Ap);
      b += (p*alf);  r -= (Ap*alf);  rho_2 = rho_1;
         rho_1 = r*r;
   }
   delete space;
}
```

This subroutine checks input parameters and allocates its own explicit work space, using new and delete. It accumulates the solution directly into b. It quits when the magnitude of r is less than eps times the input magnitude of b. The algorithm in this form requires previous values of r*r one (rho_1) and two (rho_2) iterations back. The loop is allowed to exceed slightly the theoretically maximum n iterations.

4.3.1 Review Question

Identify the real_vector assignment operator (=) in the code above and suggest an alternative to using it.

Answer: It occurs in Ap = A*p. We could write a member function real_
vector& real_vector::byM (const sparse&, const real_vector&);
analogous to the byc() function, and employ it as in Ap.byM(A, p);.

4.3.2 Comparison

The following example is set up to apply the foregoing three methods to the same small problem:

```
{   double y[4] = {1.,1.,1.,1.};
    real_vector b(4), q(y,4);
    sparse A(4,4,10);
    for(int i=1; i<=4; i++) A(i,i) = (double)i;
    for(int i=1; i<4;  i++) A(i+1,i) = A(i,i+1) = 1.;
    print_matrix( A );                                    //6
    b = A * q;
    b.dumpall();                                          //8
// TEST CODE GOES HERE
    b.dumpall();                                          //10
}
```

Line 6 prints out sparse matrix A, which is

```
|1|1|0|0|
|1|2|1|0|
|0|1|3|1|
|0|0|1|4|
```

Line 8 prints out the input vector b = A * q;, which the reader can verify is

```
|2|4|5|5
```

The test code for the first case (steepest descent) is

```
unsigned Q;
Q = steepest_descent (A, b, 1.e-10);
printf(" Q %d\n", Q);
```

The printf statement reports the number of iterations, and line 10 prints the output result contained in b:

```
Q 90
|0.99998|1.00001|0.999993|1
```

The value of tol input to steepest_descent is 10^{-10}. The subroutine returns when the squared magnitude of the residual r*r has decreased below that. So the final value of x returned in b differs from the correct answer at the level of 10^{-5}, and it required 90 iterations to get there!

The test code for the second case (conjugate gradient 1) is

```
double Q; Q = CG_Version_One (A, b);
printf(" Q %G\n", Q);
```

The number of iterations in `CG_Version_One` is always `b.N()` (i.e., four). The `printf` statement reports the final value of `r*r`, and line 10 prints the output result contained in b:

```
Q 2.09623E-29
|1|1|1|1
```

The squared residual returned is essentially round-off error, and the answer is correct.

The test code for the third case (conjugate gradient 2) is

```
Pos_Def_Con_Grad (A, b);,
```

and a print statement `r.dumpall();` is included within the subroutine itself. This test displays the residual vector r at each stage of iteration, and then the correct result:

```
k=1:|0.675079|0.687697|-0.299685|-0.520505
k=2:|0.128485|-0.0643534|-0.192175|0.192263
k=3:|0.0467142|-0.04357|0.0309931|-0.0148228
k=4:|-2.22045e-16|-9.29812e-16|-2.328e-15|-2.9126e-15
output b:|1|1|1|1
```

In the final iteration, residual **r** has been annihilated to the level of round-off error.

4.4 EXTENSION TO GENERAL MATRICES

The steepest descent and conjugate gradient methods incorporate the restrictive assumption that matrix **A** is positive definite and symmetric. However, these methods can be applied to more general matrices with a bit of preprocessing. Given **Ax** = **b**, multiply both sides from the left by $\mathbf{A}^T$: $\mathbf{A}^T\mathbf{Ax} = \mathbf{A}^T\mathbf{b}$. The product matrix $(\mathbf{A}^T\mathbf{A})$ is symmetric and nonnegative definite by construction, even if **A** is rectangular with more rows than columns! This is sufficient to apply the conjugate-gradient method to the modified equation.

The theoretical distinction between positive definite and nonnegative definite is that in the latter case, we are only guaranteed that $\mathbf{p}_k^T(\mathbf{A}^T\mathbf{A})\mathbf{p}_k \geq 0$, where $\mathbf{p}_k$ is the direction vector arising in stage k of the conjugate-gradient iteration. In other words, the crucial denominator (`p*Ap`) can vanish. If it does not, the solution **x** obtained for the preprocessed equation is also the exact solution of the original equation $\mathbf{Ax} = \mathbf{b}$. If this denominator does degenerate to zero upon reaching iteration k, say, the interim result $\mathbf{x}_k$ accumulated up to that point is theoretically a *least-squares* solution of the original equation.

4.4.1 Example

We incorporate the following additional code as a test case in the code for the previous comparison (Section 4.3.2):

```
sparse AtA(4,4,16);
    for(int i=1; i<=4; i++)                              //2
        for(int j=1; j<=4; j++)
            for(int k=1; k<=4; k++)
                AtA(i,j) += A.getval(k,i)*A.getval(k,j); //5
print_matrix( AtA );

b = b * A;                                               //8
b.dumpall();
Pos_Def_Con_Grad (AtA, b);
```

Lines 2 through 5 initialize the product matrix $\mathbf{A}^T\mathbf{A}$, which is printed out as

```
|2|3|1|0|
|3|6|5|1|
|1|5|11|7|
|0|1|7|17|
```

This is symmetric, of course, and less sparse than $\mathbf{A}$. Line 8 computes $\mathbf{A}^T\mathbf{b}$, in the form of $(\mathbf{b}^T\mathbf{A})^T$, which is printed out as

```
|6|15|24|25
```

Then `Pos_Def_Con_Grad` is applied to $\mathbf{A}^T\mathbf{A}$ and $\mathbf{A}^T\mathbf{b}$ and prints out

```
k=1:|2.2948|3.42696|0.21351|-2.8119
k=2:|0.541137|0.229797|-0.955119|0.649163
k=3:|0.0178979|-0.0136697|0.00575283|-0.0016164
k=4:|2.64996e-14|-8.82974e-16|-2.43479e-13|-5.73701e-13
output b:|1|1|1|1
```

Therefore, the extended method is demonstrated to produce the same answer in a case where the original problem was easily solvable.

4.5 BICONJUGATE GRADIENT

It was outlined in Section 4.2 that the conjugate-gradient method is based on the theory of minimizing $f(\mathbf{x}) = \frac{1}{2}\mathbf{x}^T\mathbf{Ax} - \mathbf{x}^T\mathbf{b}$, which in turn implies that $\nabla f(\mathbf{x}) = \mathbf{Ax} - \mathbf{b} = 0$.

Thus we obtain a solution of $\mathbf{Ax} = \mathbf{b}$. The biconjugate-gradient method is based instead on the theory of minimizing the squared residual $\Phi(\mathbf{x}) = \frac{1}{2}|\mathbf{Ax} - \mathbf{b}|^2$. The corresponding gradient is $\nabla\Phi(\mathbf{x}) = \mathbf{A}^{\mathrm{T}}(\mathbf{Ax} - \mathbf{b})$. The right-hand side of this relation is the same form that appeared in Section 4.4. If we carried out the multiplication indicated, we would again have the modified matrix $\mathbf{A}^{\mathrm{T}}\mathbf{A}$ and the modified vector $\mathbf{A}^{\mathrm{T}}\mathbf{b}$. In the biconjugate-gradient approach, however, $\mathbf{A}^{\mathrm{T}}$ and $\mathbf{A}$ are carried forward in the algorithm as distinct entities.

The biconjugate-gradient method removes the restriction that $\mathbf{A}$ must be positive definite. It has two advantages compared to working with the product $\mathbf{A}^{\mathrm{T}}\mathbf{A}$. The results obtained using the product matrix and the conjugate-gradient method are doomed to be less accurate. The product matrix is likely to be significantly less sparse than $\mathbf{A}$ itself.

The biconjugate-gradient method that I have coded retains the restriction that $\mathbf{A}$ must be symmetric:

```
void Sym_Indef_Bicon_Grad( const sparse& A,
   real_vector& b)
{
   unsigned n = A.N();   if(A.M() != n || b.N() != n)
      exit(1);
   double* space = new double [5*n];
   memset(space, 0, 5*n*sizeof(double));
   real_vector r(space,n), s(space+n,n), p(space+n*2,n),
               q(space+n*3,n), Ap(space+n*4,n);
   double alf, bet, rho_1, rho_2, eps = 1.e-10;
   eps = eps*eps*(b*b);
   r = b; b.init(); s = r*A; rho_2 = s*r;
   p = r; q = A*p;  alf = rho_2 / (q*q);
   b += (p*alf);   r -= (q*alf);   s -= ((q*A)*alf);
      rho_1 = s*r;

   for (unsigned k=2; k<=n+3; k++)
   {
      if(r*r < eps) break;
      bet = rho_1 / rho_2;  p *= bet;  p += r;  q *= bet;
         q += s;
      Ap = A*p; alf = rho_1 / (q*Ap);
      b += (p*alf);   r -= (Ap*alf);  s -= ((q*A)*alf);
      rho_2 = rho_1;  rho_1 = s*r;
   }
   delete space;
}
```

Compared with `Pos_Def_Con_Grad`, this subroutine contains two additional work vectors: s to contain $\mathbf{A}^{\mathrm{T}}\mathbf{r}$ and q to contain $\mathbf{A}^{\mathrm{T}}\mathbf{p}$. This algorithm is said to be equivalent to the positive definite version, with dot products of the form $\mathbf{r}^T\mathbf{r}$ superseded by the form $\mathbf{r}^T\mathbf{A}\mathbf{r}$ [25].

4.5.1 Example

Subroutine `Sym_Indef_Bicon_Grad` was inserted as an additional test case into the comparison code of Section 4.3.2. With a statement `r.dumpall();` incorporated within the k loop itself, the following printout was obtained, comparable in this case to the results for `Pos_Def_Con_Grad`:

```
k=1:|0.699042|0.747606|-0.20383|-0.420657
k=2:|0.168132|-0.00793222|-0.192985|0.149673
k=3:|0.0535651|-0.0415592|0.0183553|-0.00554122
k=4:|-6.52256e-16|-2.0331e-15|-4.85029e-15|-7.43416e-15
output b:|1|1|1|1
```

4.5.2 Review Question

Compare and contrast $\mathbf{x}^T\mathbf{A}$ and $\mathbf{A}^T\mathbf{x}$.

Answer: The row vector that results in the first case is the transpose of the column vector that results in the second case if we are distinguishing row vectors from column vectors. In both cases each component of the resultant vector is the dot product of $\mathbf{x}$ with a column of $\mathbf{A}$. The *crucial* fact is that the number of components in $\mathbf{x}$ must equal the number of rows in $\mathbf{A}$. Therefore, x*A models $\mathbf{x}^T\mathbf{A}$ and $(\mathbf{A}^T\mathbf{x})^T$.

4.6 LEAST SQUARES

Section 4.4 implies that if we are given the equation $\mathbf{A}\mathbf{x} = \mathbf{b}$, where $\mathbf{A}$ is rectangular ($m \times n$) with more rows than columns ($m > n$), the solution of the auxiliary problem $(\mathbf{A}^T\mathbf{A})\mathbf{x} = \mathbf{A}^T\mathbf{b}$ amounts to a least-squares solution of the original equation. In Section 6.3 we will compare and contrast several methods of least-squares solution and identify this one as the *normal equations* approach.

In this book I prefer to emphasize methods that do not require preparatory calculations, such as forming the normal matrix $(\mathbf{A}^T\mathbf{A})$. If $\mathbf{A}$ is sparse, we strive to avoid modifying it at all, let alone *squaring* it. In Chapter 6 I describe a more elegant approach for applying conjugate-gradient solutions to least-squares problems. We are instructed to work a different auxiliary problem: solving the $(m + n) \times (m + n)$ system

$$\left[\begin{array}{c|c} \mathbf{I} & \mathbf{A} \\ \hline \mathbf{A}^T & \mathbf{0} \end{array}\right]\left[\begin{array}{c} \mathbf{r} \\ \hline \mathbf{x} \end{array}\right] = \left[\begin{array}{c} \mathbf{b} \\ \hline \mathbf{0} \end{array}\right] \quad \text{or} \quad \mathbf{B}\mathbf{x}' = \mathbf{b}'$$

This is an example of partitioned matrix notation. It shows how a large matrix is to be constructed out of smaller ones. $\mathbf{I}$ is the $m \times m$ identity matrix, and $\mathbf{0}$ is an $n \times n$

matrix of zeros. The top row states $\mathbf{r} + \mathbf{Ax} = \mathbf{b}$ (i.e., $\mathbf{r} = \mathbf{b} - \mathbf{Ax}$), which is the definition of the residual vector. The bottom row reads $\mathbf{A}^T\mathbf{r} = 0$. The two together imply that $\mathbf{A}^T(\mathbf{b} - \mathbf{Ax}) = 0$, which is the condition for minimizing $|\mathbf{Ax} - \mathbf{b}|^2 = |\mathbf{r}|^2$. The problem $\mathbf{Bx'} = \mathbf{b'}$ is appropriate input for a conjugate-gradient method.

In Section 6.3 an example is presented for determining the parameters of a straight line that best fits a set of 10 data points, in the least-squares sense. The augmented matrix $\mathbf{B}$ and right-hand side, $\mathbf{b'}$, for that problem are

$$
\mathbf{B} =
\left[
\begin{array}{cccccccccc|cc}
1 & & & & & & & & & & -5 & 2 \\
& 1 & & & & & & & & & -1 & 4 \\
& & 1 & & & & & & & & 2 & 6 \\
& & & 1 & & & & & & & 3 & 7 \\
& & & & 1 & & & & & & 10 & 11 \\
& & & & & 1 & & & & & 9 & 11 \\
& & & & & & 1 & & & & 1 & 5 \\
& & & & & & & 1 & & & 1 & 6 \\
& & & & & & & & 1 & & 7 & 9 \\
& & & & & & & & & 1 & 4 & 8 \\
\hline
-5 & -1 & 2 & 3 & 10 & 9 & 1 & 1 & 7 & 4 & & \\
2 & 4 & 6 & 7 & 11 & 11 & 5 & 6 & 9 & 8 & &
\end{array}
\right],
\quad
\mathbf{b'} =
\left[
\begin{array}{c}
1 \\ 1 \\ 1 \\ 1 \\ 1 \\ 1 \\ 1 \\ 1 \\ 1 \\ 1 \\ \hline 0 \\ 0
\end{array}
\right]
$$

The point I wish to emphasize is that the numbers in the last two rows and columns of $\mathbf{B}$ are the raw data points themselves. Despite the formidable appearance of the partitioned matrix, the mechanics of setting up this problem are made trivial by our straightforward manner of handling `sparse` matrices. The code to set up and solve this example is

```
{   double data[20] = {-5., 2.,-1., 4., 2., 6., 3., 7.,
                       10.,11.,9.,11., 1., 5., 1., 6.,
                        7., 9., 4., 8.};
    matrix A(data,10,2);
    sparse B(12,12,50);
    for(int i=1; i<=10; i++){ B(i,i) = 1.;
       for(int j=1; j<=2; j++)
          B(j+10,i) = B(i,j+10) = A(i,j); }

    real_vector b(12); b.init() += 1.; b(11) = b(12) = 0.;

    Pos_Def_Con_Grad( B, b);
    b.dumpall();
}
```

The last line here prints out the answer:

```
|-0.026678| 0.0732902|0.0480755|-0.0271233|0.0476302|
   0.0775528
| 0.123274|-0.0771074|0.0728449|-0.102322 |-0.125183|
   0.200382
```

The first 10 entries (**r**) are the best-fit residuals of the problem. The last two entries (**x**) are the parameters of the least-squares straight line. These parameters are the same values as in Section 6.3.1, where the problem is solved by a different method.

4.7 SUMMARY AND CONCLUSIONS

Definitions

Symmetric: $\mathbf{A}^T = \mathbf{A}$.
Positive definite: $\mathbf{r}^T \mathbf{A} \mathbf{r} > 0$ for all nontrivial $\mathbf{r}$.
Nonnegative definite or positive semidefinite: $\mathbf{r}^T \mathbf{A} \mathbf{r} \geq 0$.

Gram–Schmidt. If the rows of **A** are linearly independent, Gram_Schmidt (A); makes them orthonormal: A[i]*A[i] is 1 and A[i]*A[j] is 0.

Conjugate Gradient. If **A** is symmetric and positive definite, and the equation to be solved is $\mathbf{Ax} = \mathbf{b}$, Pos_Def_Con_Grad(A, b); overwrites solution **x** onto the right-hand side, **b**, and does not change **A**.

Biconjugate Gradient. If **A** is symmetric and the equation to be solved is $\mathbf{Ax} = \mathbf{b}$, Sym_Indef_Bicon_Grad(A, b); overwrites solution **x** onto right-hand side, **b**, and does not change **A**.

Least-Squares Application. If **A** is $m \times n$, with $m > n$, to obtain a least-squares solution of the problem $\mathbf{Ax} = \mathbf{b}$, construct the built-up problem

$$\left[\begin{array}{c|c} \mathbf{I} & \mathbf{A} \\ \hline \mathbf{A}^T & \mathbf{0} \end{array} \right] \left[\begin{array}{c} \mathbf{r} \\ \mathbf{x} \end{array} \right] = \left[\begin{array}{c} \mathbf{b} \\ \mathbf{0} \end{array} \right]$$

that is, $\mathbf{Bx}' = \mathbf{b}'$, and apply a conjugate-gradient subroutine to **B** and **b**'. The residuals **r** are returned as well as the answer **x**.

5 Triangular Matrices

In this chapter I present methods for solving the matrix equation $\mathbf{Ax} = \mathbf{b}$ in the important special case that $\mathbf{A}$ is triangular. We say that $\mathbf{A}$ is *upper triangular* if all the entries *below* its main diagonal are zero, and *lower triangular* if all the entries *above* its main diagonal are zero. (Lower- and upper-triangular matrices are sometimes designated left- and right-triangular, respectively.) Triangular matrices are important because they correspond to systems of equations in which the solution is obvious and simple to implement. The methods we will see later for solving more general systems of equations mainly involve forcing their corresponding matrices into triangular form.

5.0.1 Example

Suppose that your grandfather has just made the final payment of principal and interest, in the amount of $183.44, on his 8% 30-year mortgage. Estimate the original amount of the loan.

A 30-year mortgage repayment scheme is structured as 360 monthly installments of equal size s, allocated partly to interest and partly to retiring the balance, b. For the final payment, $s = b(1 + x)$, where $x = 0.08/12$, the monthly interest rate. More generally, $b_{now} - b_{next} = s - xb_{now}$; the reduction in balance from now to the next payment equals the amount by which s exceeds the interest now due. This leads to an upper-triangular system of 360 equations in which the last four equations are

$$(1 + x)\, b_{357} - b_{358} = s$$
$$(1 + x)\, b_{358} - b_{359} = s$$
$$(1 + x)\, b_{359} - b_{360} = s$$
$$(1 + x)\, b_{360} = s$$

It is immediately apparent that $b_{360} = s/(1 + x)$, and that from there we could in principle work backward to b_1, the initial balance: $b_{359} = (s + b_{360})/(1 + x)$, $b_{358} = (s + b_{359})/(1 + x)$, $b_{357} = (s + b_{358})/(1 + x)$, and so on. We could code a few lines to carry out this recursion, but it will be more instructive to illustrate a standard triangular solver using this uncomplicated example.

The matrix $\mathbf{A}$ for this problem is of dimensions 360 by 360, but sparse. The last four rows of the last four columns are

$$\begin{bmatrix} 1+x & -1 & & \\ & 1+x & -1 & \\ & & 1+x & -1 \\ & & & 1+x \end{bmatrix}$$

In other words, $\mathbf{A}$ contains $(1+x)$ everywhere on the main diagonal, and -1 everywhere on the first superdiagonal. The unknown $\mathbf{x}$ is a vector representing the sequence of monthly balances: $[b_1, b_2, \ldots, b_{359}, b_{360}]^\mathrm{T}$. The right-hand side, $\mathbf{b}$, is a vector of dimension 360, and each of its entries is the same constant payment, s. The code to solve this problem by a general method is

```
{   sparse A(360,360,719);
    real_vector b(360);
    double factr, s = 183.44;   factr = 1.+(.08/12.);
    for(int i=1; i<=360; i++){ A(i,i) = factr;
       b(i) = s; }                                          //4
    for(int i=1; i<=359; i++)  A(i,i+1) = -1.;              //5
    b.Usolve( A );                                          //6
    b.dumpall(5);                                           //7
}
```

Line 4 initializes each diagonal element of A to `factr`, representing $(1+x)$, and each component of b to the constant payment value s. Line 5 sets each super-diagonal element of A to -1. Line 6 calls the `real_vector` member function Usolve, which carries out the recursion and overwrites the resulting sequence of balances onto b; Usolve, the subject of the next section, does not modify A. Line 7 writes out the first five values in the solution, which are

|24999.8|24983.1|24966.2|24949.2|24932.1

Therefore, we estimate that Grandfather's original loan balance was $25,000.00. The result is inexact because of rounding to the nearest penny.

5.1 BACKWARD SOLVERS

Upper-triangular systems of equations are solved recursively by substituting solved values into unsolved equations working backward from the final equation. For each row of the corresponding matrix, it is necessary to divide by the diagonal element. If $\mathbf{Ux} = \mathbf{b}$, $x_i = (b_i - \Sigma_{(j>i)} u_{ij}x_j)/u_{ii}$. The summation is of known values of x_j (i.e., $j > i$). The following subroutine implements this algorithm for a sparse upper-triangular matrix:

```
real_vector& real_vector::Usolve(const sparse& U)
{
   if(n != U.ncols) exit(1);
   element* elem;  unsigned i,j,k;   double Uii;
   if ((Uii = U.getval(n,n)) == 0.) exit(1); (*this)(n)
      /= Uii;
   for(i=n-1; i>=1; i--){                              //6
      if ((Uii = U.getval(i,i)) == 0.) exit(1);
      elem = U.row[i-1];
      while ((k = elem->next) != 0){ elem = U.e+k;   //9
         if ((j = elem->col) > i)
            (*this)(i) -= (elem->value)*((*this)(j));
      }
      (*this)(i) /= Uii;
   }
   return *this;
}
```

This is a real_vector member function, invoked as in b.Usolve(U); b contains the right-hand-side data **b** on input, and the solution **x** is overwritten onto it. Within the code, b is represented by (*this). The for() loop beginning in line 6 is the row-by-row backward recursion. The while() loop beginning in line 9 traverses each row as in Section 3.2.2, looking for nonzero elements to subtract. Each diagonal element is required to be nonzero, and only previously solved rows ($j > i$) are included in the subtraction.

In the conventions that I follow in my code, a lower-triangular matrix is assumed to contain all ones on its main diagonal, so that actual storage for the main diagonal is not required. This practice permits one lower-triangular matrix and one upper-triangular matrix to coexist within the bounds of one square matrix. Apart from that, the transpose of a lower-triangular matrix is an upper-triangular matrix, so that a backward solution will work. If a problem is stated as $\mathbf{x}^T\mathbf{L} = \mathbf{b}^T$, where **L** is lower triangular, it can be solved as $\mathbf{L}^T\mathbf{x} = \mathbf{b}$, where $\mathbf{L}^T$ is upper triangular. Because of the storage convention, a special subroutine is required:

```
real_vector& real_vector::TLsolve(const sparse& s)
{
   if(n != s.mrows) exit(1);
   element* elem;  unsigned i,j,k;
   for (j=n-1; j>=1; j--){
      elem = s.col[j-1];
      while ((k = elem->mext) != 0){ elem = s.e+k;
```

```
      if ((i = elem->row)   >  j)
          (*this)(j) -= (elem->value)*((*this)(i));
    }
  }
  return *this;
}
```

Compared to `Usolve`, the roles of rows and columns are interchanged, reflecting the implied transposition of the matrix. This code is simpler because diagonal element `Uii` is not involved.

5.2 FORWARD SOLVERS

Normally, a lower-triangular matrix **L** appears in the context **Lx** = **b**, corresponding to a system of equations

$$
\begin{aligned}
x_1 &= b_1 \\
l_{21}x_1 + x_2 &= b_2 \\
l_{31}x_1 + l_{32}x_2 + x_3 &= b_3 \\
l_{41}x_1 + l_{42}x_2 + l_{43}x_3 + x_4 &= b_4, \quad \text{etc.}
\end{aligned}
$$

One manner of solving this system is perfectly clear: $x_1 = b_1$, $x_2 = b_2 - l_{21}x_1$, $x_3 = b_3 - l_{31}x_1 - l_{32}x_2$, $x_4 = b_4 - l_{41}x_1 - l_{42}x_2 - l_{43}x_3$, and so on. This is the row-by-row approach we followed in the backward solvers. To solve each row in its turn, we accessed all the previously solved x_j. There is an alternative, however; as each new x_j becomes known, we can presubtract its contribution $l_{ij}x_j$ from each of the succeeding b_i. This amounts to a column-by-column procedure. By the time we get to column i, we have already carried out $x_i = b_i - \sum_{j<i} l_{ij}x_j$. The prime example of a forward solver based on this approach is

```
real_vector& real_vector::Lsolve(const sparse& s)
{
   if(n != s.ncols) exit(1);
   element* elem;   unsigned i,j,k;   double x;
   for(j=1; j<n; j++){
      if((x = (*this)(j)) == 0.) continue;              //6
      elem = s.col[j-1];
      while ((k = elem->mext) != 0){ elem = s.e+k;      //8
         if ((i = elem->row) > j)
            (*this)(i) -= (elem->value) * x;            //10
      }
```

```
    }
    return *this;
}
```

This subroutine assumes that lower-triangular sparse s contains ones on its main diagonal, but no attempt is made to access them. This is a real_vector member function that overwrites the solution onto the input. The columnwise forward recursion means that each component (*this)(j) is finalized just as we get to it. Line 6 bears some explanation; x is the finalized output value of component j of the input–output real_vector. If it is 0, there is nothing more to do with it; continue in C and C++ means to branch back to the for() statement without executing the rest of the statements within the loop. If x is not zero, line 8 scans column j looking for nonzero coefficients l_{ij} to incorporate into the weighted subtraction on line 10.

To handle the case of a transposed upper-triangular matrix when the problem is stated in the form $\mathbf{U}^T\mathbf{x} = \mathbf{b}$, a forward solver is required that employs the diagonal elements of $\mathbf{U}$ as divisors. Such a subroutine is

```
real_vector& real_vector::TUsolve(const sparse& s)
{
    if(n != s.mrows) exit(1);
    element* elem;  unsigned i,j,k;  double Uii, x;
    if ((Uii = s.getval(1,1)) == 0.) exit(1);
        x = (ptr[0] /= Uii);
    for(i=1; i<n; i++){
        if(x != 0.){
            elem = s.row[i-1];
            while ((k = elem->next) != 0){ elem = s.e+k;
                if ((j = elem->col)  >  i)
                    ptr[j-1] -= (elem->value) * x;
            }
        }
        if ((Uii = s.getval(i+1,i+1)) == 0.) exit(1);
        x = (ptr[i] /= Uii);
    }
    return *this;
}
```

Like the previous three solvers, TUsolve is a real_vector member function. It directly accesses real_vector protected members ptr and n. Class real_vector in its entirety is a friend of class sparse. That explains why all four solvers are allowed access to sparse private members e, mrows, ncols, row, and col. Structure element is entirely public. There are no particular restrictions on using expressions such as elem->next once you have gained access to (*elem), which belongs to s.

C++ technicalities aside, this code is more complicated than `Lsolve` because it divides each x by `Uii` to finalize it, and it must therefore require that no diagonal element is zero. Compared to `Lsolve`, the roles of rows and columns are interchanged, reflecting the implied transposition of the matrix.

5.3 SPLINE INTERPOLATION

A traditional spline is a flexible drafting tool that a naval architect employs to draw a fair curve through fixed points outlining a ship's hull. By extension, a mathematical spline is an algorithm for defining a maximally smooth curve that passes through a given set of fixed points. The variety of spline that we examine is termed a *cubic spline* [30]. This algorithm provides an interesting example of solution by forward and backward recursion.

We are given a sequence of points (x_k, y_k) in a plane, with $x_k > x_{k-1}$. Each interval $d_k \equiv x_k - x_{k-1}$ is variable. The algorithm prescribes a kind of piecewise interpolation, interval by interval. Consider the interval between x_{k-1} and x_k. To simplify the notation, define $u \equiv (x - x_{k-1})/d_k$ and $1 - u \equiv (x_k - x)/d_k$. In this interval, then, *linear* interpolation between the two endpoints takes the appealingly simple form $y(x) = y_k u + y_{k-1}(1 - u)$. To generalize this linear interpolation to cubic interpolation, we need one additional parameter c_k provided for each point. The form of the cubic interpolation within each interval then becomes

$$y(x) = (y_k - c_k)u + (y_{k-1} - c_{k-1})(1 - u) + c_k u^3 + c_{k-1}(1 - u)^3$$

Science comes into play through the criteria governing the c_k's. To begin with, $c_k = (d_k^2/6)g_k$ and $c_{k-1} = (d_k^2/6)g_{k-1}$. (Yes, d_k is the same in both instances.) Each g_k is the value of the second derivative of the interpolated curve at the corresponding x_k. By requiring that the slope (first derivative) of the interpolated curve at each point (x_k, y_k) be the same whether we approach the point from the left or the right, the following form of equation is obtained:

$$A_k g_{k-1} + B_k g_k + C_k g_{k+1} = D_k$$

where

$$A_k = \frac{d_k}{6}$$

$$B_k = \frac{d_k + d_{k+1}}{3}$$

$$C_k = \frac{d_{k+1}}{6}$$

$$D_k = \frac{y_{k+1} - y_k}{d_{k+1}} - \frac{y_k - y_{k-1}}{d_k}$$

The only unknowns in all this are the g_k. In the form of a matrix equation, this system becomes, say, $\mathbf{Tg} = \mathbf{d}$, where $\mathbf{g} = [g_1, \ldots, g_n]^T$, $\mathbf{d} = [D_1, \ldots, D_n]^T$, and $\mathbf{T}$ is the *tridiagonal* matrix

$$
\mathbf{T} = \begin{bmatrix}
B_1 & C_1 & & & \\
A_2 & B_2 & C_2 & & \\
& A_3 & B_3 & C_3 & \\
& & \ddots & \ddots & \ddots \\
& & & A_n & B_n
\end{bmatrix}
$$

To be clear about this, the B_k occupy the main diagonal; the A_k are on the subdiagonal, and the C_k are on the superdiagonal. I have taken the number of points to be $n + 2$, labeled 0 through $n + 1$, and I have set g_0 and g_{n+1} to zero. We have n equations in n unknowns.

The specialized way of solving a tridiagonal system such as this prescribes a forward and a backward recursion employing temporary variables W_k and S_k. On the forward recursion, set $W_1 = B_1$ and $S_1 = D_1$. Then for k values from 2 through n, compute

$$
W_k = B_k - \frac{A_k C_{k-1}}{W_{k-1}}
$$

$$
S_k = D_k - \frac{A_k S_{k-1}}{W_{k-1}}
$$

Each row in turn becomes

$$
W_k g_k + C_k g_{k+1} = S_k
$$

The last row of the matrix then yields an immediate solution, $g_n = S_n/W_n$. From this point we work backward from $n - 1$ to 1, solving

$$
g_k = \frac{S_k - C_k g_{k+1}}{W_k} \qquad \text{Q.E.D.}
$$

Earlier in this chapter we saw that forward recursion is connected with lower-triangular matrices and that backward recursion is connected with upper-triangular matrices. Indeed, the forward recursion here solves the matrix equation $\mathbf{Ls} = \mathbf{d}$, where $\mathbf{s} = [S_1, \ldots, S_n]^T$ and $\mathbf{L}$ is the lower-triangular matrix having ones on the main diagonal and $L_{ij} = A_i/W_j$ on the subdiagonal ($j = i - 1$). Specifically,

$$
\begin{bmatrix}
1 & & & \\
A_2/W_1 & 1 & & \\
& A_3/W_2 & 1 & \\
& & \ddots & \ddots
\end{bmatrix}
\begin{bmatrix}
S_1 \\ S_2 \\ S_3 \\ \vdots
\end{bmatrix}
=
\begin{bmatrix}
D_1 \\ D_2 \\ D_3 \\ \vdots
\end{bmatrix}
\Rightarrow
\begin{cases}
S_1 = D_1 \\
S_2 = D_2 - A_2 S_1/W_1 \\
S_3 = D_3 - A_3 S_2/W_2 \\
\vdots
\end{cases}
$$

Furthermore, the backward recursion solves $\mathbf{Ug} = \mathbf{s}$, where $\mathbf{U}$ is the upper-triangular matrix having $U_{ii} = W_i$ on the main diagonal and $U_{ij} = C_i$ on the superdiagonal $(j = i + 1)$. Specifically,

$$\begin{bmatrix} \ddots & \ddots & & \\ & W_{n-2} & C_{n-2} & \\ & & W_{n-1} & C_{n-1} \\ & & & W_n \end{bmatrix} \begin{bmatrix} \vdots \\ g_{n-2} \\ g_{n-1} \\ g_n \end{bmatrix} = \begin{bmatrix} \vdots \\ S_{n-2} \\ S_{n-1} \\ S_n \end{bmatrix}$$

$$\Rightarrow \begin{cases} \vdots \\ g_{n-2} = (S_{n-2} - C_{n-2}g_{n-1})/W_{n-2} \\ g_{n-1} = (S_{n-1} - C_{n-1}g_n)/W_{n-1} \\ g_n = S_n/W_n \end{cases}$$

This is a particular instance of matrix *factorization*. We have $\mathbf{Ug} = \mathbf{s} = \mathbf{L}^{-1}\mathbf{d}$, symbolically. Multiplying through by $\mathbf{L}$, we obtain $\mathbf{LUg} = \mathbf{d}$, and we conclude that $\mathbf{LU} = \mathbf{T}$. Tridiagonal systems are easy to factorize.

5.3.1 Exercise

Assuming that $w_k = b_k - a_k c_{k-1}/w_{k-1}$, verify the matrix multiplication

$$\begin{bmatrix} 1 & & & \\ a_2/w_1 & 1 & & \\ & a_3/w_2 & 1 & \\ & & a_4/w_3 & 1 \end{bmatrix} \times \begin{bmatrix} w_1 & c_1 & & \\ & w_2 & c_2 & \\ & & w_3 & c_3 \\ & & & w_4 \end{bmatrix} = \begin{bmatrix} b_1 & c_1 & & \\ a_2 & b_2 & c_2 & \\ & a_3 & b_3 & c_3 \\ & & a_4 & b_4 \end{bmatrix}$$

To crystallize all the foregoing mathematics, here is a subroutine to fit a cubic spline through a set of points, using Lsolve and Usolve:

```
void spline_fit( double x[], double y[], double g[],
    unsigned nint)
{
    unsigned n = nint-1;
    sparse T(n, n, n*3-2);
    real_vector d(g+1,n);
    for(int k=1; k<=n-1; k++){                       //6
        T(k+1,k) = (x[k+1]-x[k])/6.;                 //A(k+1)
        T(k,k+1) = (x[k+1]-x[k])/6.;}                //C(k)
    for(int k=1; k<=n; k++){                         //9
        d(k)   = (y[k+1]-y[k])/(x[k+1]-x[k])         //D(k)
               - (y[k]-y[k-1])/(x[k]-x[k-1]);
        T(k,k) = (x[k]-x[k-1]+x[k+1]-x[k])/3.;}      //B(k)
```

```
    for(int k=2; k<=n; k++){                         //13
        T(k,k)  -= T(k,k-1)*T(k-1,k)/T(k-1,k-1); //W(k)
        T(k,k-1) /= T(k-1,k-1);      }             //A(k)/W(k-1)
    d.Lsolve( T ).Usolve( T );
}
```

Arrays x, y, and g define the spline, with x and y (plus the first and last entries of g) initialized by the caller. The argument nint in the call list is the number of intervals, one less than the length of x, y, and g. The dimension of tridiagonal matrix T is n, one less than nint. Vector d overlays g, omitting the first and last entries.

Most of the code is concerned with setting up the problem. The matrix coefficients are stored in sparse T. The loop beginning on line 6 initializes the off-diagonal elements of T. We note, if we had not noticed already, that $C_k = A_{k+1}$. The loop starting on line 9 initializes the right-hand-side d and the diagonal elements of T. The line labeled //B(k) retains a redundancy, so that the code may parallel the theory. The loop that begins in line 13 modifies the diagonal and subdiagonal of the matrix as if it had been factorized in accordance with the exercise above.

The line d.Lsolve(T).Usolve(T); models $\mathbf{U}^{-1}\mathbf{L}^{-1}\mathbf{d}$. The diagonal and the superdiagonal of T belong to the upper-triangular factor $\mathbf{U}$, and the subdiagonal belongs to the lower-triangular factor $\mathbf{L}$, whose diagonal is assumed to be all ones. (A notation I admire is L\U for a matrix in this condition.) The result is written onto d, which is the same as g[1] through g[n].

An example of how spline_fit() can be applied is shown by the following code:

```
{  double x[7] = {0., 1., 1.5, 2.1, 2.8, 3.7, 5.};
   double y[7] = {0., 1., 2., 3., 3., 2., 1.};
   double g[7] = {0., 0., 0., 0., 0., 0., 0.};

   spline_fit( x, y, g, 6);

   for(double X=0.; X<=5.; X+=.1)
       PLOT_CURVE( X, splind( x, y, g, 6, X));
}
```

The seven data points and the cubic spline curve that fits through them are displayed in Fig. 5.1.

After spline_fit() determines the g[] coefficients, the subroutine that evaluates the cubic spline is

```
double splind( double x[], double y[], double g[],
        unsigned nint, double X)
{
    double d, u, v, w, cku, ckv, Y;
    if(X > x[nint]) return y[nint];
    if(X <= x[0] ) return y[0];
```

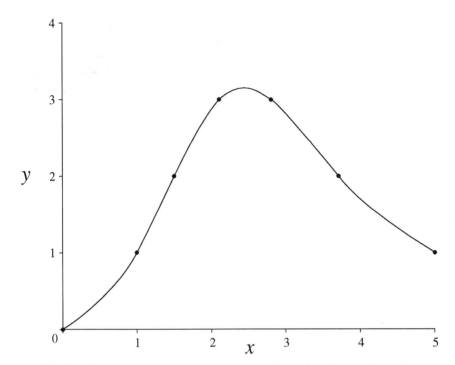

Fig. 5.1 Seven data points and a smooth curve interpolated by a cubic spline.

```
for(unsigned k=1; k<=nint; k++){
    if(X > x[k]) continue;                            //9
    d = x[k] - x[k-1];   u = (X - x[k-1])/d;    v = 1. - u;
    w = d*d/6.;             cku = g[k]*w*u;
        ckv = g[k-1]*w*v;
    Y = y[k]*u - cku + y[k-1]*v - ckv + cku*u*u
        + ckv*v*v;                                     //12
    break; }
    return Y;
}
```

The code in line 12 parallels the formula stated at the end of the second paragraph of Section 5.3, with v corresponding to $1 - u$. Line 9 determines which interval contains the input value of X. Of course, if g[] is input as all zeros, this subroutine carries out linear interpolation between pairs of points.

Line 9 guarantees that if x[k] and x[k-1] are the same, evaluation will never be attempted in interval k. This leads to a useful extension of basic spline methodology. We can incorporate intentional discontinuities into a set of x, y, and g arrays submitted to splind(). The right end of one continuous spline and the left end of a second continuous spline can share a common x value if this value is entered twice in consecutive entries of array x. Subroutine splind() will continue to operate in its normal manner, but the curve plotted will show a discontinuity in slope, curvature, or even value at the designated x location.

Basic spline methodology is easily extended from one function of one variable to curves in multidimensional space. Consider an ordered set of points $\mathbf{x}_k$ in two or three dimensions. Define a new parameter t, which is the cumulative chord length of the curve that fits through the $\mathbf{x}_k$: $t_k \equiv \sum_{j=1}^{k} |\mathbf{x}_j - \mathbf{x}_{j-1}|$, with $t_0 = 0$. Then fit each of the spatial components of $\mathbf{x}$ as a separate spline, taking t as the independent variable.

The following example demonstrates this approach in two dimensions. This code generates the closed curve shown in Fig. 5.2.

```
{   double  x[27] = {4.,4.3,5.7,6.,6.,13.,13.,13.3,14.7,
                     15.,15.,16.3,16.3,15.,14.,13.,11.,
                     9.,8.,8.,7.4,7.4,6.,4.,2.7,3.,4.};
    double  y[27] = {6.,5.3,5.3,6.,6.,6.,6.,5.3,5.3,6.,
                     6.,6.5,7.3,8.7,9.6,10.,10.3,10.,9.7,
                     9.7,8.8,8.8,8.6,8.1,6.9,6.3,6.};
    double gx[27] = {0.,0.,0.,0.,0.,0.,0.,0.,0.,0.,
                     0.,0.,0.,0.,0.,0.,0.,0.,0.,0.,
                     0.,0.,0.,0.,0.,0.};
```

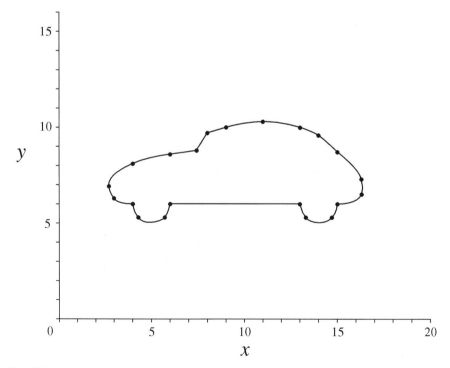

Fig. 5.2   Closed curve with intentional breaks in slope, formed as if by cubic spline interpolation.

```
double gy[27] = {0.,0.,0.,0.,0.,0.,0.,0.,0.,0.,
                 0.,0.,0.,0.,0.,0.,0.,0.,0.,0.,0.,
                 0.,0.,0.,0.,0.,0.};
double  t[27]; t[0] = 0.;
(more...)
```

These arrays are dimensioned for 27 points. Figure 5.2 shows only 21 distinct points, but six of these are recorded twice to provide intentional discontinuities between continuous spline segments. The reader will note consecutive identical values in the x and y arrays. The independent variable t is computed by the following loop:

```
for(int  k=1;  k<27;  k++)
   t[k]  =  t[k-1]  +  sqrt(  (x[k]-x[k-1])*(x[k]-x[k-1])
                          +  (y[k]-y[k-1])*(y[k]-y[k-1]));
```

The strategy is to fit x and y separately as functions of t. Within the 27 points are four groups to be fit as smooth curves:

```
spline_fit( t,     x,     gx,     3); //front wheel
spline_fit( t,     y,     gy,     3);
spline_fit( t+6,   x+6,   gx+6,   3); //rear wheel
spline_fit( t+6,   y+6,   gy+6,   3);
spline_fit( t+10,  x+10,  gx+10,  8); //trunk and top
spline_fit( t+10,  y+10,  gy+10,  8);
spline_fit( t+21,  x+21,  gx+21,  5); //hood and front
spline_fit( t+21,  y+21,  gy+21,  5);
```

The 27 points include two straight-line segments not requiring spline_fit. The segmented curve that results from this can be plotted as if it is a single spline:

```
for(double T=0.;  T<=t[26];  T+=.1)
   PLOT_CURVE( splind( t, x, gx, 26, T),
               splind( t, y, gy, 26, T) );
}
```

(The name PLOT_CURVE is illustrative only and does not represent the software I actually used.)

5.4 ROW AND COLUMN PERMUTATIONS

The matrix factorization methods that we will encounter later in the book are often more effective when applied not to arbitrary matrices but to matrices having their rows or columns carefully reordered. The convention is that if **P** and **Q** are *permutation* matrices, **PA** symbolizes **A** with its rows reordered and **AQ** represents **A** with its columns rearranged. The result of reordering columns and rows together is symbolized **PAQ**. Each permutation matrix itself appears like an identity matrix with the rows and columns rearranged, so that the ones no longer occupy the main diagonal. Each 1 remains the only entry in its respective row and column, however. The transpose of a permutation matrix is its own inverse: $\mathbf{P}^T\mathbf{P} = \mathbf{QQ}^T = \mathbf{I}$.

Symbolically, when we obtain the LU decomposition of the modified matrix **PAQ**, we write **LU = PAQ**. If the problem to be solved is **Ax = b**, we infer that

$$\mathbf{PAx} = \mathbf{Pb}$$

$$\mathbf{PAQQ}^T\mathbf{x} = \mathbf{Pb}$$

$$\mathbf{LUQ}^T\mathbf{x} = \mathbf{Pb}$$

$$\mathbf{Q}^T\mathbf{x} = \mathbf{U}^{-1}\mathbf{L}^{-1}\mathbf{Pb}$$

$$\mathbf{x} = \mathbf{QU}^{-1}\mathbf{L}^{-1}\mathbf{Pb}$$

In words, apply **P** to **b** before `Lsolve` and apply **Q** to the result after `Usolve`.

Row and column permutations are symbolized as matrices, but they are usually implemented more parsimoniously. I define a structure

```
struct pivot
{
    unsigned* R;   unsigned* C;
    unsigned m, n;

    pivot() {R = C = NULL;   m = n = 0;}
    pivot(unsigned, unsigned);
    void dumpall (unsigned = 0) const;
};
```

whose principal constructor is

```
pivot::pivot(unsigned i, unsigned j)
{
    m = i; n = j; R = new unsigned [m+n]; C = R + m;
    for (unsigned k=1; k<=m; k++) R[k-1] = k;
    for (unsigned k=1; k<=n; k++) C[k-1] = k;
}
```

Two arrays of `unsigned` integers, R and C, are initialized to 1 through m and 1 through n, respectively. Then whenever a subroutine swaps two rows of a `matrix` or `sparse`, it also swaps the two corresponding entries of R:

```
void pivot::swaprows (const unsigned i, const unsigned j)
{
```

```
    unsigned k;
    k = R[j-1]; R[j-1] = R[i-1]; R[i-1] = k;
}
```

Similarly, whenever two columns of a matrix or sparse are exchanged, the two corresponding entries of C are exchanged:

```
void pivot::swapcols (const unsigned i, const unsigned j)
{
    unsigned k;
    k = C[j-1]; C[j-1] = C[i-1]; C[i-1] = k;
}
```

The end result is that R[i-1] contains the original row number of the row that is currently numbered row i, and C[j-1] contains the original column number of the column that is now column j.

To model **Pb** (i.e., to shuffle the components of the right-hand-side vector **b** into the same order as the rows of the modified matrix), we move to position i the component initially at R[i-1]:

```
real_vector& real_vector::Map (const unsigned R[],
    double* buf)
{   unsigned q = 0;
    if (buf == NULL) { buf = new double [n];
        checkptr(buf); q = n;}
    memcpy(buf, ptr, n*sizeof(double));
    for (unsigned i=0; i<n; i++) ptr[i] = *(buf+R[i]-1);
    if(q) delete buf;
    return *this;
}
```

This is a real_vector member function. It is declared with a default (double*=NULL) for buf, so that if no buffer is provided in the call list, Map allocates and deletes its own. The input ptr array is copied into buf. Then each component is stored back in ptr in the order determined by array R. The for loop uses C-style indexing.

The result vector $\mathbf{Q}^T\mathbf{x}$ is produced with its components shuffled into the same order as the columns of the modified matrix, so the need is to put them back into the order given in the original problem. This is the inverse of the previous mapping, in a sense, and it is implemented as

```
real_vector& real_vector::Pam (const unsigned C[],
    double* buf)
{   unsigned q = 0;
    if (buf == NULL) { buf = new double [n];
        checkptr(buf); q = n;}
```

```
    memcpy(buf, ptr, n*sizeof(double));
    for (unsigned i=0; i<n; i++) *(ptr+C[i]-1) = buf[i];
    if(q) delete buf;
    return *this;
}
```

By way of review, recall that if `x` is a `real_vector`, then `ptr[i]` and `*(ptr+i)` are the same `double`, namely, `x(i+1)`.

We will see that a complete solution of $\mathbf{Ax} = \mathbf{b}$, when $\mathbf{A}$ is factorized as $\mathbf{L\backslash U}$ with `pivot P`, takes the form

```
b.Map(P.R).Lsolve(A).Usolve(A).Pam(P.C);
```

5.5 SUMMARY AND CONCLUSIONS

Upper-Triangular Matrices. If $\mathbf{U}$ is upper triangular and $\mathbf{Ux} = \mathbf{b}$, `b.Usolve ( U );` overwrites solution `x` onto `b`. If $\mathbf{U}$ is upper triangular and $\mathbf{x^T U} = \mathbf{b^T}$, `b. TUsolve(U);` overwrites solution `x` onto `b`.

Lower-Triangular Matrices. If $\mathbf{L}$ is lower triangular and $\mathbf{Lx} = \mathbf{b}$, `b.Lsolve ( L );` overwrites solution `x` onto `b`. If $\mathbf{L}$ is lower triangular and $\mathbf{x^T L} = \mathbf{b^T}$, `b. TLsolve( L );` overwrites solution `x` onto `b`.

The main diagonal of a lower-triangular matrix is assumed to consist of all ones and is therefore not addressed.

Row and Column Permutations

```
    pivot p; contains
```
        `p.m`   how many rows in $\mathbf{A}$.
        `p.n`   how many columns in $\mathbf{A}$.
        `p.R [i-1]` original number of current row *i*.
        `p.C [j-1]` original number of current column *j*.

If the problem $\mathbf{Ax} = \mathbf{b}$ is solved using row and column exchanges in $\mathbf{A}$, `b.Map ( p.R );` shuffles the components of $\mathbf{b}$ into the same order as the rows of $\mathbf{A}$; `x.Pam( p.C );` unshuffles the components of $\mathbf{x}$ from the order of the columns of $\mathbf{A}$.

Spline Interpolation. If `x[]` and `y[]` are the coordinates of `n+1` points, with the `x[]` entries in increasing order, `spline_fit( x, y, g, n);` computes the coefficients `g[]` defining a cubic spline. Then `double Y = splind( x, y, g, n, X);` computes the value of `Y` obtained by cubic-spline interpolation at location `X`.

6 Householder Matrix Methods

A *Householder transformation* is a matrix of a special form that has the power to zero out all the elements below the first in the first column of a target matrix. (Of course, the transformation has side effects on the remaining columns.) This power may seem too limited to be impressive in itself, but it provides the foundation for several useful methods for factorizing and diagonalizing dense matrices.

The special form of a Householder matrix is written as $\mathbf{I} - 2\mathbf{v}\mathbf{v}^T/\mathbf{v}^T\mathbf{v}$. Here $\mathbf{I}$ is the identity matrix (all ones on the main diagonal, zeros elsewhere) and $\mathbf{v}$ is called a *Householder vector*. The form $\mathbf{v}^T\mathbf{v}$ is the squared length of $\mathbf{v}$, and the other way around $\mathbf{v}\mathbf{v}^T$ is a matrix whose ijth element is a product of vector components v_iv_j. All matrices involved here are $n \times n$, if n is the order of the target matrix.

It remains to be specified how $\mathbf{v}$ is obtained. If vector $\mathbf{x}$ represents the first column of the target matrix and $\mathbf{e}$ is a vector with an initial 1 its only nonzero component, then $(\mathbf{I} - 2\mathbf{v}\mathbf{v}^T/\mathbf{v}^T\mathbf{v})\mathbf{x} = \mu\mathbf{e}$ if $\mathbf{v} = \mathbf{x} + \mu\mathbf{e}$, and $\mu = \pm(\mathbf{x}^T\mathbf{x})^{1/2}$. These relationships are shown quite concretely in the following code:

```
temp_real_vector house (const matrix& A, const unsigned j)
{//G&VL 5.1.1 p196
    real_vector s (A.M());
    for(unsigned i = 0; i < A.M(); i++) s[i] = A[i] (j);
    double mu = sqrt(s*s);
    if( mu != 0.){
        if(s(1) < 0.) mu = -mu;
        double beta = 1./(s(1) + mu);
        s *= beta;
    }
    s(1) = 1.;
    return temp_real_vector(s);
}
```

Argument A is the target matrix, and argument j allows the target column to be other than the first. The Householder vector is returned as a temp_real_vector. The sign of mu is chosen to avoid cancellation in the denominator of beta. The returned vector is scaled so that its first entry is 1.

With $\mathbf{v}$ thus computed, $(\mathbf{I} - 2\mathbf{vv}^T/\mathbf{v}^T\mathbf{v})\,\mathbf{A} = \mathbf{A} + \mathbf{vw}^T$, where $\mathbf{w} = \beta\mathbf{A}^T\mathbf{v}$ and $\beta = -2/\mathbf{v}^T\mathbf{v}$. The effect on $\mathbf{A}$ of the Householder matrix is only a subtraction of an outer product. Matrix-by-matrix multiplication is not required, only vector-by matrix:

```
matrix& matrix::row_house (const real_vector& x)
{//G&VL 5.1.2 p197; includes stashing x
    double beta = x * x;  beta = -2./beta;              //3
    plus_outer( x, (x*(*this))*= beta );               //4
    for (unsigned i=1; i<mrows; i++) v[i][0] = x[i]; //5
    return *this;
}
```

This is a `matrix` member function, and I coded x for the input vector because v is already a predefined member of `matrix`. Line 3 computes and divides by the norm of x, which is presumed nonzero. Line 4 performs the update of the target matrix and is equivalent to `A.plus_outer(x,(x*A)*beta)`. Line 5 stores the Householder vector in the part of the target column that has just been zapped, in anticipation of using it later in `Qsolve()`. More precisely, it stores components 2 through `mrows`, knowing that $x(1) = 1$.

6.0.1 Example

```
{   double data[10] = {1.,2.,3.,4.,5.,6.,7.,8.,9.,10.};
    real_vector v, c(data,10);
    submatrix A (c,1);
    v = house (A,1);
    A.row_house(v);
}
```

In this code, A is a one-column matrix version of c, which in turn is essentially a `real_vector` alias for array `data[]`. With line 5 of row_house suppressed, the following results can be printed out:

```
v norm 1.3795
```

row:	A before:	House v:	A after:
1	1	1	-19.6214
2	2	0.0969865	-3.38705e-16
3	3	0.14548	-2.21828e-16
4	4	0.193973	-6.7741e-16
5	5	0.242466	-1.13277e-15
6	6	0.29096	-4.43656e-16
7	7	0.339453	-8.9902e-16
8	8	0.387946	-1.35482e-15
9	9	0.436439	-1.81018e-15
10	10	0.4849	-2.26555e-15

The Householder vector v has an initial entry 1, and $(\mathbf{v}^T\mathbf{v})^{1/2}$ is 1.3795. Entries 2 through 10 of v are proportional to the corresponding initial values in A. Entries 2 through 10 of A are annihilated, to the level of round-off error. Entry 1 of modified A is equal to $-(\mathbf{c}^T\mathbf{c})^{1/2}$.

6.1 QR FACTORIZATION

The QR factorization of $\mathbf{A}$ ($m \times n$) is $\mathbf{A} = \mathbf{QR}$, where $\mathbf{R}$ is upper triangular. Some authors call this QU to maintain a consistent notation for an upper-triangular matrix. A need not be square as long as its number of rows at least equals its number of columns ($m \geq n$). Then $\mathbf{R}$ is $m \times n$ and $\mathbf{Q}$ is $m \times m$. $\mathbf{Q}$ is an orthogonal matrix, meaning that $\mathbf{Q}^T\mathbf{Q} = \mathbf{I}$; its transpose is its inverse. $\mathbf{Q}$ itself is the product of orthogonal matrices:

$$\mathbf{Q}^T\mathbf{A} = \mathbf{R} = \mathbf{Q}_n\,\mathbf{Q}_{n-1}\cdots\mathbf{Q}_2\,\mathbf{Q}_1\,\mathbf{A}; \quad \text{so} \quad \mathbf{Q} = \mathbf{Q}_1^T\,\mathbf{Q}_2^T\cdots\mathbf{Q}_{n-1}^T\,\mathbf{Q}_n^T$$

Each $\mathbf{Q}_k$ represents a Householder transformation $(\mathbf{I} - 2\mathbf{v}\mathbf{v}^T/\mathbf{v}^T\mathbf{v})_k$, where k designates the column from which $\mathbf{v}$ is derived. The strategy is that each successive transformation zeros one additional column of $\mathbf{A}$ (below the main diagonal):

```
matrix& matrix::HouseholderQR()
{//G&VL 5.2.1 p212
    for(unsigned i=1; i<=ncols; i++){        //3
        submatrix C (*this,i,i);             //4
        C.row_house( house(C,1) );    }      //5
    return *this;
}
```

This `matrix` member function is invoked as in `A.HouseholderQR()`. Line 3 controls a loop that targets each column of `matrix` A in succession. Line 4 defines `submatrix` C as the part of A below and to the right of `A(i,i)`. Line 5 creates a Householder vector based on the first column of C and then applies the corresponding transformation to C and therefore A. After `ncols` passes through the loop, A has factor $\mathbf{R}$ stored on and above its main diagonal, and the essential part of each $\mathbf{v}$ stored (by `row_house`) below the diagonal.

QR factorization can be used in solving equations. To solve $\mathbf{Ax} = \mathbf{b}$, for example, knowing that $\mathbf{A} = \mathbf{QR}$, and that $\mathbf{Q}$ is an orthogonal transformation matrix, we can write $\mathbf{Rx} = \mathbf{Q}^T\mathbf{b}$. This suggests that upper-triangular $\mathbf{R}$ will be grist for a backward-solution mill once we have obtained $\mathbf{Q}^T\mathbf{b}$. We do not have $\mathbf{Q}$ itself, because only the Householder vectors $\mathbf{v}$ were saved at each stage of the QR decomposition.

$\mathbf{Q}^T$ is the product of factors $\mathbf{Q}_k^T$, each of the form $[\mathbf{I} - 2\mathbf{v}\mathbf{v}^T/(\mathbf{v}^T\mathbf{v})]_k^T$. Now $\mathbf{v}^T\mathbf{v}$ is a scalar; $\mathbf{I}$ and $\mathbf{v}\mathbf{v}^T$ are symmetrical. Therefore, $\mathbf{Q}_k^T = \mathbf{Q}_k$, and $\mathbf{Q}_k^T\mathbf{b} = \mathbf{b} - 2\mathbf{v}(\mathbf{v}^T\mathbf{b})/(\mathbf{v}^T\mathbf{v})$. This is the effect of the Householder transformation `row_house` that we observed for a one-column matrix in the example in Section 6.0.1. However, because the vectors **v** are concealed within **A** by `HouseholderQR()`, we will need the following specialized code:

```
real_vector& real_vector::Qsolve (const matrix& A)
{//Apply Q stored as house vectors to *this
    unsigned i, j; double alfa, beta;
    if(n != A.M()) exit(1);
    for(j=1; j<=A.N(); j++){                              //5
        beta = 1.; alfa = (*this)(j);
        for(i=n; i>j; i--){
            beta += A(i,j)*A(i,j);        //v*v
            alfa += A(i,j)*(*this)(i);  //v*b
        }
        alfa *= 2.; alfa /= beta;         //2vb/vv
        (*this)(j) -= alfa;                 //b -= (2vb/vv)v  //12
        for (i=n; i>j; i--) (*this)(i) -= A(i,j)*alfa;  //13
    }
    return *this;
}
```

This is a `real_vector` member function to be applied as `b.Qsolve(A)`, where b is a right-hand-side vector and A has been factored by `HouseholderQR`. The subroutine extracts the vectors **v** from **A** and applies the corresponding Householder transformations. It is not assumed that **A** is square, but the dimension of **b** must equal the number of rows in **A**. The loop beginning in line 5 examines each column of A in order. Scalar variables `alpha` and `beta` accumulate v^Tb and v^Tv, respectively. Lines 12 and 13 subtract $v \times 2(v^Tb/v^Tv)$ from **b**.

The result is ready to be put into a backward solver: `b.Usolve(A)`. We will need a new version of `Usolve`, however. The one we saw in Section 5.1 took a `sparse` argument. A suitable version for upper-triangular matrices in `matrix` form is

```
real_vector& real_vector::Usolve (const matrix& A)
{//Solve Rx = Qb where R is upper triangular
    unsigned i, j, r; double Uii;
    r = A.N();
    for(i=r; i<n; i++) ptr[i] = 0.;                      //5
    if((Uii = A(r,r)) != 0.)(*this)(r) /= Uii;
        else               (*this)(r) = 0.;             //7
    for(i=r-1; i>0; i--)
    {
        for(j=i+1; j<=r; j++) (*this)(i) -= A(i,j)*
            (*this)(j);
        if((Uii = A(i,i)) != 0.)(*this)(i) /= Uii;
            else               (*this)(i) = 0.;   //11
    }
    return *this;
}
```

Compared to `Usolve(const   sparse&)`, this subroutine incorporates some additional features. It allows the length of `b` to exceed the number of columns of `A`. Lines 5, 7, and 11 zero any entry in `x` that corresponds to a zero diagonal element of `A`. The basic computation, $x_i = (b_i - \sum_{j>i} u_{ij}x_j)/u_{ii}$, is the same.

6.1.1 Example

The following code sets up and solves a matrix equation of the form $\mathbf{Ax} = \mathbf{b}$ using QR factorization. Matrix `A` is the same as matrix `e` in the Gram–Schmidt example (Section 4.1.1). Vector `x` is all ones so that the statement `b = A*x;` creates a right-hand-side $\mathbf{b}$ yielding a known solution. The `dumpall()` calls print out the pertinent data:

```
{double y[16] = {1.,0.,0.,0.,2.,3.,0.,0.,4.,5.,6.,0.,7.,
                8.,9.,10.};
   matrix A(y,4,4);      A.dumpall();
   real_vector x(4), b(4);
   x.init() += 1.;       x.dumpall();
   b = A*x;              b.dumpall();
   A.HouseholderQR();    A.dumpall();
   b.Qsolve(A);          b.dumpall();
   b.Usolve(A);          b.dumpall();    }
```

A initially is

```
1|1|0|0|0
2|2|3|0|0
3|4|5|6|0
4|7|8|9|10
```

x is all ones:

```
|1|1|1|1
```

b initially is **Ax**:

```
|1|5|15|34
```

A stores **Q\R** after `HouseholderQR()`:

```
1|-8.3666|-9.80087|-10.3985|-8.3666
2|0.213525|-1.39386|-0.061494|1.43486
3|0.427049|0.353975|-2.97786|-1.03707
4|0.747336|0.293529|0.351327|-5.18321
```

$\mathbf{Q}^T\mathbf{b}$ results from Qsolve:

```
|-36.9326|-0.020498|-4.01492|-5.18321
```

$\mathbf{R}^{-1}\mathbf{Q}^T\mathbf{b}$, the answer, results from Usolve:

```
|1|1|1|1
```

6.2 RANK DEFICIENCY

Matrix **A** in the foregoing example (Section 6.1.1) is 4 by 4, and its four columns and four rows are linearly independent. The terminology is that **A** has full rank. The QR method is able to respond appropriately to matrices somewhat less perfect than that. To begin with, **A** can be rectangular with more rows than columns, $m > n$. In that case, $m - n$ of the rows might be weighted sums of the others, but the matrix could still have full *column* rank. QR can produce an informative result even for rectangular matrices with deficient column rank.

Consider the matrix **A** corresponding to the code

```
double y[12] = {1.,2.,3.,4.,5.,6.,7.,8.,9.,10.,11.,12.};
matrix A(y,4,3);   A.dumpall();
```

A has four rows and three columns and is printed out as

```
1|  1|  2|  3
2|  4|  5|  6
3|  7|  8|  9
4|10|11|12
```

Furthermore, only two of the three columns of **A** are linearly independent. Column 3 is twice column 2, less column 1. In other words, the column rank of this matrix is deficient by one. When HouseholderQR() is applied to **A**, the **Q\R** result is

```
1|-12.8841|  -14.5916|-16.2992
2|0.288099|  -1.04132|-2.08263
3|0.504174|-0.289442|4.94571e-16
4|0.720248|  -0.75328|0.332274
```

We know that $\mathbf{Q}^T$ wipes out everything below the main diagonal in **A**. (Of course, this is reversible: $\mathbf{Q}\mathbf{Q}^T\mathbf{A} = \mathbf{A}$.) Since $m > n$, the last $m - n$ rows of **A** *in all columns* have been zeroed out (and overwritten by components of Householder vectors). Each of the fully deleted rows represents the left-hand side of an equation that has somehow vanished. What happens to the corresponding right-hand-side entries? The following code prints out a right-hand-side vector b before and after $\mathbf{Q}^T$ is applied to it:

```
double z[4]   = {1.,2.,3.,4.};
real_vector b(z,4);   b.dumpall();
b.Qsolve(A);          b.dumpall();
```

Before, **b** is $|1|2|3|4|$. After, $\mathbf{Q}^T\mathbf{b}$ is

$$|-5.43305|-0.69421|-4.65464e-17|8.44561e-17|$$

We notice first that the fourth right-hand-side component has been essentially ze-roed, consistent with zeroing the left-hand-side coefficients for the fourth row. In other words, the fourth row (or equation) is no longer a part of the problem. We also observe that the third component has been eliminated. This deletion is syn-chronized with the vanishing of the third diagonal element of **R**. This is how rank deficiency manifests itself and why we are justified to zero each component of the backward solution that corresponds to a diagonal zero in **R**.

Something has to be done about round-off error. Computed numbers that are zero in theory actually retain a small value, such as $4.94571e-16$ for r_{33}. One con-venient approach is demonstrated in

```
unsigned matrix::col_rank (double drop_tol)
{
   unsigned r = ncols;
   for(unsigned i=0; i<ncols; i++)
      if( fabs( v[i][i] ) < drop_tol ) { v[i][i] = 0.;
         r--; }
   return r;
}
```

This `matrix` member function examines each diagonal element of a `matrix`. If the absolute value is below a specified *drop tolerance*, the element is zeroed and the rank of the matrix is reduced by one. This function fits in among the other QR com-ponents as shown here:

```
A.HouseholderQR();
printf(" Rank %u\n",
A.col_rank( 1.e-12 ));
b.Qsolve(A).Usolve(A);   b.dumpall();
```

This code yields

```
Rank 2
|-0.333333|0.666667|0|0
```

Mechanically, at least, we have found a legitimate basis for replacing a potential zero divisor with a zero resultant. In the next section we examine what meaning should be ascribed to this.

6.2.1 Exercise

Verify the foregoing solution by matrix multiplication:

$$\begin{bmatrix} 1 & 2 & 3 \\ 4 & 5 & 6 \\ 7 & 8 & 9 \\ 10 & 11 & 12 \end{bmatrix} \begin{bmatrix} -\frac{1}{3} \\ \frac{2}{3} \\ 0 \end{bmatrix} = \begin{bmatrix} 1 \\ 2 \\ 3 \\ 4 \end{bmatrix}$$

6.3 LEAST-SQUARES APPLICATIONS

In Section 6.2, the demonstration problem had effectively two unknowns but four equations, and yet the outcome was, fortuitously, an exact solution. In retrospect, this was possible because the four equations were *consistent*, albeit redundant. It is as if the right-hand side were the result of working the exercise in Section 6.2.1 in advance. More generally, when the number of equations exceeds the number of unknowns ($m > n$), the equations are inconsistent. The system $\mathbf{Ax} = \mathbf{b}$ is said to be *overdetermined*, and at best an approximate solution can be obtained.

The QR method applied to an overdetermined system produces a *least-squares* solution. That is, the resulting value of $\mathbf{x}$ is that which minimizes $[(\mathbf{Ax} - \mathbf{b})^{\mathrm{T}}(\mathbf{Ax} - \mathbf{b})]^{1/2}$, the Euclidean length of the residual. (I define residual $\mathbf{r} = \mathbf{b} - \mathbf{Ax}$ as in Section 4.2.) Least squares is a criterion that minimizes the misfit of an approximation, as measured by the residual.

The theory of least squares proposes to minimize the squared residual function $\Phi(\mathbf{x}) = \frac{1}{2}|\mathbf{Ax} - \mathbf{b}|^2$, just like the biconjugate gradient method (Section 4.5). The minimum value occurs at a zero of the corresponding gradient $\nabla\Phi = \mathbf{A}^{\mathrm{T}}(\mathbf{Ax} - \mathbf{b})$. There are at least three ways of manipulating the basic requirement $\mathbf{A}^{\mathrm{T}}(\mathbf{Ax} - \mathbf{b}) = 0$ to exploit different matrix computational methods.

The *normal equations* approach works the problem in the form $(\mathbf{A}^{\mathrm{T}}\mathbf{A})\mathbf{x} = \mathbf{A}^{\mathrm{T}}\mathbf{b}$. The *normal matrix* $\mathbf{A}^{\mathrm{T}}\mathbf{A}$ is actually constructed, and the right-hand side is literally modified to $\mathbf{A}^{\mathrm{T}}\mathbf{b}$. The normal matrix is symmetric and positive definite. It can be factorized very reliably by the Cholesky method. If $\mathbf{A}$ is $m \times n$, $\mathbf{A}^{\mathrm{T}}\mathbf{A}$ is only $n \times n$.

A second approach undertakes to solve the $(m + n) \times (m + n)$ system

$$\left[\begin{array}{c|c} \mathbf{I} & \mathbf{A} \\ \hline \mathbf{A}^T & \mathbf{0} \end{array}\right]\left[\begin{array}{c} \mathbf{r} \\ \hline \mathbf{x} \end{array}\right] = \left[\begin{array}{c} \mathbf{b} \\ \hline \mathbf{0} \end{array}\right] \quad \text{or} \quad \mathbf{Bx}' = \mathbf{b}'$$

This is an example of partitioned matrix notation. It shows how a large matrix is to be constructed out of smaller matrices. $\mathbf{I}$ is the $m \times m$ identity matrix, and $\mathbf{0}$ is an $n \times n$ matrix of zeros. The meaning is that we will simultaneously solve the matrix equations $\mathbf{r} + \mathbf{Ax} = \mathbf{b}$ (top row) and $\mathbf{A}^T\mathbf{r} = 0$ (bottom row). The two together imply that $\mathbf{A}^T(\mathbf{b} - \mathbf{Ax}) = 0$, Q.E.D. The built-up matrix (call it $\mathbf{B}$) is explicitly symmetric. The problem $\mathbf{Bx}' = \mathbf{b}'$ is appropriate input for the conjugate gradient method, as described in Section 4.6. Result $\mathbf{x}'$ overwrites input $\mathbf{b}'$, and input $\mathbf{B}$ is not modified.

The third way is QR. All we need to do is recognize that when the system of equations is overdetermined $(m > n)$, the solution produced by QR *is* a least-squares solution. The upper-triangular factor $\mathbf{R}$ is the result of applying $\mathbf{Q}^T$ to $\mathbf{A}$. We noted that $\mathbf{Q}^T$ zeros out the bottom $m - n$ rows of $\mathbf{A}$, and that $\mathbf{R}$ is, in effect, partitioned as

$$\mathbf{Q}^T\mathbf{A} = \mathbf{R} = \left[\begin{array}{c} \mathbf{R}_n \\ \hline \mathbf{0} \end{array}\right] \begin{array}{l} n \\ m - n \end{array}$$

where $\mathbf{R}_n$ represents the $n \times n$ upper-triangular part of $\mathbf{R}$. Similarly, $\mathbf{Q}^T$ applied to $\mathbf{b}$ yields a partitioned result:

$$\mathbf{Q}^T\mathbf{b} = \left[\begin{array}{c} \mathbf{c} \\ \hline \mathbf{d} \end{array}\right] \begin{array}{l} n \\ m - n \end{array}$$

The key is that the $\mathbf{Q}$ transformation preserves the length of any vector it operates on; the length of $\mathbf{Qr}$ or $\mathbf{Q}^T\mathbf{r}$ is the length of $\mathbf{r}$. Therefore,

$$|\mathbf{r}|^2 = |\mathbf{Ax} - \mathbf{b}|^2 = |\mathbf{Q}^T\mathbf{Ax} - \mathbf{Q}^T\mathbf{b}|^2 = |\mathbf{R}_n\mathbf{x} - \mathbf{c}|^2 + |\mathbf{d}|^2$$

The interpretation of this is that the $\mathbf{x}$ we obtain in the form $\mathbf{R}_n^{-1}\mathbf{c}$ is the least squares solution, and that $|\mathbf{d}|^2$ is the squared minimum residual.

Where $\mathbf{A}^T\mathbf{A}$ is called the *normal matrix*, $\mathbf{A}$ by itself is called the *design matrix*. In obtaining a least-squares solution, applying QR (or SVD, described later) to the design matrix is a feasible alternative to solving the normal equations.

6.3.1   Example (Linear Regression)

The familiar form of a straight line in two dimensions is $y = \alpha x + y_0$, where α is the slope and y_0 is the y-intercept. An alternative, more convenient form is $x/x_0 + y/y_0 = 1$, where x_0 is the x-intercept. In the simplest problem of linear regression, we are given a number of points (x_i, y_i) and are required to find the parameters of the line that best fits the data in a least-squares sense. The dimensions of this problem are $m \times 2$, where m is the number of data points. The unknown $\mathbf{x}$ is interpreted as $\mathbf{x} = [(1/x_0), (1/y_0)]^T$. Each data point (x_i, y_i) becomes a row (the ith) of matrix $\mathbf{A}$. The right-hand-side vector $\mathbf{b}$ is just a column of m ones. Figure 6.1 presents a set of 10 such data points.

```
{   double data[20] = {-5., 2.,-1., 4., 2., 6., 3., 7.,
                       10.,11.,9.,11., 1., 5., 1., 6.,
                       7., 9., 4., 8.};
    matrix A(data,10,2);                    A.dumpall();
    A.HouseholderQR();                      A.dumpall();
    printf(" Rank %u\n", A.col_rank( 1.e-12 ));
    real_vector b(10);   b.init() += 1.;    b.dumpall();
    b.Qsolve(A).Usolve(A);                  b.dumpall();
}
```

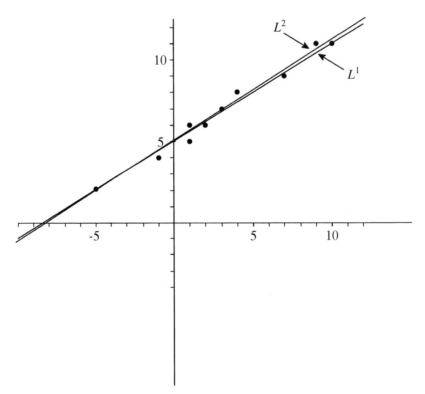

Fig. 6.1 Ten data points and a straight-line fit by linear regression under the least-squares criterion (L^2), compared to the L^1 criterion (see Chapter 11).

In this code excerpt, A is the design matrix, 10 rows by two columns. Column 1 holds the x data values and column 2 holds the y data values. Here is the content of A before and after HouseholderQR():

```
 1|-5| 2                     1|   16.9411| 19.7154
 2|-1| 4                     2| 0.0455766|-12.8181
 3| 2| 6                     3|-0.0911532|0.248798
 4| 3| 7                     4|  -0.13673|0.259725
 5|10|11                     5| -0.455766|0.166005
 6| 9|11                     6|  -0.41019|0.211814
 7| 1| 5                     7|-0.0455766|0.237871
 8| 1| 6                     8|-0.0455766|0.294607
 9| 7| 9                     9| -0.319036| 0.18996
10| 4| 8                    10| -0.182306|0.270652
Rank 2
```

The right-hand-side real_vector b is initially all ones. Here is b before and after Qsolve() and Usolve():

```
|1|1|1|1|1|1|1|1|1|1
```

```
|-0.125183|0.200382|0|0|0|0|0|0|0|0
```

The first two entries are the reciprocals of the axis intercepts. Therefore, the best-fit line has $x_0 = -7.988$ and $y_0 = 4.99$. This line is shown in Fig. 6.1 labeled L^2.

6.3.2   Exercise

Verify that the following represents the normal-equation setup of the two-dimensional linear regression problem:

$$(A^TA)x = A^Tb, \quad \text{where} \quad A^TA = \begin{bmatrix} \sum x_i^2 & \sum x_i y_i \\ \sum x_i y_i & \sum y_i^2 \end{bmatrix} \quad \text{and} \quad A^Tb = \begin{bmatrix} \sum x_i \\ \sum y_i \end{bmatrix}$$

The equivalent design-matrix setup requires less preparation of the data.

6.3.3   Review Question

Q^Tb contains the least-squares residuals (r) in its d partition, but Usolve zeros it out. What if we want to know this information?

Answer: After b.Qsolve(A) but before b.Usolve(A), define d to be the final eight entries of b and print out its Euclidean norm:

```
b.Qsolve(A);
real_vector d( &(b(3)), 8);
printf(" |d| %G\n", sqrt(d*d) );
b.Usolve(A);
```

Yielding

```
|d|  0.233091
```

6.4 EIGENSTUFF

The German adjective *eigen* translates to *inherent*. In English, we prepend *eigen* to seemingly any noun connected with diagonalizing a matrix. A diagonalized matrix is equivalent to a solved problem: Each row i effectively reads $\lambda_i x_i = b_i$, so that $x_i = b_i/\lambda_i$, where λ_i is the value of the diagonal element, called an *eigenvalue*. The operations that transform a matrix to diagonal form work a corresponding transformation of the right-hand-side vector, **b**.

The *eigenvectors* of a matrix **A** are special vectors $\mathbf{w}_i$ that satisfy the condition $\mathbf{Aw}_i = \lambda_i \mathbf{w}_i$, where λ_i is an eigenvalue. In words, the effect of multiplying an eigenvector by matrix **A** is the same as multiplying it by a scalar. In general, there is a one-to-one correspondence between eigenvectors and eigenvalues. There should be as many of each as the order n of the matrix.

The method I describe in this section is applicable to symmetric matrices, which are necessarily square. Their eigenvalues are guaranteed real. Their eigenvectors span the n-dimensional space. General rectangular matrices are best handled by singular value decomposition, which I describe in Chapter 7.

The reduction of a symmetric matrix to diagonal form proceeds in two phases. First, the matrix is converted to symmetric tridiagonal form by Householder transformations. This is as far as one can go with exact noniterative methods. Then the symmetric tridiagonal matrix is diagonalized by an efficient but fallible iterative process.

Formally, if **A** is real, symmetric, and $n \times n$, there exists a real orthogonal matrix **U** that produces $\mathbf{U}^T\mathbf{AU} = \mathbf{diag}(\lambda_1, \lambda_2, \ldots, \lambda_n)$, where $\lambda_1 \geq \lambda_2 \geq \cdots \geq \lambda_n$. The notation **diag**() designates a diagonal matrix with the values indicated along its main diagonal. Putting the eigenvalues in order of decreasing size is a convention, not an intrinsic feature of the basic process. The object of the following development is to implement a very good approximation of **U**.

In Section 6.0.1 we saw that `row_house` applied a Householder transformation in the sense of $\mathbf{Q}^T\mathbf{A}$. A companion subroutine that we did not see, `col_house`, yields the transposed result $\mathbf{AQ}$. Tridiagonalization is based on the symmetric Householder transformation $\mathbf{Q}^T\mathbf{AQ}$, employing a Householder vector generated as in the following code:

```
temp_real_vector sym_house (matrix& A)
{//G&VL p196 applied to leading row & column (2:n)
    real_vector s (A.M()-1);                              //3
    for(unsigned i = 0; i < s.N(); i++) s[i] = A[i+1] (1);
    double mu = sqrt(s*s);
    if( mu != 0.){
        if(s(1) < 0.) mu = -mu;                          //7
```

```
      double beta = 1./(s(1) + mu);
      s *= beta;
   }
   s(1) = 1.;                                              //10
   A(2,1) = A(1,2) = -mu;   // sub\superdiag              //11
   for(unsigned i = 2; i <= s.N(); i++)                   //12
      A[i][0] = A[0][i] = s(i);
   return temp_real_vector(s);
}
```

Lines 3 through 10 of symm_house parallel the corresponding lines of house. The vector s here is one entry shorter, and its leading element corresponds to the *second* entry of column 1. The effect of $\mathbf{Q}^T\mathbf{A}\mathbf{Q}$ on the leading row and column of the matrix should be to symmetrically zero all elements past the sub- and superdiagonal. The loop that begins in line 12 therefore can overwrite the essential part of s onto the last $n-2$ entries of both column 1 and row 1 of the matrix.

This subroutine also implements the effect of the transformation on the sub- and superdiagonal elements themselves, which is to set them equal to plus or minus the norm of the original subdiagonal column, μ. Whatever sign is chosen for mu in line 7, the opposite sign should be used in setting the sub- and superdiagonal elements, as in line 11 [14, equation 5.1.2].

The reduction of a symmetric matrix to the form of a tridiagonal symmetric matrix by successive Householder transformations is performed by

```
matrix& matrix::HouseTridiag()
{//G&VL p420; algorithm 8.2.1: symmetric QR
   if(mrows != ncols) exit(1);
   double* space = new double [2*ncols];
   real_vector v(space,ncols), w(space+ncols,ncols);
   double beta;
   for(unsigned j=1; j<ncols-1; j++){
      --v; --w;
      submatrix C(*this,j,j);
      v = sym_house(C);
      beta = v * v;
      submatrix D(*this,j+1,j+1);
      w  = D * v;
      w *= (-2./beta);
      w -= (v * ((w * v) / beta));
      D.plus_outer(w,v).plus_outer(v,w);              //16
   }
   delete space;
   return *this;
}
```

The use of submatrix here makes a couple of points obvious. First, when applied to matrix A, the algorithm steps down the main diagonal from A(1,1) to A(ncols-2, ncols-2). Second, the matrix D to which vector v is applied is smaller than the matrix C from which v is derived. That is why sym_house fixed the off-diagonal elements in the leading row and column.

In mathematical notation, line 16 reads $\mathbf{D}' = \mathbf{D} + \mathbf{w}\mathbf{v}^T + \mathbf{v}\mathbf{w}^T$. This $\mathbf{w}$ has a built-in minus sign from (-2./beta). The effect of plus_outer is sometimes called a *rank-one update*; two successive applications therefore make a *rank-two update*.

6.4.1 Example

I suppressed the loop in sym_house() that stores the Householder vector (line 12) and ran the following test code:

```
{   double data[16] = { 1., 5., 8., 0., 5., 2., 6., 9.,
                        8., 6., 3., 7., 0., 9., 7., 4. };
    matrix A(data,4,4);   A.dumpall();
    A.HouseTridiag();     A.dumpall();
}
```

This printed out

```
1| 1| 5| 8| 0
2| 5| 2| 6| 9
3| 8| 6| 3| 7
4| 0| 9| 7| 4
```

```
1|        1|-9.43398|        0|        0
2|-9.43398| 8.11236|-10.9256|        0
3|        0|-10.9256| 5.25039|-2.21931
4|        0|        0|-2.21931|-4.36275
```

The two Householder vectors were $[1 \mid 0.554248 \mid 0]^T$ and $[1 \mid -0.816913]^T$.

6.5 GIVENS TRANSFORMATION

The theme of this chapter has been to describe the Householder transformation and demonstrate how it leads to concise methods for QR factorization and for symmetric tridiagonalization. At this juncture on the path to full diagonalization, we abandon the Householder route and go by way of the Givens approach. Recall that the Householder transformation was designed to zero out all entries in a column of a matrix below a selected initial element. By contrast, a Givens transformation is designed to zero out just one entry of a pair selected from an arbitrary column. The simplest representation of a Givens transformation is a 2×2 matrix operation,

$$\begin{bmatrix} c & -s \\ s & c \end{bmatrix} \begin{bmatrix} a \\ b \end{bmatrix} = \begin{bmatrix} * \\ 0 \end{bmatrix} \equiv \mathbf{G} \begin{bmatrix} a \\ b \end{bmatrix}$$

This expression is formally similar to a spatial rotation, and the parameters c and s suggest cosine and sine, respectively. The asterisk means that we don't care about the top row of the result. Instead, we impose a requirement that $c^2 + s^2 = 1$. The second row represents the equation $sa + cb = 0$. Taken together, these criteria imply that $(1 + b^2/a^2)\, c^2 = 1$, so that $c = a/(a^2 + b^2)^{1/2}$ and $s = -b/(a^2 + b^2)^{1/2}$.

The first few lines of subroutine `givens_2x2_prepost()` compute c and s, given a and b, with precautions to avoid numerical overflow:

```
void givens_2x2_prepost( matrix& T, unsigned k, double
   a, double b)
{//c and s per G&VL p202; algorithm 5.1.5:
   double c, s, r, t;
   if(b == 0.) return; //{c = 1.; s = 0.;}
     else{
       if(fabs(b) > fabs(a)){
         r = -a/b; s = 1./sqrt(1.+r*r); c = s*r;}
         else{ r = -b/a;  c = 1./sqrt(1.+r*r);  s = c*r;}
     }
   (more...)
```

The remaining code in `givens_2x2_prepost()` applies a Givens rotation to rows k and k+1 of matrix T (as if premultiplying by **G**), and the same rotation to columns k and k+1 (as if postmultiplying by $\mathbf{G}^{\mathrm{T}}$). An awkward side effect arises when such a transformation is applied to an initially tridiagonal matrix, for example,

$$\mathbf{G} \begin{bmatrix} 1 & 2 & & \\ 2 & 3 & 4 & \\ & 4 & 5 & 6 \\ & & 6 & 7 \end{bmatrix} \mathbf{G}^{\mathrm{T}} = \begin{bmatrix} 1' & 2' & * & \\ 2' & 3' & 4' & \\ * & 4' & 5 & 6 \\ & & 6 & 7 \end{bmatrix}$$

If the Givens transformation mixes rows 1 and 2, and columns 1 and 2, as shown, an undesired off-diagonal term, indicated as *, is introduced. To get rid of it, a second Givens transformation is applied, mixing rows 2 and 3 and columns

2 and 3. To get rid of the spurious term introduced by the second transformation, a third transformation is applied, and so on. The process of chasing the unwanted term out of the matrix is implemented in the loop beginning in line 8 of the following subroutine:

```
void alg_822( matrix& T )
{//G&VL p423 symmetric QR step with implicit shift
    double d, mu, a, b; unsigned k, n = T.N();
    d = ( T(n-1,n-1) - T(n,n) ) * .5;
    a = T(n,n-1)*T(n,n-1); mu = sqrt(d*d+a); if
        (d < 0.) mu = -mu;
    mu = d + mu; mu = T(n,n) - a/mu;
    a = T(1,1) - mu; b = T(2,1);
    for (k=1; k<n; k++)                              //8
    {
        givens_2x2_prepost( T, k, a, b);
        if(k > n-2) break;
        a = T(k+1,k); b = T(k+2,k);
    }
}
```

The science in this subroutine is how the initial values of a and b are determined *prior* to line 8. These values are what would diagonalize the trailing 2×2 submatrix of T, if it could be separated out. Repeated application of alg_822() *will* diagonalize the trailing 2×2 submatrix of symmetric tridiagonal matrix T, which fact is the basis of

```
void alg_823( matrix& A )
{//G&VL p424 Symmetric QR Diagonalization
    unsigned i, n;   double e=1.0e-12;
    submatrix T(A,1,1);
    while( (n=T.N()) > 1 ){   i = n-1;
        alg_822( T );
        if(fabs(T(i+1,i)) <= (fabs(T(i,i))+fabs
            (T(i+1,i+1))) * e){
            T(i+1,i) = T(i,i+1) = 0.;   --T;
        }
    }
}
```

This subroutine calls alg_822() repeatedly until the off-diagonal term T(n,n-1) is indistinguishable from zero. Then it reduces the order of the matrix and repeats the procedure.

6.5.1 Example

I applied `alg_823()` to a tridiagonal matrix as follows:

```
{   double data[16] = { 1.,  2.,  0.,  0.,
                        2.,  3.,  4.,  0.,
                        0.,  4.,  5.,  6.,
                        0.,  0.,  6.,  7. };
    matrix A(data,4,4);        A.dumpall();
    alg_823( A );              A.dumpall();
}
```

The statements `A.dumpall();` printed out the matrix before and after diagonalization:

```
1|1|2|0|0
2|2|3|4|0
3|0|4|5|6
4|0|0|6|7

1|-2.48479|        0|        0|        0
2|        0|0.704565|        0|        0
3|        0|        0|4.93655|        0
4|        0|        0|        0|12.8437
```

In the final result, the diagonal elements are the eigenvalues of the matrix, in reverse order:

$$\lambda(\mathbf{A}) = \{12.8437, 4.93655, .704565, -2.48479\}.$$

It is conventional to assign label λ_1 to the greatest eigenvalue (12.8437), which was also the first to emerge from the iterations.

In the source files, there is a version `givens_2x2_symmetric()` that neither reads from nor writes to the tridiagonal input matrix above its main diagonal.

6.6 SUMMARY AND CONCLUSIONS

QR Factorization. If $\mathbf{A}$ is $m \times n$, with $m \geq n$, then `A.HouseholderQR();` factorizes $\mathbf{A} = \mathbf{QR}$, where $\mathbf{R}$ is upper triangular ($m \times n$) and $\mathbf{Q}$ is orthogonal ($m \times m$, $\mathbf{Q}^T\mathbf{Q} = \mathbf{I}$). $\mathbf{R}$ is stored into the upper-triangular part of A and $\mathbf{Q}$ is represented as Householder vectors stored below the main diagonal of A. If $\mathbf{Ax} = \mathbf{b}$, the solution $\mathbf{x} = \mathbf{R}^{-1}\mathbf{Q}^T\mathbf{b}$ is implemented in the form `b.Qsolve(A).Usolve(A);` so that $\mathbf{x}$ overwrites $\mathbf{b}$. The effective rank of $\mathbf{A}$ may be determined by running `A.col_rank(tol);` between factorization and solution.

Least Squares. If the system $\mathbf{Ax} = \mathbf{b}$ is overdetermined, `b.Qsolve(A).` `Usolve(A);` after $\mathbf{Q\backslash R}$ factorization returns the solution $\mathbf{x}$ that minimizes $|\mathbf{Ax} - \mathbf{b}|^2$. The components of $\mathbf{x}$ are returned in the first r components of b, where r is the rank of $\mathbf{A}$.

Linear Regression. Each data point becomes a row of $(m \times n)$ matrix $\mathbf{A}$, and $\mathbf{b}$ is a vector of m ones. The system $\mathbf{Ax} = \mathbf{b}$ is overdetermined. The QR solution minimizes $\sum_{i,j} (b_i - a_{ij}/\xi_j)^2$, where ξ_j is the j-axis intercept. The $(\xi_j)^{-1}$ values are returned as the first n components of $\mathbf{x}$.

Eigenvalues. If $\mathbf{A}$ is symmetric, the expression `alg_823( A.HouseTridiag` `( ) );` makes $\mathbf{A}$ diagonal with its eigenvalues along the main diagonal and zeros elsewhere. `HouseTridiag()` applies Householder transformations, and `alg_823()` uses Givens transformations. Compare `LanczosTridiag()` and an alternative version of `alg_823()` in Chapter 7.

7 Singular Value Decomposition

Singular value decomposition (SVD) is a general approach to obtaining eigenvalues and eigenvectors that is not restricted to symmetric or even square matrices. We have already seen the trick that if matrix $\mathbf{A}$ is rectangular, the product $\mathbf{A}^T\mathbf{A}$ is square and symmetric. The SVD approach instead works directly with $\mathbf{A}$. Specifically, it accomplishes the diagonalization

$$\mathbf{U}^T\mathbf{A}\mathbf{V} = \mathbf{diag}(w_1, \ldots, w_p) \equiv \mathbf{W}$$

If $\mathbf{A}$ is $m \times n$, then $\mathbf{U}$ is $m \times m$ and $\mathbf{V}$ is $n \times n$. Matrix $\mathbf{W}$ is formally $m \times n$, but only its p diagonal elements w_i are nonzeros, where p is the lesser of m or n. The transformations $\mathbf{U}$ and $\mathbf{V}$ are orthogonal (i.e., $\mathbf{U}^T\mathbf{U} = \mathbf{I}_m$ and $\mathbf{V}^T\mathbf{V} = \mathbf{I}_n$, where the subscript on the identity matrix distinguishes its size). Therefore, $\mathbf{A} = \mathbf{U}\mathbf{W}\mathbf{V}^T$.

The columns $\mathbf{u}_j$ of $\mathbf{U}$ and $\mathbf{v}_j$ of $\mathbf{V}$ are termed left and right singular vectors respectively. The columns $\mathbf{v}_j$ of $\mathbf{V}$ are the eigenvectors of $\mathbf{A}^T\mathbf{A}$ and the columns $\mathbf{u}_j$ of $\mathbf{U}$ are the eigenvectors of $\mathbf{A}\mathbf{A}^T$. The respective eigenvalues are w_j^2 (i.e., the *squares* of the singular values). The singular values w_j themselves are analogous to eigenvalues for the dual eigenproblems $\mathbf{A}\mathbf{v}_j = w_j\mathbf{u}_j$ and $\mathbf{A}^T\mathbf{u}_j = w_j\mathbf{v}_j$. The expression $\mathbf{A} = \mathbf{U}\mathbf{W}\mathbf{V}^T$ is the equivalent of $\mathbf{A} = \sum w_j(\mathbf{u}_j\mathbf{v}_j^T)$. Recalling that the outer product $\mathbf{u}\mathbf{v}^T$ of two vectors is a matrix of rank one, we might as well call $(\mathbf{u}_j\mathbf{v}_j^T)$ an eigenmatrix. If the summation $\sum w_j(\mathbf{u}_j\mathbf{v}_j^T)$ omits the q smallest singular values, we obtain the best approximation to $\mathbf{A}$ that can be had for rank $(p - q)$.

The eigenvalues of the normal matrix $\mathbf{A}^T\mathbf{A}$ are the squares of the singular values of $\mathbf{A}$ itself. The square of a small number is, of course, more difficult to distinguish from round-off error than the number itself. However, this consideration alone should not dissuade the reader from forming and working with the normal matrix, at least as a prelude to singular value computations.

7.1 JACOBI TRANSFORMATION

The SVD method I will describe makes good use of the fact that each row of a `matrix` is a `real_vector`. Consider applying the Givens 2×2 matrix from Section 6.5 to a $2 \times n$ matrix:

$$\begin{bmatrix} c & -s \\ s & c \end{bmatrix}\begin{bmatrix} \mathbf{x}^T \\ \mathbf{y}^T \end{bmatrix} = \begin{bmatrix} c\mathbf{x}^T & -s\mathbf{y}^T \\ s\mathbf{x}^T & +c\mathbf{y}^T \end{bmatrix}$$

In this context, this is called a *Jacobi transformation*. The only difference is that $\mathbf{x}^T$ and $\mathbf{y}^T$ are row vectors with n components. The objective of the algorithm is to set c and s so that the rows of the transformed matrix are orthogonal, to wit,

$$(c\mathbf{x}^T - s\mathbf{y}^T)(s\mathbf{x} + c\mathbf{y}) = 0 = cs\mathbf{x}^T\mathbf{x} + (c^2 - s^2)\mathbf{x}^T\mathbf{y} - cs\mathbf{y}^T\mathbf{y}$$
$$\equiv cs\alpha + (c^2 - s^2)\gamma - cs\beta = cs(\alpha - \beta) + (c^2 - s^2)\gamma$$

If we take seriously the idea that c and s are the cosine and sine of an unknown angle θ, then $cs = \frac{1}{2}\sin 2\theta$ and $c^2 - s^2 = \cos 2\theta$. Therefore, formally, $\cot 2\theta = (\beta - \alpha)/2\gamma$. Let us denote $\xi \equiv (\beta - \alpha)/2\gamma$, for short. Then additional trigonometric identities yield $\tan\theta = \text{sign}(\xi)/[|\xi| + (1 + \xi^2)^{1/2}]$, $c = (1 + \tan^2\theta)^{-1/2}$, and $s = c\tan\theta$.

These formulas are encoded in the first few lines of subroutine `Jacobi`:

```
unsigned Jacobi (real_vector& x, real_vector& y,
    // [ETC] )
{
    double e = 1.0e-12;
    double alfa = x*x; if( sqrt(alfa) <= e ) return 0;
    double beta = y*y; if( sqrt(beta) <= e ) return 0;
    double gama = x*y; if( fabs(gama) <= sqrt(alfa*beta)*e )
        return 0;
    double xi = 0.5*(beta-alfa)/gama;
    double t = 1./(fabs(xi)+sqrt(1.+xi*xi));
    double c = 1./sqrt(1.+t*t);
    double s = t*c;   if( xi < 0.) s = -s;
    (more...)
```

If α, β, or γ is zero or less than a specified threshold, no action is necessary, and the subroutine returns zero as an indicator of this fact. Otherwise, c and s are evaluated as indicated above. This formulation is numerically sound even if `xi` (ξ) vanishes.

7.1.1 Example

Let $\mathbf{x}$ be $[3 \quad 5]^T$ and $\mathbf{y}$ be $[8 \quad 1]^T$. Figure 7.1 shows these as points or vectors in a plane. Then $\alpha = \mathbf{x}^T\mathbf{x} = 34$, $\beta = \mathbf{y}^T\mathbf{y} = 65$, and $\gamma = \mathbf{x}^T\mathbf{y} = 29$. Therefore, $\cot 2\theta = 31/58 = 0.53448$ and $\theta = (61.876°)/2 = 30.938°$. Consequently, $c = 0.8577$ and $s = 0.5141$. Applying the transformation, $\mathbf{x}' = c\mathbf{x} - s\mathbf{y} = [-1.540 \quad 3.775]^T$ and $\mathbf{y}' = s\mathbf{x} + c\mathbf{y} = [8.404 \quad 3.428]^T$. The transformed vectors $\mathbf{x}'$ and $\mathbf{y}'$ are also shown in Fig. 7.1, where they appear to be perpendicular to each other. The reader can verify that $\mathbf{x}'^T\mathbf{y}' = -12.94 + 12.94 = 0$.

To change $\mathbf{y}$ to $\mathbf{y}'$, the transformation rotated the vector 15° and increased its length. To change $\mathbf{x}$ to $\mathbf{x}'$, the transformation rotated the vector 53° and reduced its length. The sum of squares $\mathbf{x}^T\mathbf{x} + \mathbf{y}^T\mathbf{y}$ *is* preserved. The point is that the transformation

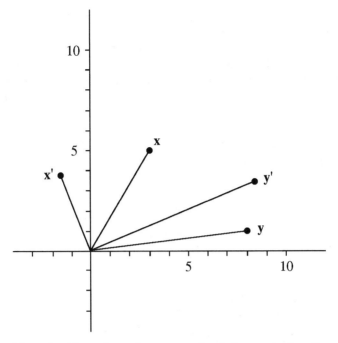

Fig. 7.1 After a Jacobi transformation, vectors $\mathbf{x}'$ and $\mathbf{y}'$ are mutually orthogonal.

is not a geometrical rotation and that the Jacobi angle θ is not a physical angle in Fig. 7.1. If one vector is a multiple of the other, $\mathbf{y} = a\mathbf{x}$, say, the Jacobi transformation yields $\mathbf{x}' = 0$ and $\mathbf{y}' = \mathbf{x}(1 + a^2)^{1/2}$.

Recall that Gram–Schmidt orthogonalization (Section 4.1) started with a set of linearly independent vectors spanning a space and from this produced a set of mutually orthogonal vectors, each normalized to unit length. The simplest SVD algorithm is likewise an exercise in orthogonalization. However, it uses the Jacobi transformation rather than the projection method of Gram–Schmidt.

To make the concept concrete, consider what happens in the case of matrix $\mathbf{A}$, $m \times n$, $m > n$, if we undertake to make its rows mutually orthogonal. Begin by writing the defining equation of SVD in the form $\mathbf{U}^{\mathrm{T}}\mathbf{A} = \mathbf{W}\mathbf{V}^{\mathrm{T}}$. The product matrix $\mathbf{W}\mathbf{V}^{\mathrm{T}}$ has the interesting form

$$
\mathbf{W}\mathbf{V}^{\mathrm{T}} = \begin{bmatrix} w_1\mathbf{v}_1^{\mathrm{T}} \\ \cdots \\ w_n\mathbf{v}_n^{\mathrm{T}} \\ \hline \mathbf{0} \end{bmatrix} \begin{matrix} n \\ \\ \\ \hline m-n \end{matrix}
$$

The first n rows of this matrix are the transposed columns of $\mathbf{V}$, row vectors $\mathbf{v}_j^{\mathrm{T}}$, mutually orthogonal by hypothesis, each multiplied by the corresponding singular value w_j. The last $m - n$ rows are zero. The plan of action is to subject matrix $\mathbf{A}$ recursively to a sequence of Jacobi transformations, $\mathbf{A}_{k+1} = \mathbf{J}_k\mathbf{A}_k$, until n (at most) of its rows are mutually orthogonal and the remainder are zero. We will then identify $\mathbf{WV}^T = \mathbf{J}_N \cdots \mathbf{J}_1\mathbf{A}$. Since $\mathbf{WV}^T = \mathbf{U}^T\mathbf{A}$, we will also identify $\mathbf{U}^T = \mathbf{J}_N \cdots \mathbf{J}_1$, where N is the total number of Jacobi transformations applied. We will accumulate $\mathbf{U}^T$ by applying the sequence of transformations $\mathbf{J}_N \cdots \mathbf{J}_1$ to an identity matrix at the same time that we transform $\mathbf{A}$ (i.e., $\mathbf{U}^T = \mathbf{J}_N \cdots \mathbf{J}_1\mathbf{I}$).

This plan of action is reflected in the code for subroutine Jacobi. In the call list, x and y are intended to be two rows of $\mathbf{A}_k$, and p and q are intended to be the two corresponding rows of $\mathbf{I}_k$. If the subroutine returns a 1, it indicates that transformation $\mathbf{J}_k$ has been applied.

```
unsigned Jacobi(real_vector& x, real_vector& y,
                real_vector& p, real_vector& q)
{//Greenstadt (in R&W) p85
// Compute c and s from x and y, as above; then

// Apply J to x and y:
   for(unsigned i=0; i<x.N(); i++){
      t = x[i]; x[i] = x[i]*c - y[i]*s; y[i] = y[i]*c
         + s*t;}

// Apply J to p and q:
   for(unsigned i=0; i<p.N(); i++){
      t = p[i]; p[i] = p[i]*c - q[i]*s; q[i] = q[i]*c
         + s*t;}
   return 1;
}
```

In this subroutine I use element-by-element loops rather than real_vector arithmetic and real_vector temporaries. The vector lengths x.N() and p.N() are generally different.

The SVD subroutine that calls Jacobi is straightforward:

```
void SVD (matrix& A, matrix& I, real_vector& w)
{//G&VL p456, transposed
   unsigned i, j, k, m = A.M(); double norm,
      e = 1.0e-12;

   for(i=0; i<m; i++){                                    //5
      do{k = 0;
         for(j=i+1; j<m; j++)                             //7
```

```
              k += Jacobi( A[j], A[i], I[j], I[i]);
        }while (k>0);

        norm = sqrt(A[i]*A[i]);                        //11
        if(norm > e){ w[i] = norm;
            A[i] *=(1./norm); }                        //12
            else     { w[i] = 0.;    A[i].init();
                I[i].init(); }
//      A.dumpall();
    }
    return;
}
```

The loop beginning in line 5 selects each row of A in sequence and makes it or-thogonal to each of the higher-numbered rows. The loop beginning in line 7 may be repeated in its entirety a number of times until Jacobi returns 0 for all values of j. At line 11, A[i] represents a row of $\mathbf{WV}^T$ and I[i] represents a row of $\mathbf{U}^T$. The matrix $\mathbf{W}$ is represented as a real_vector w containing the diagonal elements w_i. Line 12 therefore divides A[i] by w[i]. If the apparent norm of a row A[i] is less than a specified threshold, the row, its singular value, and the cor-responding row I[i] are zeroed.

When SVD returns, the rows of A ($\mathbf{V}^T$) are the columns $\mathbf{v}_j$ of $\mathbf{V}$, and the rows of I ($\mathbf{U}^T$) are the columns $\mathbf{u}_j$ of $\mathbf{U}$. Since theoretically, $\mathbf{A} = \sum w_j(\mathbf{u}_j\mathbf{v}_j^T)$, $\mathbf{A}$ can be re-built as in

```
matrix Q(mrows,ncols);
for(j=0; j<mrows; j++) Q.plus_outer( I[j], (A[j]*w[j]) );
```

7.1.2 Example

Recall from Section 4.1.1 that the Gram–Schmidt method applied to a particular matrix made an identity matrix of it. SVD applied to the same matrix produces quite a different result. The test case is

```
{   double y[16] = {1.,0.,0.,0.,2.,3.,0.,0.,4.,5.,6.,0.,
                    7.,8.,9.,10.};
    matrix A(y,4,4);  A.dumpall();
    real_vector w(4);
    matrix I(4,4);   for(int i=0; i<4; i++) I[i][i] = 1.;
    SVD(A,I,w);
    w.dumpall();
    A.dumpall();
    I.dumpall();
```

The input matrix A or **A** is

```
1|1|0|0|0
2|2|3|0|0
3|4|5|6|0
4|7|8|9|10
```

The output vector of singular values w representing **W** is

```
|0.819481|2.38028|4.90009|18.8322
```

The output matrix A representing $\mathbf{V}^{\mathrm{T}}$ is

```
1|0.810849|-0.580089|-0.0573508|-0.0522582
2|0.323563| 0.524088|-0.785159 | 0.0645356
3|0.215688| 0.355051| 0.254088 |-0.873417
4|0.43739 | 0.512609| 0.56185  | 0.479841
```

The output matrix I representing $\mathbf{U}^{\mathrm{T}}$ is

```
1|0.989467 |-0.144689|-0.0014093|-0.00428246
2|0.135934 | 0.932405|-0.334526 | 0.0153613
3|0.0440171| 0.305409| 0.849482 |-0.427982
4|0.0232256| 0.128111| 0.408009 | 0.903647
```

No remarkable pattern is obvious in these results, except perhaps that the singular values seem to be in ascending order. We can check the validity of the results by reconstructing the input matrix, as in

```
matrix Q(4,4);
for(int i=0; i<4; i++) Q.plus_outer( I[i], (A[i]*w[i]));
Q.dumpall();
```

The result Q contains the reconstruction of input **A**:

```
1|1|-3.32091e-16|-2.08844e-16|8.15185e-17
2|2|3|-1.16302e-15|-1.91795e-16
3|4|5|6|6.15176e-16
4|7|8|9|10
```

The only difference is that round-off error appears where we expect zeros. Finally, reconstruction of $\mathbf{A}^\mathrm{T}$ is effected by

```
    matrix T(4,4);
    for(int i=0; i<4; i++) T.plus_outer( (A[i]*w[i]),
        I[i]);
    T.dumpall();
}
```

The result T of this code contains the reconstruction of $\mathbf{A}^\mathrm{T}$, again with round-off error:

```
1|1|2|4|7
2|-3.32091e-16|3|5|8
3|-2.08844e-16|-1.16302e-15|6|9
4|8.15185e-17|-1.91795e-16|6.15176e-16|10
```

7.2 THE PSEUDOINVERSE

Consider once more the matrix equation $\mathbf{Ax} = \mathbf{b}$. Since we now know how to compute the SVD $\mathbf{A} = \mathbf{UWV}^\mathrm{T}$, formally we have a solution $\mathbf{x} = \mathbf{A}^{-1}\mathbf{b} = \mathbf{VW}^{-1}\mathbf{U}^\mathrm{T}\,\mathbf{b}$. The construct $\mathbf{VW}^{-1}\mathbf{U}^\mathrm{T}$ is known as the Moore–Penrose solution, or the pseudoinverse. The beauty of it is that the same formulation applies whether we have a full-rank problem or a least-squares case. We can even choose to restrict the solution to a particular subspace of the eigenmatrix set. All we need to do is agree that a zero singular value w_i is a signal to omit that value and its associated singular vectors from all summations. With that understood, the solution can be written

$$\mathbf{x} = \sum_{w_i \neq 0} \mathbf{v}_i \frac{1}{w_i} \mathbf{u}_i^\mathrm{T} \mathbf{b}$$

In this expression, $\mathbf{v}_i$ is a column of $\mathbf{V}$, and $\mathbf{u}_i$ is the like-numbered column of $\mathbf{U}$. The projection of $\mathbf{b}$ onto $\mathbf{u}_i$ is the scalar product $\mathbf{u}_i^\mathrm{T}\mathbf{b}$.

In terms of code, assuming that A as input to SVD represents $\mathbf{A}$ as in Section 7.1.2, and that x and b are represented as real_vectors, this expression can be implemented as

```
    for(i=0; i<mrows; i++)
        if(w[i] != 0.)
            x += A[i] * (( I[i] * b ) * (1./w[i]) );
```

Figure 7.2a shows schematically the relationships among the dimensions of $\mathbf{A}$, $\mathbf{x}$, and $\mathbf{b}$ in the least-squares problem $\mathbf{Ax} = \mathbf{b}$. Figure 7.2b relates the dimensions of

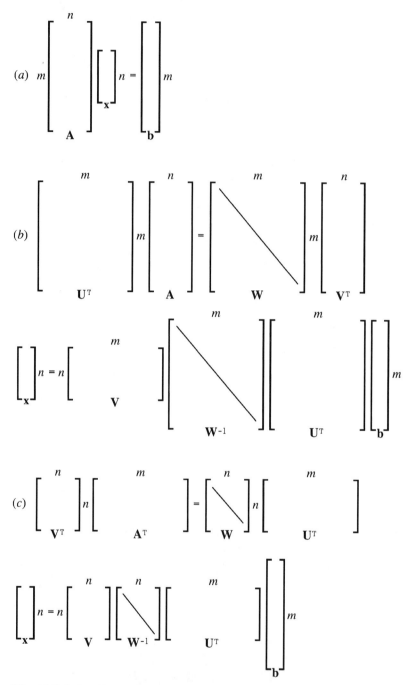

Fig. 7.2   (*a*) Relationship among the dimensions of **A**, **x**, and **b** in the overdetermined system **Ax** = **b**; (*b*) dimensions of **A**, **U**, **V**, and **W** in straightforward SVD; (*c*) dimensions of **A**, **U**, **V**, and **W** in transposed SVD.

A, **U**, **V**, and **W** that result when **A** is input to SVD(A,I,w). Recall that $\mathbf{V}^T$ overwrites **A** and $\mathbf{U}^T$ overwrites **I**. So A[i] corresponds to $\mathbf{v}_i$ and I[i] * b corresponds to $\mathbf{u}_i^T\mathbf{b}$, in the foregoing code.

For reasons I will demonstrate shortly, in a problem such as **Ax** = **b**, I prefer to input $\mathbf{A}^T$ (as A) to SVD(A,I,w), exploiting the relationship $\mathbf{V}^T\mathbf{A}^T = \mathbf{W}\mathbf{U}^T$. The interpretation that applies in this case is shown in Fig. 7.2c. When SVD finishes, I[i] corresponds to $\mathbf{v}_i$ and A[i] corresponds to $\mathbf{u}_i$. Therefore, the solution for **x** by means of the pseudoinverse takes the following form:

```
for(i=0; i<ncols; i++)
    if(w[i] != 0.)
        x += I[i] * (( A[i] * b ) * (1./w[i]) );
```

Here A[i] has ncols rows, because it was initialized by $\mathbf{A}^T$ rather than **A**.

7.2.1 Example

This example compares and contrasts the straight and transposed versions of the pseudoinverse solution of the same problem as in Section 6.3.1. The following code initializes the design matrix and its transpose:

```
{   double data[20] = {-5., 2.,-1., 4., 2., 6., 3., 7.,
                       10.,11.,9.,11., 1., 5., 1., 6.,
                       7., 9., 4., 8.};
    matrix A(data,10,2);
    A.dumpall();
    matrix At(2,10);
    for(int i=1; i<=2; i++) for(int j=1; j<=10; j++)
        At(i,j) = A(j,i);
    At.dumpall();
```

The statement A.dumpall(); prints out **A**:

```
 1| -5|  2
 2| -1|  4
 3|  2|  6
 4|  3|  7
 5| 10| 11
 6|  9| 11
 7|  1|  5
 8|  1|  6
 9|  7|  9
10|  4|  8
```

The statement `At.dumpall();` prints out $\mathbf{A}^\mathrm{T}$:

```
1|-5|-1| 2| 3|10| 9| 1| 1| 7| 4
2| 2| 4| 6| 7|11|11| 5| 6| 9| 8
```

The following code sets up and solves the linear-regression least-squares problem by applying SVD to the design matrix $\mathbf{A}$:

```
matrix I(10,10);  for(int i=0; i<10; i++) I[i][i] = 1.;
real_vector w(10);
SVD(A,I,w);
A.dumpall();
w.dumpall();
I.dumpall();
```

After `SVD(A,I,w);` we find $\mathbf{V}^\mathrm{T}$ in `A`:

```
 1|0|0
 2|0|0
 3|0|0
 4|0|0
 5|0.56127|0.827633
 6|0|0
 7|-0.827633|0.56127
 8|0|0
 9|0|0
10|0|0
```

We note that only two rows are nonzero, and that their locations are not obvious. At the same time, the result for $\mathbf{W}$ (in `w`) shows corresponding nonzero entries:

```
|0|0|0|0|27.9196|0|7.77775|0|0|0
```

The result for $\mathbf{U}^\mathrm{T}$ is contained in `I` and is similarly structured:

```
 1|0|0|0|0|0|0|0|0|0|0
 2|0|0|0|0|0|0|0|0|0|0
 3|0|0|0|0|0|0|0|0|0|0
 4|0|0|0|0|0|0|0|0|0|0
 5|-0.0412285|0.0984705|0.218066|0.267813|0.527108
  | 0.507005 |0.16832  |0.197963|0.407512|0.317559
 6|0|0|0|0|0|0|0|0|0|0
 7|0.676379 |0.395065|0.220161|0.185914  |-0.270304
  |-0.163893|0.254408|0.326571|-0.0953999| 0.151667
```

```
 8|0|0|0|0|0|0|0|0|0|0|0
 9|0|0|0|0|0|0|0|0|0|0|0
10|0|0|0|0|0|0|0|0|0|0|0
```

With **U**, **V**, and **W** thus in hand, we define a **b** containing all ones, as in Section 6.3.1 and obtain the pseudoinverse solution as follows:

```
real_vector x(2), b(10); x.init(); b.init() += 1.;
for(int i=0; i<10; i++)
   if(w[i] != 0.)
      x += A[i] * ( (I[i] * b) * (1./w[i]) );
printf("Answer = "); x.dumpall();
```

Yielding: `Answer  =  |-0.125183|0.200382`. A quick comparison shows that this is the same result as obtained in Section 6.3.1 by QR factorization of the design matrix.

The advantage of subjecting the transpose of **A** to SVD in a least-squares problem with many more rows than columns lies in a more compact formulation without a large proportion of zeros in the results. The following code sets up and solves the same least-squares problem by applying SVD to the transposed design matrix $\mathbf{A}^T$:

```
matrix I2(2,2); I2(1,1) = I2(2,2) = 1.;
real_vector w2(2);
SVD(At,I2,w2);
At.dumpall();
w2.dumpall();
I2.dumpall();
```

The dimensions of the auxiliary arrays are 2 rather than 10. After `SVD(At,I2,w2);` we find that `At` contains $\mathbf{U}^T$:

```
1|-0.676379|-0.395065|-0.220161|-0.185914|0.270304
 | 0.163893|-0.254408|-0.326571|0.0953999|-0.151667
2|-0.0412285|0.0984705|0.218066|0.267813|0.527108
 |  0.507005|  0.16832|0.197963|0.407512|0.317559
```

The corresponding result for **W** is contained in `w2`:

```
|7.77775|27.9196
```

Finally, `I2` contains the result for $\mathbf{V}^T$:

```
1|0.827633|-0.56127
2|0.56127 |0.827633
```

The corresponding pseudoinverse solution makes two passes through its main loop rather than 10. We begin by reinitializing the same x and b as before:

```
x.init(); b.init() += 1.;
for(int i=0; i<2; i++)
    if(w2[i] != 0.)
        x += I2[i] * ( (At[i] * b) * (1./w2[i]) );
printf("Answer = "); x.dumpall();
}
```

Yielding: `Answer = |-0.125183|0.200382`. The correct result, again.

My preference for solving least-squares problems of the parameter-fitting type is to apply SVD() to the transpose of the design matrix. This approach does not require the user to deal with redundant zeros.

7.3   APPLICATION TO TWO-DIMENSIONAL IMAGES

At the start of this chapter I suggested that the outer product of a pair of singular vectors $(\mathbf{u}_j \mathbf{v}_j^T)$ can be called an eigenmatrix. We have seen several demonstrations that the weighted summation of eigenmatrices $\sum w_j (\mathbf{u}_j \mathbf{v}_j^T)$ reproduces the original input matrix. When the input matrix represents a two-dimensional image, the eigenmatrices are often referred to as *eigenimages*. This term connotes the decomposition and reconstruction of images by SVD.

In the following code excerpts, a matrix $\mathbf{A}^T$ (as A) is defined whose pattern of zeros and nonzeros, when graphed, makes a recognizable image. SVD is applied and reduces this image to a very few singular vectors. The corresponding eigenimages, when summed together, then reconstitute the original image.

```
{   matrix A(96,128);
    for(int i=16; i<32; i++) for(int j=48; j<72; j++)
        A(i,j) = 1.0;
    for(int i=32; i<64; i++) for(int j=24; j<96; j++)
        A(i,j) = 1.0;
    for(int i=64; i<80; i++) for(int j=48; j<72; j++)
        A(i,j) = 1.0;
    plot_matrix( A );
```

The graph of $\mathbf{A}^T$ is shown in Fig. 7.3a. Rows 16 through 79 contain ones, plotted as black, and the pattern is widest in rows 32 through 63. Figure 7.3b shows the graph of the identity matrix $\mathbf{I}$ (I), which is initialized as follows:

```
matrix I(96,96);  for(int i=0; i<96; i++) I[i][i] = 1.;
plot_matrix( I );
```

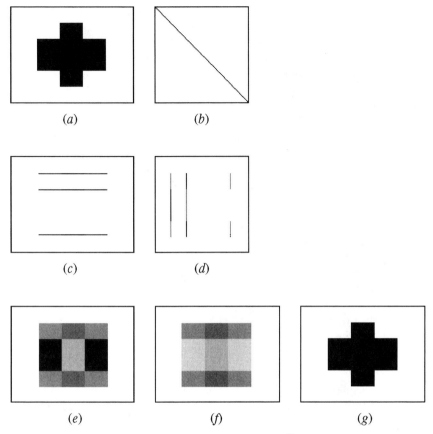

Fig. 7.3   Two-dimensional SVD problem: (*a*) input matrix $\mathbf{A}^\mathrm{T}$; (*b*) identity matrix $\mathbf{I}$; (*c*) computed matrix $\mathbf{U}^\mathrm{T}$ replaces $\mathbf{A}^\mathrm{T}$; (*d*) computed matrix $\mathbf{V}$ replaces $\mathbf{I}$; (*e*) eigenimage $w_{16}v_{16}u_{16}^\mathrm{T}$; (*f*) eigenimage $w_{32}v_{32}u_{32}^\mathrm{T}$; (*g*) the sum of (*e*) and (*f*) reproduces (*a*).

Diagonal matrix $\mathbf{W}$ (as `real_vector` w) is defined and SVD is applied:

```
real_vector w(96);
SVD(A,I,w);
w.dumpall();
```

After `SVD()`, w contains

```
|0|0|0|0|0|0|0|0|0|0|0|0|0|0|0|0|51.2066|0|0|0|0|0|0|0|0|0
|0|0|0|0|0|0|0|21.2105|0|0|0|0|0|0|0|0|0|0|0|0|0|0|0|0|0|0
|0|0|0|0|0|0|0|0|0|0|0|0|0|0|0|0|0|0|0|0|0|0|0|0|0|0
|0|0|0|0|3.84596e-12|0|0|0|0|0|0|0|0|0|0|0|0|0|0|0|0|0|0|0|0
```

The nonzero values correspond to $w_{16} = 51.2066$, $w_{32} = 21.2105$, and $w_{77} = 3.84596 \times 10^{-12}$. Figure 7.3c shows the corresponding matrix $\mathbf{U}^T$ (A after SVD), and Fig. 7.3d displays $\mathbf{V}$ (I after SVD, transposed). We see $\mathbf{u}_{16}$ and $\mathbf{v}_{16}$ corresponding to w_{16}, together with $\mathbf{u}_{32}$ and $\mathbf{v}_{32}$ corresponding to w_{32}. The variation in gray shading indicates a variation in the values of the nonzeros. Both negative and positive values are represented.

It is instructive to note that w_{77}, $\mathbf{u}_{77}$, and $\mathbf{v}_{77}$ are artifacts. They result from the fact that setting e = 1.e-12 in Jacobi tolerates a residual error that is quite small, but still distinguishable from round-off error. So w_{77}, $\mathbf{u}_{77}$, and $\mathbf{v}_{77}$ are generated to absorb the residual error. Setting thresholds can be tricky.

Only eigenimages 16 and 32 are significant in the SVD of $\mathbf{A}^T$. They are defined and displayed by the following code:

```
matrix Q(96,128);   Q.plus_outer( (I[15]*w[15]), A[15]);
plot_matrix( Q );

matrix T(96,128);   T.plus_outer( (I[31]*w[31]), A[31]);
plot_matrix( T );

T.plus_outer( (I[15]*w[15]), A[15]);
plot_matrix( T );
}
```

Figure 7.3e displays the weighted eigenimage $w_{16}\mathbf{v}_{16}\mathbf{u}_{16}^T$, and Fig. 7.3f displays the weighted eigenimage $w_{32}\mathbf{v}_{32}\mathbf{u}_{32}^T$. Figure 7.3g shows the sum of these two, which obviously matches the original $\mathbf{A}^T$, Fig. 7.3a. In other words, the information contained in Fig. 7.3a can be distilled down to two pairs of singular vectors. It is a simple image.

7.3.1 Review Question

What is the rank of $\mathbf{A}^T$ (Fig. 7.3a) in the foregoing example?

7.4 INDIRECT SVD METHODS

A singular value decomposition can be computed without necessarily employing an SVD algorithm per se. I stated at the beginning of this chapter that singular value decomposition amounts to solving the coupled eigenproblems $\mathbf{A}\mathbf{v}_j = w_j\mathbf{u}_j$ and $\mathbf{A}^T\mathbf{u}_j = w_j\mathbf{v}_j$. We can make this explicit with partitioned-matrix notation, for example,

$$\left[\begin{array}{c|c} \mathbf{0} & \mathbf{A} \\ \hline \mathbf{A}^T & \mathbf{0} \end{array}\right]\left[\frac{\mathbf{u}_j}{\mathbf{v}_j}\right] = w_j\left[\frac{\mathbf{u}_j}{\mathbf{v}_j}\right]$$

The top row of the built-up matrix equation reads $\mathbf{A}\mathbf{v}_j = w_j\mathbf{u}_j$, and the bottom row reads $\mathbf{A}^T\mathbf{u}_j = w_j\mathbf{v}_j$. Q.E.D. With this construction, we have come full circle and expressed SVD as a symmetric eigenvalue problem! Specifically, if

$$\mathbf{B} = \begin{bmatrix} \mathbf{0} & \mathbf{A} \\ \hline \mathbf{A}^T & \mathbf{0} \end{bmatrix} \quad \text{and} \quad \mathbf{q}_j = \begin{bmatrix} \mathbf{u}_j \\ \hline \mathbf{v}_j \end{bmatrix}$$

the problem to be solved is $\mathbf{B}\mathbf{q}_j = w_j\mathbf{q}_j$. This is the same form as the problem attacked in Section 6.4.

The method applied to the symmetric eigenproblem in Section 6.4 proceeds in two stages. First, matrix member function HouseTridiag() makes a symmetric matrix tridiagonal, and then function alg823() diagonalizes the tridiagonal matrix.

7.4.1 Example

This example applies the symmetric eigenvalue method from Chapter 6 to the same data as in the SVD example in Section 7.1.2:

```
{  double y[16] = {1.,0.,0.,0.,2.,3.,0.,0.,4.,5.,6.,0.,
                   7.,8.,9.,10.};
   matrix A(y,4,4);
   matrix B(8,8);
   for(int i=1; i<=4; i++)              //4
       for(int j=1; j<=4; j++)          //5
           B(i,j+4) = B(j+4,i) = A(i,j); //6
   B.dumpall();
```

The matrix A is the same as in Section 7.1.2. The contents of A and its transpose are copied into built-up matrix B in lines 4 through 6. So B initially contains

```
1|0|0|0|0|1|0|0|0
2|0|0|0|0|2|3|0|0
3|0|0|0|0|4|5|6|0
4|0|0|0|0|7|8|9|10
5|1|2|4|7|0|0|0|0
6|0|3|5|8|0|0|0|0
7|0|0|6|9|0|0|0|0
8|0|0|0|10|0|0|0|0
```

Built-up matrix B is explicitly symmetric, even though it lacks a nonzero main diagonal. It is fair game for

```
   B.HouseTridiag();
   B.dumpall();
```

which yields

```
1|0|-1|0|0|0|0|0|0
2|-1|0|8.30662|0|0|0|0|0
3|0|8.30662|0|-16.6781|0|0|0|0
4|0|0|-16.6781|0|-2.93868|0|0|0
5|0|0|0|-2.93868|0|-4.07597|0|0
6|0|0|0|0|-4.07597|0|-2.14011|0
7|0|0|0|0|0|-2.14011|0|-2.64786
8|0|0|0|0|0|0|-2.64786|0
```

For clarity, I have taken the liberty of editing round-off error to 0 on the main diagonal. Finally,

```
    alg_823( B );
    B.dumpall();
}
```

yields

```
1|-18.8322|0|0|0|0|0|0|0
2|0|18.8322|0|0|0|0|0|0
3|0|0|-4.90009|0|0|0|0|0
4|0|0|0|4.90009|0|0|0|0
5|0|0|0|0|-2.38028|0|0|0
6|0|0|0|0|0|-0.819481|0|
7|0|0|0|0|0|0|0.819481|0
8|0|0|0|0|0|0|0|2.38028
```

compared to the result w from the example in Section 7.1.2:

```
|0.819481|2.38028|4.90009|18.8322 .
```

What this shows is generally true of this method. The eigenvalues appearing in the diagonalized built-up matrix are the same as the singular values of the initial SVD problem, but they are repeated with both algebraic signs.

As the $+$ and $-$ eigenvalues of the symmetric problem are related to the singular values of the SVD problem, the eigenvectors of the symmetric problem are related predictably to the singular vectors of the SVD problem. If $\mathbf{Av} = w\mathbf{u}$ and $\mathbf{A}^T\mathbf{u} = w\mathbf{v}$ for some singular value w and singular vectors $\mathbf{u}$ and $\mathbf{v}$, the built-up problem will have solutions $\mathbf{Bq}_+ = w\mathbf{q}_+$ and $\mathbf{Bq}_- = -w\mathbf{q}_-$, where $\mathbf{q}_+ = [\mathbf{u} \ \mathbf{v}]^T/\sqrt{2}$, and $\mathbf{q}_- = [\mathbf{u} \ -\mathbf{v}]^T/\sqrt{2}$. Thus $\mathbf{q}_+^T\mathbf{q}_- = 0$ and $\mathbf{q}_+^T\mathbf{q}_+ = \mathbf{q}_-^T\mathbf{q}_- = 1$. Orthonormality is maintained.

7.4.2 Power Method

This method, simple in concept, can be effective in finding the eigenvectors that correspond to the largest eigenvalues of a matrix. Start with an arbitrary vector $\mathbf{x}$, which is an unknown weighted sum of eigenvectors: $\mathbf{x} = a_1\mathbf{q}_1 + a_2\mathbf{q}_2 + a_3\mathbf{q}_3 + \cdots$. Simply multiply this N times by the matrix in question and divide through by w_1^N, where w_1 is the largest eigenvalue: $\mathbf{B}^N\mathbf{x} = w_1^N (a_1\mathbf{q}_1 + a_2(w_2/w_1)^N\mathbf{q}_2 + a_3(w_3/w_1)^N\mathbf{q}_3 + \cdots)$. After this is renormalized to unit length, the components $\mathbf{q}_j$ other than $\mathbf{q}_1$ are reduced by a factor of $(w_j/w_1)^N$. In the limit, only $\mathbf{q}_1$ survives. For this algorithm to work well, the initial vector $\mathbf{x}$ must contain a substantial amount of $\mathbf{q}_1$. The following subroutine implements a basic power iteration method. It makes an eigenvector out of x and returns its eigenvalue:

```
double Power_Method (const matrix& A, real_vector& x)
{//After G&VL p351 (7.3.3)
   double l, eps=1.e-12, o = 0., s = 1.;
   real_vector q(x.N()); q = x;

   for(int i=0; i<4*(x.N()); i++){
      l = sqrt(q*q); if(l < eps) break;
      x = (q *= (s/l));
      l = x * (q = A * x);
      if(abs(l-o) < eps) break;  o = l;
      s = (l > 0. ? 1. : -1.);
   }
   q.zap();
   return l;
}
```

For a demonstration, I declared a matrix Z(2,8); and initialized its top row to something close to $[\mathbf{u}\ \mathbf{v}]^T$ as determined in Section 7.1.2, rows 4 of $\mathbf{U}^T$ and $\mathbf{V}^T$. The bottom row of Z was initialized to alternating ones and zeros. Then I ran

```
lam = Power_Method( B, Z[0] ); cout << lam << endl; //1
Gram_Schmidt( Z ); //2
lam = Power_Method( B, Z[1] ); cout << lam << endl; //3
Z.dumpall();
```

which printed out

```
18 8322
-18.8322
1|0.01642|0.09059|0.2885|0.639|0.3093|0.36245|0.39727|
   0.33928
2|0.01642|0.09058|0.2885|0.6389|-0.3093|-0.36249|
   -0.3973|-0.33931
```

Line 1 makes Z[0] an eigenvector with eigenvalue 18.8322. Line 2 makes Z[1] initially orthogonal to Z[0], and line 3 reduces it to an eigenvector with eigenvalue -18.8322. We observe that the rows of Z show the expected $q_{\pm}$ form. We also see that round-off error would be an issue in further elaboration of this approach.

7.5   LANCZOS METHOD

The Lanczos strategy for the symmetric eigenproblem is like the Householder strategy in that we first tridiagonalize a symmetric matrix and then we diagonalize the tridiagonal matrix. The difference lies in the tridiagonalization step. Like the conjugate gradient method, the Lanczos approach requires only matrix $\times$ vector products, and it never modifies the input matrix. This is a decisive advantage when dealing with large sparse matrices.

A basic Lanczos tridiagonalization algorithm is embodied in the subroutine

```
unsigned LanczosTridiag (const sparse& A, real_vector& diag,
                                          real_vector& sub1)
```

In the call list, A is the symmetric input matrix, while diag and sub1 are vectors provided by the caller to receive the diagonal and subdiagonal of the tridiagonal output matrix. An alternative version of the subroutine accepts const matrix& instead of const sparse&. The subroutine works with three internal vectors, each of length A.N(): v, w, t. The results are quite sensitive to how w is initialized. There are three scalars: alfa, beta, and eps. If the output of the subroutine is conceptually a symmetric tridiagonal matrix **T**, then diag(i) corresponds to t_{ii} and sub1(i) corresponds to $t_{i,i-1}$, provided that $i > 1$. Entry diag(1) is handled as a special case, and the main loop recursively fills the other entries in order:

```
v += A * w;
diag(1) = alfa = w * v;   sub1(1) = 0;
for(j=2; j<=A.N(); j++)
{
    v -= w * alfa;
    sub1(j) = beta = sqrt( v * v );
    if(beta < eps) break;
    t = v;  v = w * (-beta);   w = t * (1./beta);
    v += A * w;
    diag(j) = alfa = w * v;
}
```

The output vectors are input to a diagonalization routine such as alg_823() to determine the eigenvalues. To obtain eigenvectors as well as eigenvalues, it would be necessary to store each iteration of w, called the *Lanczos vectors*. They can serve as input to an additional process (not presented here) that produces eigenvectors.

As with the power method, applying the Lanczos method to high-order matrices requires confronting the problem that round-off error degrades the orthogonality of purported eigenvectors [2]. The following code applies the Lanczos method to our ongoing symmetric eigenvalue problem. Matrix B is set up as in the example in Section 7.4.1. Then

```
real_vector diag(8), sub1(8);  unsigned k;
k = LanczosTridiag( B, diag, sub1 );
printf("k = %d\n", k);
diag.dumpall(); sub1.dumpall();
alg_823( diag, sub1 );
diag.dumpall(); sub1.dumpall();
```

After LanczosTridiag(), sub1 is not the same as the subdiagonal of the previous result from B.HouseTridiag() (q.v.):

```
k = 8
diag: |0|0|0|0|0|0|0|0
sub1: |0|3.60555|12.3319|13.8513|2.90229|4.28483|0.757386
      |0.841155
```

Nevertheless, alg_823(diag, sub1) produces neatly ordered correct pairs of eigenvalues:

```
|18.8322|-18.8322|4.90009|-4.90009|2.38028|-2.38028|
    0.819481|-0.819481
|0|0|0|0|0|0|0|0
```

7.6 SUMMARY AND CONCLUSIONS

Singular Value Decomposition. The standard depiction of SVD is the canonical form $U^T A V = diag(w_1, \dots, w_p)$. The orthogonal transformations U and V are applied as shown and diagonalize A. Matrix A can then be decomposed as $A = \sum w_j (u_j v_j^T)$, where u_j and v_j are corresponding columns of U and V, respectively.

Pseudoinverse. If the problem to be solved is $Ax = b$, then SVD leads to the solution $x = A^{-1}b = VW^{-1}U^T b$. ($W$ represents the diagonal matrix of singular values.) This expression is equivalent to $x = \sum_{w_i \neq 0} v_i (1/w_i)(u_i^T b)$. Zero singular values are omitted from the summation.

Implementation. If A is $m \times n$, with $m > n$, work with its transpose: SVD(At, I, w); so that matrix At is $n \times m$, matrix I is $n \times n$, and real_vector w is length n. When SVD() finishes, $\mathbf{U}^{\mathrm{T}}$ overwrites $\mathbf{A}^{\mathrm{T}}$, $\mathbf{V}^{\mathrm{T}}$ overwrites $\mathbf{I}$, and $\mathbf{w}$ contains the singular values. Therefore, the solution of $\mathbf{Ax} = \mathbf{b}$ takes the form

```
for(int i=0; i<n; i++)
   if(w[i] != 0.)
      x += I[i]*((At[i] * b)*(1./w[i]));
```

Indirect Methods. Singular value decomposition can be expressed as a symmetric eigenproblem:

$$\left[\begin{array}{c|c} \mathbf{0} & \mathbf{A} \\ \hline \mathbf{A}^{\mathrm{T}} & \mathbf{0} \end{array}\right]\left[\begin{array}{c} \mathbf{u}_j \\ \hline \mathbf{v}_j \end{array}\right] = w_j \left[\begin{array}{c} \mathbf{u}_j \\ \hline \mathbf{v}_j \end{array}\right]$$

If $\mathbf{A}$ is large and sparse, indirect eigenvalue methods such as Power_Method() and LanczosTridiag() may be helpful. For smaller $\mathbf{A}$, HouseTridiag() (Section 6.4) is applicable.

8 Cholesky Decomposition

In this chapter we present a method of factorizing a symmetric matrix into the product of a triangular matrix and its transpose. This method is especially suitable for sparse matrices because it can be arranged to minimize the creation of additional nonzeros. Symmetric sparse matrices show up in many practical problems, and this approach is quite valuable despite its apparent restrictions.

If matrix $\mathbf{A}$ is symmetric, we shall see that it can be factorized as $\mathbf{A} = \mathbf{LDL}^{\mathrm{T}}$. $\mathbf{L}$ is a lower-triangular matrix, and $\mathbf{D}$ is diagonal. $\mathbf{D}$ is included between $\mathbf{L}$ and its transpose so that $\mathbf{L}$ may have all ones on its main diagonal, as we assumed in Chapter 5 regarding lower-triangular matrices. Cholesky decomposition in the narrow sense requires that $\mathbf{A}$ is also positive definite, so that the square root can be taken of each element of $\mathbf{D}$. Then the decomposition of $\mathbf{A}$ can be structured as $\mathbf{A} = (\mathbf{LD}^{1/2})\,(\mathbf{D}^{1/2}\mathbf{L}^{\mathrm{T}})$ (i.e., $\mathbf{CC}^{\mathrm{T}}$, where $\mathbf{C} = \mathbf{LD}^{1/2}$). The form $\mathbf{A} = \mathbf{CC}^{\mathrm{T}}$ is the definition of Cholesky factorization in the narrow sense. In this chapter we concentrate on the more general form $\mathbf{LDL}^{\mathrm{T}}$.

It is instructive to work out a small example. Assume that $\mathbf{LDL}^{\mathrm{T}}$ takes the shape

$$
\mathbf{LDL}^{\mathrm{T}} =
\begin{bmatrix}
1 & & & \\
a_1 & 1 & & \\
b_1 & b_2 & 1 & \\
c_1 & c_2 & c_3 & 1
\end{bmatrix}
\begin{bmatrix}
d_1 & & & \\
& d_2 & & \\
& & d_3 & \\
& & & d_4
\end{bmatrix}
\begin{bmatrix}
1 & a_1 & b_1 & c_1 \\
& 1 & b_2 & c_2 \\
& & 1 & c_3 \\
& & & 1
\end{bmatrix}
$$

$$
(\mathbf{LD})\mathbf{L}^{\mathrm{T}} =
\begin{bmatrix}
d_1 & & & \\
d_1 a_1 & d_2 & & \\
d_1 b_1 & d_2 b_2 & d_3 & \\
d_1 c_1 & d_2 c_2 & d_3 c_3 & d_4
\end{bmatrix}
\begin{bmatrix}
1 & a_1 & b_1 & c_1 \\
& 1 & b_2 & c_2 \\
& & 1 & c_3 \\
& & & 1
\end{bmatrix}
$$

$$
=
\begin{bmatrix}
d_1 & d_1 a_1 & d_1 b_1 & d_1 c_1 \\
d_1 a_1 & d_2 + d_1 a_1 a_1 & d_2 b_2 + d_1 a_1 b_1 & d_2 c_2 + d_1 a_1 c_1 \\
d_1 b_1 & d_2 b_2 + d_1 a_1 b_1 & d_3 + d_1 b_1 b_1 + d_2 b_2 b_2 & d_3 c_3 + d_1 b_1 c_1 + d_2 b_2 c_2 \\
d_1 c_1 & d_2 c_2 + d_1 a_1 c_1 & d_3 c_3 + d_1 b_1 c_1 + d_2 b_2 c_2 & d_4 + d_1 c_1 c_1 + d_2 c_2 c_2 + d_3 c_3 c_3
\end{bmatrix}
$$

A close reading reveals that this product matrix is explicitly symmetric. It can therefore be equated to any symmetric matrix of the same size, for example,

$$
\mathbf{A} =
\begin{bmatrix}
a_{11} & a_{12} & a_{13} & a_{14} \\
a_{21} & a_{22} & a_{23} & a_{24} \\
a_{31} & a_{32} & a_{33} & a_{34} \\
a_{41} & a_{42} & a_{43} & a_{44}
\end{bmatrix},
\qquad \text{where } a_{ij} = a_{ji}
$$

If we equate corresponding elements of these two matrices, starting at the top left, we can solve for $\mathbf{L}$ and $\mathbf{D}$. Specifically,

$$d_1 = a_{11}$$

$$a_1 = \frac{a_{21}}{d_1}$$

$$d_2 = a_{22} - d_1 a_1^2$$

$$b_1 = \frac{a_{31}}{d_1}$$

$$b_2 = \frac{a_{32} - d_1 a_1 b_1}{d_2}$$

$$d_3 = a_{33} - d_1 b_1^2 - d_2 b_2^2 \quad \text{etc.}$$

The pattern is clear. If we proceed row by row from top to bottom, and from left to right within each row, each element of $\mathbf{L}$ and $\mathbf{D}$ can be solved for in terms of elements already determined. The general formulas, denoting an element of $\mathbf{L}$ as l_{ij}, are

$$l_{ij} = \frac{a_{ij} - \sum_{k<j, j<i} d_k l_{ik} l_{jk}}{d_j}$$

$$d_i = a_{ii} - \sum_{j<i} d_j l_{ij}^2$$

These formulas do not access elements of $\mathbf{A}$ above its main diagonal.

My $\mathbf{LDL}^{\mathrm{T}}$ factorization subroutine is a `sparse` member function that leaves the input $\mathbf{A}$ untouched and writes result $\mathbf{L}$ to a separate `sparse` matrix. The elements of diagonal $\mathbf{D}$ are stored into a `real_vector`:

```
void sparse::LDLt (const sparse& A, real_vector& d);
```

After `L`, `A`, and d have been appropriately set up, the subroutine call is

```
L.LDLt( A, d);.
```

One further observation is pertinent to the concise implementation of `LDLt()`. In the formulas above, it is worthwhile to isolate the products of the form $l_{ij}d_j$ as distinct entities. That is,

$$l_{ij}d_j = a_{ij} - \sum_{k<j, j<i} (l_{ik}d_k) l_{jk}$$

Clearly, the current value of $l_{ij}d_j$ is constructed from a_{ij} and from previous values $l_{ik}d_k$ in the same row, in leftward columns, $k < j$, multiplied by corresponding values of l_{jk} from a previous row, $j < i$. Similarly,

$$d_i = a_{ii} - \sum_{j<i} (l_{ij}d_j)\, l_{ij}$$

The value of d_i for each row is constructed from a_{ii} and from leftward values of $l_{ij}d_j$ in the same row.

The source code for subroutine LDLt() begins as follows:

```
void sparse::LDLt (const sparse& A, real_vector& d)
{
    unsigned i,j,k,l,r;  double lij, lij_dj,  diagi;
    element *elem, *prev;
    real_vector tmp (ncols);  tmp.init();
    for (i=1; i<=d.N(); i++) d(i) = A.getval(i,i);
    (more...)
```

Pointers elem and prev are of type element. They will be used in accessing nonzeros in **A** and **L**, respectively. Work vector tmp is defined and initialized to hold up to a full row of results. The main diagonal of **A** is copied into d. Then rows 1 and 2 of the factorization are handled as a special case:

```
    lij_dj = A.getval(2,1);
    if(lij_dj != 0.){
        lij = lij_dj / d(1);
        d(2) -= lij * lij_dj;
        stash(2,1) = lij; }
    (more...)
```

The last line of this stores l_{21} into **L**. The main loop of the subroutine processes rows 3 through mrows in increasing order:

```
    for (i=3; i<=mrows; i++)
    {
        diagi = d(i);

//      Dump row i of A into tmp, checking j < i:
        elem = A.row[i-1];
        while((k = elem->next) != 0){ elem = A.e+k;
            if((j = elem->col) >= i) continue;
            tmp(j) = elem->value;  }

//      Process row i from left to right:
        for (j=1; j<i; j++)
```

```
        {
            if (tmp(j) == 0.) continue;
            if ( d(j)  == 0.) continue;
                // (redundant, theoretically)
            lij_dj = tmp(j); lij = lij_dj / d(j);   tmp(j)
                = 0.;                                    //27
            diagi -= lij * lij_dj;

//          Combine lij_dj and previous lij from this
//              column:
            prev = col[j-1];
            while ((l = prev->mext) != 0){ prev = e+1;
                r = prev->row;   tmp(r) -= lij_dj *
                    (prev->value);
            }
            stash(i,j) = lij;                            //35
        }
        d(i) = diagi; // This row is now final
    }
    tmp.zap();
    return;
}
```

The organization of the main loop is referred to as a *Doolittle algorithm*. As soon as each new value of $l_{ik}d_k$ is determined, its contribution to the summation $\sum(l_{ik}d_k)l_{jk}$ for each column j to its right (i.e., $j > k$) is distributed. This is guided by retrieving all previous nonzero l_{jk} values in the same column k. Each `lij_dj` value is completely determined just before it is accessed, as `tmp(j)`. It is through this mechanism that the value of l_{ij} can become nonzero even if the corresponding a_{ij} value was zero.

8.0.1 Example

This example applies `LDLt()` to the same symmetric matrix as in the example in Section 6.4.1 demonstrating `HouseTridiag()`. In the present case, array `data` is two-dimensional, and `sparse A` is initialized element by element:

```
{   double data[4][4] = {{ 1., 5., 8., 0.},
                         { 5., 2., 6., 9.},
                         { 8., 6., 3., 7.},
                         { 0., 9., 7., 4.} };
    sparse A(4,4,16); sparse L(4,4,16); real_vector d(4);
    for(int i=1; i<=4; i++)
        for(int j=1; j<=4; j++)
```

```
        if(data[i-1][j-1] != 0.) A(i,j) = data[i-1] [j-1];
    print_matrix( A );
    L.LDLt( A, d);
    print_matrix( L );
    d.dumpall();
```

Input **A** is printed out as

```
|1|5|8|0|
|5|2|6|9|
|8|6|3|7|
|0|9|7|4|
```

Outputs **L** and **D** are printed out as

```
|0|0|0|0|
|5|0|0|0|
|8|1.47826|0|0|
|0|-0.391304|0.587045|0|
```

```
|1|-23|-10.7391|11.2227
```

Factor **L** is indeed lower triangular, with an undefined main diagonal. Two of the diagonal elements in **D** are negative. Therefore, **A**, although symmetric, is clearly not positive definite.

Finally, the result is verified by carrying out the multiplication **LDL**^{T}:

```
    for(int i=1; i<=4; i++) L(i,i) = 1.;
    LDLt_test( L, d );
}
```

yielding

```
|1|
|5|2|
|8|6|3|
|0|9|7|4|
```

This matches the lower-triangular part of the input matrix **A**.

8.0.2 Review Question

In the source code for LDLt(), each final value of lij is completely determined in line 27. However, this value is not stashed into **L** until line 35. What is the reason for this delay?

Answer: The value of `lij` for the current row `i` must not be stored before the column traversal in lines 31 through 33 is completed; else it would be detected erroneously among the previous values l_{rj}, $r < i$. This traversal is examining column j of **L**.

Note also that since `LDLt()` is a member function of `sparse`, items such as `mrows`, `ncols`, `col`, and `stash()` implicitly pertain to `*this` (i.e., **L**). As a member function, `LDLt()` also has direct access to `A.row` and `A.e`.

8.0.3   Sidebar

Utility subroutine `LDLt_test()` is an exception to the rule that the diagonal of a lower-triangular matrix is never accessed. Instead, this subroutine *requires* the caller to initialize the main diagonal of **L** to all ones. Therefore, the matrix-multiplication loop it executes can be uncomplicated and definitive:

```
void LDLt_test (const sparse& L, const real_vector& D)
{//evaluates L*D*Lt; caller sets L(i,i) = 1.
   unsigned i,j,k,n=D.N();   double aij;
   if(L.N() != n || L.M() != n)
     { printf("!!!!! Incompatible Dimensions !!!!!\n");
        return; }
   for(i=1; i<=n; i++){
      for(j=1; j<=i; j++){    aij =  0.;
         for(k=1; k<=i; k++)
            aij += L.getval(i,k) * D(k) * L.getval(j,k);
         cout << '|' << aij;
      }
      cout << "|\n";
   }
}
```

This subroutine enforces the condition that `L` be dimensionally square and that `D` have the same dimension as `L`. It uses the traditional C `printf()` function to write an error message and the newer C++ `cout` method to print the results in a flexible format.

8.1   POSITIVE DEFINITENESS AND PIVOTING

The Doolittle implementation of Cholesky factorization is convenient to compute, but it obfuscates an interesting theoretical property, namely, that the propagation of $(l_{ik}d_k)l_{jk}$ into subsequent rows and columns is essentially a rank-one outer-product update.

At the beginning of this chapter, an example was worked out in which $\mathbf{LDL}^T$ was shown to be

$$\begin{bmatrix} d_1 & d_1a_1 & d_1b_1 & d_1c_1 \\ d_1a_1 & d_2 + d_1a_1a_1 & d_2b_2 + d_1a_1b_1 & d_2c_2 + d_1a_1c_1 \\ d_1b_1 & d_2b_2 + d_1a_1b_1 & d_3 + d_1b_1b_1 + d_2b_2b_2 & d_3c_3 + d_1b_1c_1 + d_2b_2c_2 \\ d_1c_1 & d_2c_2 + d_1a_1c_1 & d_3c_3 + d_1b_1c_1 + d_2b_2c_2 & d_4 + d_1c_1c_1 + d_2c_2c_2 + d_3c_3c_3 \end{bmatrix}.$$

If we erase everything from this that does not have a subscript value 1, we obtain

$$\begin{bmatrix} d_1 & d_1a_1 & d_1b_1 & d_1c_1 \\ d_1a_1 & +d_1a_1a_1 & +d_1a_1b_1 & +d_1a_1c_1 \\ d_1b_1 & +d_1a_1b_1 & +d_1b_1b_1 & +d_1b_1c_1 \\ d_1c_1 & +d_1a_1c_1 & +d_1b_1c_1 & +d_1c_1c_1 \end{bmatrix}.$$

The entries in the lower right 3×3 submatrix are products of elements from row 1 and column 1. In other words, if $\mathbf{q}$ denotes the 3-vector $[a_1 \ b_1 \ c_1]^T$, the structure of this matrix is

$$\left[\begin{array}{c|c} 1 & \mathbf{q}^T \\ \hline \mathbf{q} & \mathbf{q}\mathbf{q}^T \end{array}\right] d_1.$$

Consequently, the outer product $\mathbf{q}\mathbf{q}^T d_1$ is what needs to be *subtracted* when factorizing a matrix once the leftmost column is determined, and so on at each stage of reduction.

Recall that positive definiteness means that $\mathbf{r}^T\mathbf{A}\mathbf{r} > 0$ for arbitrary nonzero $\mathbf{r}$. In particular, if $\mathbf{e}_i$ is a vector of all zeros except component $e_i = 1$, then $\mathbf{e}_i^T\mathbf{A}\mathbf{e}_i = a_{ii} > 0$; each diagonal element of $\mathbf{A}$ is greater than zero. Each rank-one update step in Cholesky decomposition preserves this property. It can be shown [28, p. 296] that if $a_{ii}^{(k)}$ is the modified value of diagonal element a_{ii} at step k, then $0 < a_{ii}^{(k)} \le a_{ii}$. Each diagonal element a_{ii}, and hence d_i, can shrink but will not vanish.

If $\mathbf{A}$ possesses only the weaker property called *positive semidefiniteness* (i.e., $\mathbf{r}^T\mathbf{A}\mathbf{r} \ge 0$), a_{ii} and d_i can shrink to zero. However, this is not disastrous. It merely means that the outer-product update ($\mathbf{q}\mathbf{q}^T d_i$) becomes zero. In other words, step i of the algorithm has nothing to do. Moreover, theoretically, if d_j vanishes, so do all l_{ij} in the same column [14, p. 146].

In sparse matrix computations, the objective is to avoid introducing additional nonzero elements, insofar as possible. The number of elements in the outer product $\mathbf{q}\mathbf{q}^T$ is the square of the number of components in $\mathbf{q}$. For example, suppose that matrix $\mathbf{A}$ is

$$|1|2|3|4|5|6|7|8|9|$$
$$|2|1|0|0|0|0|0|0|0|$$

```
|3|0|1|0|0|0|0|0|0|0|
|4|0|0|1|0|0|0|0|0|0|
|5|0|0|0|1|0|0|0|0|0|
|6|0|0|0|0|1|0|0|0|0|
|7|0|0|0|0|0|1|0|0|0|
|8|0|0|0|0|0|0|1|0|0|
|9|0|0|0|0|0|0|0|0|1|
```

Then LDLt() determines that **L** is

```
|1|0|0|0|0|0|0|0|0|0|
|2|1|0|0|0|0|0|0|0|0|
|3|2|1|0|0|0|0|0|0|0|
|4|2.66667|1|1|0|0|0|0|0|
|5|3.33333|1.25|0.714286|1|0|0|0|0|
|6|4|1.5|0.857143|0.566038|1|0|0|0|
|7|4.66667|1.75|1|0.660377|0.47191|1|0|0|
|8|5.33333|2|1.14286|0.754717|0.539326|0.405797|1|0|
|9|6|2.25|1.28571|0.849057|0.606742|0.456522|0.356436|1|
```

including the ones on the main diagonal. Because row 1 and column 1 of **A** are full, their outer product fills **L** densely. On the other hand, if matrix **A′** is

```
|1|0|0|0|0|0|0|0|9|
|0|1|0|0|0|0|0|0|2|
|0|0|1|0|0|0|0|0|3|
|0|0|0|1|0|0|0|0|4|
|0|0|0|0|1|0|0|0|5|
|0|0|0|0|0|1|0|0|6|
|0|0|0|0|0|0|1|0|7|
|0|0|0|0|0|0|0|1|8|
|9|2|3|4|5|6|7|8|1|
```

its factor **L′** is determined by LDLt() to be

```
|1|0|0|0|0|0|0|0|0|0|
|0|1|0|0|0|0|0|0|0|0|
|0|0|1|0|0|0|0|0|0|0|
|0|0|0|1|0|0|0|0|0|0|
|0|0|0|0|1|0|0|0|0|0|
|0|0|0|0|0|1|0|0|0|0|
|0|0|0|0|0|0|1|0|0|0|
|0|0|0|0|0|0|0|1|0|0|
|9|2|3|4|5|6|7|8|1|
```

This is the same sparsity pattern as for **A′** itself, with no additional nonzeros. In fact, it *is* **A′**. **A** and **A′** represent the same set of equations in the same set of variables, merely sorted into a different order. Judicious rearrangement of the rows and columns of a symmetric matrix can greatly reduce the effort of factorization.

Matrix **A** is symmetric if $a_{ij} = a_{ji}$ (i.e., if row i is the transpose of column i). The symmetry of a symmetric matrix is maintained when two rows are exchanged as long as the like-numbered columns are also exchanged. To transform **A** into **A'** as above, rows 1 and 9 must be swapped at the same time as columns 1 and 9.

If symmetric **A** is also positive definite, the Doolittle algorithm preserves its positive definiteness as well as its symmetry. The diagonal divisors d_i cannot become zero. Therefore, we can rearrange the rows and columns of **A** into a sequence to reduce the creation of additional nonzeros, without incurring the risk of a zero divisor. If **A** is only positive semidefinite, we may need to test the value of each d_i and l_{ij} in the light of round-off error.

Subroutine Sym_Pivot() sorts a symmetric matrix symmetrically in order of increasing number of elements per row and column. It is intended to be used as a separate step before the matrix in question is submitted to LDLt(). The structure type pivot was introduced in Chapter 5. It is used in Sym_Pivot() to record the effect of the sorting:

```
void Sym_Pivot (sparse& A, pivot& P)
{
    unsigned k, m, p, r, count, cost;
    if((m = A.M()) != A.N() || m != P.n || m != P.m )
        exit(1);

    for(r=1; r<=m; r++)
    {
        if ((cost = A.rowcount(r)) == 0 ) continue;   p = r;
//      Find first row with least rowcount
        for(k=p+1; k<=m; k++){
            if ((count = A.rowcount(k)) >= cost ) continue;
            p = k; cost = count;
        }
        if (p == r ) continue;
        A.swaprows(r,p); A.swapcols(r,p);
        P.swaprows(r,p); P.swapcols(r,p);
    }
}
```

This subroutine checks that A and P are square and have the same dimensions. It uses sparse::rowcount() (Section 3.2.5) to determine the number of elements in each row. It calls sparse::swaprows() and sparse::swapcols() (Section 3.2.9) to carry out the exchanges. If rows and columns r and p are exchanged in A, so are the corresponding entries in P.R and P.C. All this presumes that the entire matrix **A** has been stored in A, not just its lower-triangular part.

For the sake of completeness, I note that Sym_Pivot() applied to the 9 × 9 matrix **A** above produces something slightly different from the matrix **A'**:

```
|1|0|0|0|0|0|0|0|2|
|0|1|0|0|0|0|0|0|3|
|0|0|1|0|0|0|0|0|4|
|0|0|0|1|0|0|0|0|5|
|0|0|0|0|1|0|0|0|6|
|0|0|0|0|0|1|0|0|7|
|0|0|0|0|0|0|1|0|8|
|0|0|0|0|0|0|0|1|9|
|2|3|4|5|6|7|8|9|1|
```

Sym_Pivot() swaps row 1 and column 1 with each of the other rows and columns in sequence.

8.2 CHOLESKY SOLUTIONS

In terms introduced into the discussion in Section 5.4, the effect of subroutine Sym_Pivot upon matrix **A** is that of a transformation $\mathbf{PAP}^T$ which reorders both the rows and columns of **A**, with $\mathbf{P}^T\mathbf{P} = \mathbf{I}$. If **A** is symmetric, $(\mathbf{PAP}^T)^T = \mathbf{PA}^T\mathbf{P}^T = \mathbf{PAP}^T$, and the transformed matrix is also symmetric.

If factorization is applied to the transformed matrix, $\mathbf{LDL}^T = \mathbf{PAP}^T$. If the original problem is $\mathbf{Ax} = \mathbf{b}$, the problem is transformed to $\mathbf{PAP}^T\mathbf{Px} = \mathbf{Pb}$, so that $\mathbf{LDL}^T\mathbf{Px} = \mathbf{Pb}$ and $\mathbf{x} = \mathbf{P}^T(\mathbf{L}^T)^{-1}\mathbf{D}^{-1}\mathbf{L}^{-1}\mathbf{Pb}$. The code to implement this is straightforward. Assuming that sparse A and L, real_vector b and d, and pivot P are allocated and initialized as required, the solution sequence is

```
Sym_Pivot( A, P );

L.LDLt( A, d );

b.Map(P.R).Lsolve(L).Dsolve(d).TLsolve(L).Pam(P.C);
```

The only new function here is Dsolve(d), which implements $\mathbf{D}^{-1}$:

```
real_vector& real_vector::Dsolve (const real_vector& d)
{
    if(n != d.n) exit(1);
    unsigned j;   double x;
    for (j=1; j<=n; j++)
    {
```

```
    if((x = d(j)) == 0.){ (*this)(j) = 0.; continue; }
    (*this)(j) /= x;
  }
  return *this;
}
```

A zero entry in d is taken as a signal to zero the same entry in **x**.

8.3 QUASIDEFINITE MATRICES

A particular generalization of the Cholesky decomposition is relied upon in the constrained optimization methods we will encounter in Chapters 10 and 11. In that context, partitioned matrices appear in the form

$$\mathbf{B} = \left[\begin{array}{c|c} -\mathbf{E} & \mathbf{A} \\ \hline \mathbf{A}^T & \mathbf{F} \end{array} \right]$$

If **E** and **F** are positive definite, **B** is *not* positive definite, because of the negative sign applied to **E**. Instead, **B** is an example of what one author [28, p. 297] calls quasidefinite. **B** can be factorized by using first all the pivots in the **E** partition before using any pivots from the **F** submatrix. Pivot elements within each partition can be chosen so as to minimize the creation of nonzero elements in factor **L**. Generally, this means processing the less populated rows and columns first, and the denser ones last. Moreover, if it is more economical to do so, the roles of **E** and **F** can be exchanged:

$$\mathbf{PBP}^T = \left[\begin{array}{c|c} \mathbf{F} & \mathbf{A}^T \\ \hline \mathbf{A} & -\mathbf{E} \end{array} \right]$$

In the applications of greatest interest, **E** and **F** are in fact diagonal. Cholesky factorization of the upper left partition then requires no arithmetic at all. We merely copy the diagonal elements from that partition into the corresponding locations in factor **D**. If **A** is $m \times n$, **E** is $m \times m$ and **F** is $n \times n$. The choice of whether to position **E** or **F** at the upper left will be guided by whether m or n is larger.

My library contains four variants of quasidefinite $\mathbf{LDL}^T$ factorization, reflecting whether **A** is matrix or sparse and whether **A** is lower left or upper right in the partitioned array. All versions leave **A** unmodified and require the caller to initialize diagonal **D** with the appropriate composite of **E** and **F** values. Figure 8.1 diagrams the comparative geometries of LDLt(), LDLt_QD(), and LDLt_QDt(). All are sparse member functions that output results to an initially empty **L**.

The following code implements the $\mathbf{LDL}^T$ factorization of quasidefinite **B** for diagonal **E** and **F** with **A** upper right and **A** represented as a matrix. It is a

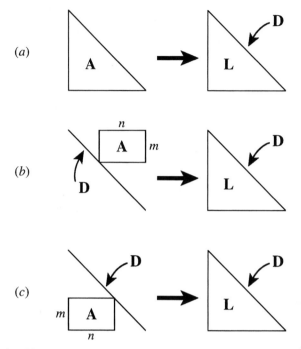

Fig. 8.1 Relationships among **A**, **L**, and **D** in three implementations of Cholesky decomposition: (*a*) LDLt(); (*b*) LDLt_QD(); (*c*) LDLt_QDt().

sparse member function that outputs **L** to an initially empty sparse:

```
void sparse::LDLt_QD (const matrix& A, real_vector& d)
{//Input A(m,n): A(j,i-m) -> L(i,j): L(m+n,m+n)
    element *prev;   unsigned i,j,l,m,r;   double lij,
       lij_dj, diagi;
    real_vector tmp (mrows);   tmp.init();
    if(((m = A.M()) + A.N()) != mrows) exit(1);

//First m rows are no-op!
    for (i=m+1; i<=mrows; i++)
       //row-by-row computation of L
    {
       diagi = d(i);
       for (j=1; j<=m; j++) tmp(j) = A(j,i-m);
          // dump A-col into tmp

       for (j=1; j<i; j++)
          // do cols in ascending order
       {
```

```
        if (tmp(j) == 0.) continue;
        if ( d(j)  == 0.) continue;
            //(redundant, theoretically)
        lij_dj = tmp(j); lij = lij_dj / d(j);
            tmp(j) = 0.;
        diagi -= lij * lij_dj;
        prev = col[j-1];               // col j of L so far
        while ((l = prev->mext) != 0){
            prev = e+l;   r = prev->row;
            tmp(r) -= lij_dj * (prev->value);
        }
        stash(i,j) = lij;
    }
    d(i) = diagi;
  }
  tmp.zap();
  return;
}
```

If A is $m \times n$, L must be dimensioned $(m + n) \times (m + n)$. The transpose of A is taken to lie in the lower-left partition. The caller is required to initialize d. The remarkable fact is that the first m rows of the algorithm then require no action! Actual work begins with row $m + 1$ of L. Each column of A is treated as a row of A^T. Apart from that, the main loop is essentially the same as in LDLt().

8.3.1 Example

In Section 6.3 on least-squares applications, it was asserted that a least-squares solution to an overdetermined system $Ax = b$ could be found by solving the partitioned matrix problem

$$\begin{bmatrix} I & A \\ \hline A^T & 0 \end{bmatrix} \begin{bmatrix} r \\ \hline x \end{bmatrix} = \begin{bmatrix} b \\ \hline 0 \end{bmatrix} \quad \text{or} \quad Bx' = b'$$

This B is sufficiently close to quasidefinite for present purposes. The following code applies LDLt_QD() to the data of the example in Section 6.3.1 structured as a partitioned matrix like B:

```
{  double data[20] = {-5., 2.,-1., 4., 2., 6., 3., 7.,
                      10.,11.,9.,11., 1.,5., 1., 6., 7.,
                       9., 4., 8.};

   matrix A(data,10,2);
   sparse L(12,12,50);    real_vector D(12);
   for(int i=1; i<=10; i++) D(i) = 1.;   D(11) = D(12) = 0.;
```

```
    L.LDLt_QD( A, D);
    print_matrix( L );
    D.dumpall();

    real_vector b(12); b.init() += 1.; b(11) = b(12) = 0.;
    b.dumpall();
    b.Lsolve(L).Dsolve(D).TLsolve(L);
    b.dumpall();
}
```

The `print_matrix( L );` statement following `LDLt_QD( A, D);` shows that L is all zeros except for its last two rows:

```
. . .
|-5|-1|2|3|10|9|1|1|7|4|0|0|
|2|4|6|7|11|11|5|6|9|8|1.16376|0|
```

For comparison, the transpose of A (i.e., A^T) is

```
|-5|-1|2|3|10|9|1|1|7|4|
|2|4|6|7|11|11|5|6|9|8|
```

Diagonal D shows nontrivial values, after processing, in its final two entries.

```
|1|1|1|1|1|1|1|1|1|1|-287|-164.303
```

The reader can verify that 287 is the sum of the squares of the elements of the first row of A^T. Result x' (as b) contains the actual solution x in its last two entries:

```
|-0.026678| 0.0732902|0.0480755|-0.0271233 |0.0476302|
    - 0.0775528
| 0.123274|-0.0771074| 0.0728449| -0.102322 |
    -0.125183|0.200382
```

These are the same numbers found previously in Sections 4.6 and 6.3.1.

Quasidefinite matrices require special handling when pivoting is applied. Assume that

$$B = \left[\begin{array}{c|c} -E & A \\ \hline A^T & F \end{array} \right]$$

and that **E** and **F** are diagonal. In my QD implementation, a single `sparse` represents both **A** and A^T. Exchanging two rows in **A** automatically exchanges two columns in A^T so that the symmetry of **B** is maintained. It remains only to exchange two diagonal entries in **E**. Similarly, exchanging two columns in **A** thereby exchanges two rows in A^T and requires the exchange of two diagonal elements in **F**. Within **A** itself, the row exchanges and column exchanges are independent.

Subroutine `Min_Deg_Pivot()` applies this strategy. The concept *minimum degree* refers to what is called the Markowitz degree of a matrix element b_{ij}, which is obtained from the number of nonzeros in row i, n_i, and the number of nonzeros in column j, m_j, as the product $(n_i - 1)(m_j - 1)$. The caller must reorder the entries in diagonals **E** and **F** using the information returned in `pivot P`.

```
void Min_Deg_Pivot (sparse& A, pivot& P)
{
    unsigned k, m, n, p, r, count, cost;
    if((m = A.M()) != P.m) exit(1);   if((n = A.N())
        != P.n) exit(1);

    for(r=1; r<=m; r++)
    {
        if ((cost = A.rowcount(r)) == 0 ) continue;  p = r;
//      Find first row with least rowcount
        for(k=p+1; k<=m; k++)
        {
            if ((count = A.rowcount(k)) >= cost ) continue;
            p = k; cost = count;
        }
        if (p == r ) continue;  A.swaprows(r,p);
            P.swaprows(r,p);
    }

    for(r=1; r<=n; r++)
    {
        if ((cost = A.colcount(r)) == 0 ) continue;  p = r;
//      Find first col with least colcount
        for(k=p+1; k<=n; k++)
        {
            if ((count = A.colcount(k)) >= cost ) continue;
            p = k; cost = count;
        }
        if (p == r ) continue;  A.swapcols(r,p);
            P.swapcols(r,p);
    }
}
```

8.4 SUMMARY AND CONCLUSIONS

Cholesky Decomposition. If **A** is symmetric, then `L.LDLt(A,d);` computes the factorization $\mathbf{A} = \mathbf{LDL}^T$. **L** is a lower-triangular matrix, and **D** is diagonal. Input A is not modified, and vector d contains the diagonal elements of **D**. The principal diagonal of L is not stored, because every value is assumed to be 1.

If

$$\mathbf{B} = \left[\begin{array}{c|c} \mathbf{E} & \mathbf{A} \\ \hline \mathbf{A}^T & \mathbf{F} \end{array}\right]$$

with **E** and **F** diagonal, then L.LDLt_QD(A,d); computes the factorization **B** = **LDL**^{T}. Vector d is input containing the diagonals of **E** and **F**, and it returns the diagonal of **D**.

If

$$\mathbf{B} = \left[\begin{array}{c|c} \mathbf{E} & \mathbf{A}^T \\ \hline \mathbf{A} & \mathbf{F} \end{array}\right]$$

with **E** and **F** diagonal, then L.LDLt_QDt(A,d); computes the factorization **B** = **LDL**^{T}. Vector d is input containing the diagonals of **E** and **F**, and it returns the diagonal of **D**.

Pivoting. If **A** is symmetric, then Sym_Pivot(A,P); applied before LDLt() may reduce the number of elements in L. Structure P is a pivot (see Section 5.4).

If

$$\mathbf{B} \text{ or } \mathbf{B}^T = \left[\begin{array}{c|c} \mathbf{E} & \mathbf{A} \\ \hline \mathbf{A}^T & \mathbf{F} \end{array}\right]$$

then Min_Deg_Pivot(A,P) applied before LDLt_QD() or LDLt_QDt() may reduce the number of elements in L.

Cholesky Solutions. Once the factorization **LDL**^{T} has been computed for a symmetric or quasidefinite matrix, the code to solve **Ax** = **b** is

b.Map(P.R).Lsolve(L).Dsolve(d).TLsolve(L).Pam(P.C);

If pivoting is omitted, the Map() and Pam() calls may be deleted.

9 Automatic Derivatives

When theory indicates a derivative, $df(x)/dx$, say, it is tacitly assumed more often than not that this expression will be approximated in code by a difference quotient, $(f(x_{i+1})-f(x_i))/(x_{i+1}-x_i)$. Call this a *numerical* derivative to distinguish it from an *analytical* derivative, which connotes a formula for $df(x)/dx$ presented in the same way as the expression for $f(x)$ itself. Past efforts to provide computer-generated analytical derivatives included programs such as FORMAC, MACSYMA and REDUCE, which manipulated the symbols of a FORTRAN-like definition of a function in order to produce a FORTRAN-like statement of its derivative (see [16]). Computerized algebra (or calculus) like this yields *explicit* analytical derivatives.

An alternative strategy is to compute analytical derivative values by *implicit* techniques based on run-time application of the chain rule to the definition of $f(x)$ alone. This approach circumvents the need for a derivative formula and is applicable to functions defined less restrictedly than by closed expressions. The advantage over numerical derivatives is a combination of precision (significant figures) and accuracy (correct value). Knuth [19, p. 338] details one implementation. A recent book [15] calls this *algorithmic differentiation*. The technique it describes records the exact sequence of floating-point operations that yields a function value, and appends to it a parallel sequence of steps that yields the corresponding derivative value.

In this chapter we present still another method for defining and computing analytical derivatives implicitly. The scheme it proposes illustrates the usefulness in scientific programming of two C++ features that have no antecedents in FORTRAN: the function pointer and the pure-virtual base class. We will also see additional examples of coding techniques familiar by now, such as overloaded operators and linked lists. This chapter provides a break from our steady diet of vectors and matrices.

9.1 POINTERS TO FUNCTIONS

The heading above reflects the sanctioned nomenclature [18, p. 118] for the C and C++ feature more loosely called *function pointers*. This is an ingenious mechanism whereby the identity of what subroutine to call at a specific point in a running program is variable. Any function with the correct return type and the specified argument list can substitute for any other.

A classic example occurs in the C standard function `qsort`. Every C compiler provides a sorting subroutine whose interface is

```
void qsort( void *list, size_t n, size_t size,
            int (*comp)(const void *, const void *) );
```

This function sorts into ascending order an array list containing n entries of size bytes. The fourth argument is the subject of interest. The syntax int (*comp) (const void *, const void *) declares that comp is a pointer to a function that takes two arguments of type void (by address) and returns an int, indicating whether the first argument is less than, equal to, or greater than the second. To invoke qsort, the caller selects a suitable comparison function and gives just its name as the fourth parameter. For example:

```
void main(){
    char *list[] = {"vat","sat","rat","pat","mat"};
    qsort( (void*)list[0], 5, 4, user_comp );
}
```

This code alphabetizes the list: mat pat rat sat vat. The caller must previously have written

```
#include <string.h>
int user_comp (const void* a, const void* b){
    return strcmp( (char*)a, (char*)b);
}
```

Comparison function user_comp is defined with the argument list and return type required by qsort, and it is merely an interface to a C library routine strcmp, whose argument list is not quite correct. The form (char*) is a *cast* that signals the compiler to treat addresses a and b as type char*. Similarly, (void*) preceding list[0] in the arguments of qsort casts char* to the specified void* type. Such machinations are needed because a C++ compiler (but not a C compiler) rigorously enforces calling list specifications.

Function pointers can be used within the declaration of a user-defined variable type. In this chapter we shall have need of

```
typedef double (*differentiable) (double);
```

This says that a variable of type differentiable is a pointer to a function whose argument is type double and whose return type is double. This is a specific form of declaration, the heart of which is the (*) embracing the name of the type being defined.

The standard mathematical functions declared in <math.h> fill the bill to be type differentiable. The syntax is something you don't see in FORTRAN:

```
#include <math.h>
typedef double (*differentiable) (double);
```

```
{
differentiable f1, f2, f3;   f1 = sin;   f2 = cos;   f3 = tan;
double x = .5;   double y = (f1(x)/f2(x))/f3(x);
   printf("%G\n", y);
}
```

This small example prints that y has final value 1.0.

We can define our own functions that meet the specifications required to be type differentiable:

```
double negsin  (double x) { return -sin(x);  }
double inv     (double x) { return 1. / x;   }
double dsqrt   (double x) { return 0.5 / sqrt(x);  }
double square  (double x) { return x * x;  }
double dsquare (double x) { return 2. * x;  }
double cube    (double x) { return x * x * x;  }
double dcube   (double x) { return 3. * x * x;  }
```

We can employ differentiable in defining additional classes. The declaration of class dif1 reads (only in part)

```
class dif1
{
   differentiable f, df;   public:

   dif1(){ f = df = NULL; }
   dif1( double(*a)(double), double(*b)(double) )
      { f = a; df = b; }
   friend differentiable value (dif1& a){ return a.f;   }
   friend differentiable deriv (dif1& a){ return a.df; }
};
```

The private members of dif1 are f and df, two pointers to functions that return double and take one double argument. The default constructor, as in dif1 g;, initializes the pointers to NULL. The principal constructor requires the names of two differentiable functions, as in dif1 sinf (sin, cos);. Then value(sinf)(x); returns sin(x) and deriv(sinf)(x); yields cos(x).

9.1.1 Example

With just the foregoing part of dif1, we can run the following example:

```
{ differentiable z;
   dif1 sinf( sin, cos );
   dif1 cosf( cos, negsin );
```

```
    double qpi = 2.*atan(1.0)/3.; //(30deg)
    cout << "1:" << value(sinf)(qpi) << endl;
    cout << "2:" << deriv(sinf)(qpi) << endl;
    cout << "3:" << value(cosf)(qpi) << endl;
    cout << "4:" << deriv(cosf)(qpi) << endl;
    z = deriv(cosf);  cout << "5:" << z(qpi)     << endl;
}
```

This example prints out various values of the sine and cosine of 30 degrees:

```
1:0.5
2:0.866025
3:0.866025
4:-0.5
5:-0.5
```

9.2   ABSTRACT BASE CLASS

In Chapter 2 we presented two cases in which one class was said to be derived from another. The applicable syntax included

```
class temp_real_vector : public real_vector
    { /*details*/ };
class submatrix : public matrix { /*details*/ };
```

In these relationships, `temp_real_vector` and `submatrix` are termed *derived* classes; `real_vector` and `matrix` are designated *base* classes. By default, a derived class receives every property of its base class implicitly, without explicit declaration. The derived class presumably possesses additional capabilities, which provide the reason for its existence.

The C++ keyword `virtual` when applied to a function defined in a base class indicates that its derived classes are allowed to define their own alternative versions of the function in question. Otherwise, the base class version is the default. The specific syntax

```
class whatever { virtual ret_type func_name (arg_type)
    = 0; };
```

makes the virtual function `func_name` *pure* virtual. This means that every derived class *must* include source code for a function that returns `ret_type` and accepts argument `arg_type` and is named `func_name`. The standard terminology for a base class consisting entirely of pure virtual functions is *abstract* base class.

I have found that a pure virtual base class is a wonderful way to unify a collection of disparate objects that have only one or two crucial properties in common.

The properties that interest us here are a value and a first derivative. My solution to the problem is

```
class C1 { public:
   virtual double operator()(double x) = 0;
   virtual double operator[](double x) = 0;
};
```

Class C1 contains no constructor, no destructor, and no members except two pure virtual functions. These functions happen to be operators. Every class derived from C1 must implement parentheses () and brackets [] to receive a double argument and return a double value. You and I agree, and the compiler need not know, that f(x) will be something's value and f[x] will be its derivative.

Class C1 comes close to modeling what a mathematician would call C^1, the set of functions with continuous first derivatives whose domain and range are the set of real numbers. However, we don't particularly rely on the property of continuity here.

With base class C1 in hand, the first order of business is to state the complete definition of class dif1:

```
class dif1 : public C1 {
   differentiable f, df;  public:

   dif1(){ f = df = NULL; }
   dif1( double(*a)(double), double(*b)(double) )
      { f = a; df = b; }
   double operator()(double x){ return f(x); }
   double operator[](double x){ return df(x);}
   double deriv( double x)     { return df(x);}
   friend differentiable value (dif1& a){ return a.f;  }
   friend differentiable deriv (dif1& a){ return a.df; }
};
```

With the two required C1 operators now available, the example in Section 9.1.1 can be rerun with output statements 1 to 5 modified as follows:

```
cout << "1:" << sinf(qpi) << endl;
cout << "2:" << sinf[qpi] << endl;
cout << "3:" << cosf(qpi) << endl;
cout << "4:" << cosf[qpi] << endl;
cout << "5:" << cosf.deriv(qpi) << endl;
```

The output is the same. The reader's attention is directed to the difference in use between member deriv(double) and nonmember deriv(dif1&).

9.2.1 Example

Here are some difl (and therefore C1) objects:

```
difl sinf ( sin,    cos );
difl cosf ( cos,    negsin );
difl logf ( log,    inv );
difl sqrtf( sqrt,   dsqrt );
difl sqf  ( square, dsquare );
difl cubf ( cube,   dcube);
difl expf ( exp,    exp );
```

The parameters within the parentheses are as defined previously.

9.3   THE CHAIN RULE

The *chain rule* of calculus says that the derivative of a sum is the sum of the derivatives. My view is that the sum of two C1 objects is itself a C1 object. So I define a class and a nonmember addition operator as follows:

```
class Sum : public C1 {
   C1 *f1, *f2;         public:
   Sum(C1& a, C1& b){ f1 = &a; f2 = &b; }
   double operator()(double x){ return (*f1)(x)
      + (*f2)(x); }
   double operator[](double x){ return (*f1)[x]
      + (*f2)[x]; }
};
inline Sum operator+ (C1& a, C1& b){ return Sum(a,b); }
```

Every object of type Sum contains two pointers to (addresses of) objects of type C1. These could be difl objects, or other Sum objects, or C1 objects of a subtype (derived class) described later. The constructor can be called explicitly to create a named object of type Sum, as in Sum poly(sqf, cubf); Thereafter, poly(x) returns the value $x^2 + x^3$ and poly[x] returns the value $2x + 3x^2$.

Another use of the Sum constructor is to be called indirectly through the addition operator for C1 objects. If we write sqf + cubf within some expression, the operator+ (sqf, cubf) calls Sum (sqf, cubf), with the result that (sqf+cubf)(x) returns the value $x^2 + x^3$ and (sqf+cubf)[x] returns the value $2x + 3x^2$.

9.3.1 Example

```
{
   Sum poly(sqf,cubf);
   cout << "1:" << poly(2.) << endl;
```

```
    cout << "2:" << poly[2.] << endl;
    cout << "3:" << (sqf+cubf)(2.) << endl;
    cout << "4:" << (sqf+cubf)[2.] << endl;
}
1:12
2:16
3:12
4:16
```

The derivative of a difference is the difference of the derivatives. The difference of two C1 objects is a C1 object. I define a Dif class and a nonmember subtraction operator exactly parallel to Sum:

```
class Dif : public C1 {
    C1 *f1, *f2;          public:
    Dif(C1& a, C1& b){ f1 = &a; f2 = &b; }
    double operator()(double x){ return (*f1)(x)
        - (*f2)(x); }
    double operator[](double x){ return (*f1)[x]
        - (*f2)[x]; }
};
inline Dif operator- (C1& a, C1& b){ return Dif(a,b); }
```

A pattern is beginning to emerge. The chain rule for a product, $f = uv$, is $df = u\,dv + v\,du$. The corresponding product class and operator for C1 objects are

```
class Prod : public C1 {
    C1 *f1, *f2;          public:
    Prod(C1& a, C1& b){ f1 = &a; f2 = &b; }
    double operator()(double x){ return (*f1)(x) *
        (*f2)(x); }
    double operator[](double x){
                return (*f1)[x]*(*f2)(x)+(*f1)(x)*
                    (*f2)[x]; }
};
inline Prod operator* (C1& a, C1& b){ return Prod(a,b); }
```

Finally, the chain rule for a quotient, $f = u/v$, is $df = (v\,du - u\,dv)/v^2$. The corresponding quotient class and operator for C1 objects are

```
class Quot : public C1 {
    C1 *f1, *f2;          public:
    Quot(C1& a, C1& b){ f1 = &a; f2 = &b; }
    double operator()(double x){ return (*f1)(x) /
        (*f2)(x); }
```

```
    double operator[](double x){ return
      ((*f1)[x] - (*f1)(x)*(*f2)[x]/
      (*f2)(x)) /(*f2)(x);}
};
inline Quot operator/ (C1& a, C1& b){ return Quot(a,b); }
```

9.3.2 Example

```
    Prod fifth (sqf,cubf);
    cout << "1:" << fifth(2.)        << endl;
    cout << "2:" << fifth[2.]        << endl;
    cout << "3:" << (sqf/cubf)(2.) << endl;
        //1/x the hard way
    cout << "4:" << (sqf/cubf)[2.] << endl;
    C1 *z;
    z = &(expf*expf);
    cout << "5:" << (*z)(2.3025851)<< endl;
    cout << "6:" << (*z)[2.3025851]<< endl;
```

```
1:32
2:80
3:0.5
4:-0.25
5:100.000001
6:200.000003
```

In this example, fifth is x^5, whose derivative is $5x^4$. sqf/cubf is the hard way of writing $1/x$, whose derivative is $-1/x^2$. (expf*expf) is e^{2x}, whose derivative is $2e^{2x}$. The natural logarithm of 10 is 2.3025851, approximately.

The syntax C1 *z; defining a pointer z to an object of type C1 arises because C++ forbids us to declare a stand-alone object of an abstract class. A pointer to such an object is acceptable, however.

9.4 CONSTANTS AND VARIABLES

We need a means of modeling how the chain rule applies when there are constants in functions, for example, $1 + 2 \cos x$. Since const is a reserved C++ keyword, we shall define

```
class Parm : public C1
{
    double c;              public:
    Parm(){ c = 0.; }
    Parm( double a ){ c = a; }
    double operator()(double x){ x; return c; }
```

```
    double operator[](double x){ x; return 0.;}
    void    operator= (double x){ c = x; }
};
```

This is a legitimate subtype of C1, because it provides the required operators, but it contains only a floating-point number, c. The default constructor, used as in Parm a;, initializes c to zero. The one-parameter constructor effectively converts a double value to a Parm: Parm one(1.0); and Parm tmp(q[j]); where q is a double array and j is defined. Subsequently, the stored value of c can be updated, because the assignment operator (=) has been overloaded: one = 2.; a = 1.; tmp = q[j]; if j has changed. The () and [] operators are required to accept double arguments, but the arguments are ignored. The statement x; is included to forfend a warning from the compiler.

The most powerful aspect of the Parm class is how it allows us to overload the arithmetic operators for a mixture of C1 and double types:

```
inline Sum operator+ (C1& a, double b){ return a
    + Parm(b); }
inline Sum operator+ (double a, C1& b){ return Parm(a)
    + b; }
inline Dif operator- (C1& a, double b){ return a
    - Parm(b); }
inline Dif operator- (double a, C1& b){ return Parm(a)
    - b; }
inline Prod operator* (C1& a, double b){ return a *
    Parm(b); }
inline Prod operator* (double a, C1& b){ return Parm(a) *
    b; }
inline Quot operator/ (C1& a, double b){ return a /
    Parm(b); }
inline Quot operator/ (double a, C1& b){ return Parm(a)/
    b; }
```

The first line of this declares that when the compiler encounters a + sign between a C1 object a and a double object b, in that order, it is to convert b into Parm(b) and invoke the + operator for two C1 objects. The second line says the same thing with a and b in the other order. The remaining lines give parallel definitions for the other arithmetic operators. These are inline definitions that we expect to be compiled without using actual call-and-return protocols.

We are now in a position to execute examples such as

```
{
    double qpi = 2.*atan(1.0)/3.; //(30deg)
    cout << "1:" << (1.0 - (2.0*(sinf*sinf)))(qpi)
        << endl;
```

```
    cout << "2:" << (1.0 - (2.0*(sinf*sinf)))[qpi]
        << endl;
    Parm one (1.0);
    cout << "3:" << (one + logf)[0.99] << endl;
    cout << "4:" << (1.0 + logf)[0.99] << endl;
}
1:0.5
2:-1.73205
3:1.0101
4:1.0101
```

The trigonometric identity $1 - 2\sin^2 x = \cos 2x$; its derivative equals $-2\sin 2x$. The derivative of $\log(x)$ is, of course, $1/x$.

The need arises to include variable x itself in expressions defining C1 objects, as simple as $1 + x$. One approach would be to define `differentiable` and `dif1` functions in the following manner:

```
double itself (double x) {return x; }
double oneval (double x) { x; return 1.0; }
{
    dif1 arg( itself, oneval );
    cout << "1:" << (arg + sqf + cubf)(3.) << endl;
    cout << "2:" << (arg + sqf + cubf)[3.] << endl;
}
```

The last two lines evaluate the value and derivative, respectively, of $x + x^2 + x^3$, for $x = 3$. (*Answer*: 39 and 34.)

Another way to approach the problem is to derive a C1 class similar to `Parm`:

```
class Variable : public C1
{
    public:
    Variable(){}
    double operator()(double x){ return x; }
    double operator[](double x){ x; return 1.;}
};
```

This class has no `private` members. Over and above the two operators that must be present in a C1-derived class, it contains only a constructor, so that we can create instances of `Variable`:

```
Variable x;
cout << "1:" << (x + sqf + cubf)(3.) << endl;
cout << "2:" << (x + sqf + cubf)[3.] << endl;
```

9.5 C^1 FUNCTIONS

It would be quite convenient if we could name each elaborate expression that we build up out of C1 objects, so that we could avoid repeating the expression. This is made feasible through the following class:

```
class C1_function : public C1
{
    C1 *f;                  public:
    C1_function()   { f = NULL; }
    C1_function(C1& a){ f = &a; }
    double operator()(double x){ return (*f)(x); }
    double operator[](double x){ return (*f)[x]; }
    void   operator= (C1&   x){ f = &x; }
};
```

This class contains only a pointer to another C1 object. It provides a default constructor so that we can declare variables and arrays of C1_function type:

```
C1_function bigfun, gradient[3], jacobian[3][3];
```

The constructor with one argument is intended for naming expressions:

```
C1_function cos2x( 1.0 - 2.0*sinf*sinf );
```

The C1_function class overloads the assignment operator (=) so that variables can be updated:

```
bigfun = cos2x;  gradient[0] = sqf;  jacobian[2][2]
   = (expf*expf);
```

9.5.1 Example

The following demonstration is based upon trigonometric identities so that we can predict the answers without having to wade through the algebra and calculus ourselves:

```
C1_function cosec( 1./sinf );
C1_function    sec( 1./cosf );
C1_function sin2x( 2.*sinf*cosf );
C1_function cos3x( 4.*cosf*cosf*cosf - 3.*cosf );
C1_function tan2x( 2.*tanf/((1.-tanf)*(1.+tanf)) );

double qpi = 2.*atan(1.0)/3.; //(30deg)
```

```
cout << "1:" << cosec(qpi) << endl;// 1/sin(30)
cout << "2:" << cosec[qpi] << endl;
    // -cos(30)/sin(30)/sin30
cout << "3:" <<    sec(qpi) << endl;// 1/cos(30)
cout << "4:" <<    sec[qpi] << endl;
    // sin(30)/cos(30)/cos(30)
cout << "5:" << sin2x(qpi) << endl;// sin(2*30)
cout << "6:" << sin2x[qpi] << endl;// 2*cos(2*30)
cout << "7:" << cos3x(qpi) << endl;// cos(3*30)
cout << "8:" << cos3x[qpi] << endl;// -3*sin(3*30)
cout << "9:" << tan2x(qpi) << endl;// tan(2*30)
cout << "10:" << tan2x[qpi] << endl;
    // 2/cos(2*30)/cos(2*30)
```

```
1:2
2:-3.4641
3:1.1547
4:0.666667
5:0.866025
6:1
7:4.29561e-16
8:-3
9:1.73205
10:8
```

The reader is invited to confirm that these values are correct. To me, it is astonishing what the compiler is performing automatically and out of sight to produce the derivative value for an expression such as tan2x.

The list of C1_function definitions above perhaps suggests the idea of accumulating a library of such things. However, despite the name, these are not callable functions. The definition of a C1_function must appear within the executable source if it is to be initialized correctly. A copy-and-paste library is indicated.

9.6 FUNCTIONS OF FUNCTIONS

Up to this point, we know how to compute automatically the derivative of any algebraic combination of constants, variables, and elemental functions. (The last term [15] describes the difl class.) We have induced the compiler to keep track of what calls what and in what order. What remains to be addressed is the case where the argument of a function is another function. This includes instances as simple as sin 2x, and it also encompasses unlimited levels of nested arguments. A special method is required.

The chain rule for functions of functions is $df(g(h(x))) = df(\#)\ dg(\#)\ dh(\#)\ dx$, where # means the present value of each respective argument. My scheme to implement this rule depends upon a derived C1 linked-list class:

```
class Chain : public C1
{
    C1     *C1ptr;
    Chain *next;
    char  *note;    public:

    Chain(){ C1ptr = NULL; next = this; note = "";}
    Chain( C1& B ){ C1ptr = &B; next = this; note = "";}
    Chain( C1& B, char* name ){ C1ptr = &B; next = this;
        note = name;}

    void setC1( C1& B){ C1ptr = &B; }
    void setnote( char* name){ note = name; }
    Chain& operator >> ( Chain& a ){ next = &a; return a; }
    friend ostream& operator << (ostream& s, Chain& q);
    double operator()(double x);
    double operator[](double x);
};
```

Each instance of Chain contains three pointers: the address of a C1 object to yield values and derivatives; the address of a Chain object, which is always initialized with the address of the present instance; and the location of an optional C string to identify this object. Two member functions are provided to update C1ptr and note. The syntax available for defining Chain objects includes the following:

```
Chain A;   A.setC1( 1.0 - 2.0*sinf*sinf );
    A.setnote("cos2x");
Chain B( 2.*sinf*sinf, "sin2x");
Chain C( tan2x );   //if tan2x already defined
```

To evaluate nested functions $f(g(h(x)))$, or their derivatives, we start with the innermost function and work outward. We can model this protocol with the precedence operator >>. For example, h >> g >> f; specifies the nesting shown. A list thus linked is then evaluated by addressing its first or innermost member, h(x) or h[x]. The tail, or outermost link, of a Chain list is recognized by the fact that next = this (i.e., it remains as it was initialized).

The output operator << is used in conjunction with cout to write a formatted list of the contents of a Chain:

```
ostream& operator << (ostream& s, Chain& q)
{
```

```
s   << "[" <<
&q << " -> " << q.next << " | " << q.C1ptr << " | "
    << q.note
    << " ]\n";
return s;
}
```

As an example:

```
Variable x;
Parm three(3.0), one(1.0), a;  a = 1.0;
Chain A(Sum(x,one));    A.setnote("x+1");
Chain B(logf);          B.setnote("ln");
Chain C(Prod(x,three)); C.setnote("x*3");
Chain D(Quot(a,sqf));   D.setnote("a/x**2");
A >> B >> C;                        // 3*ln(x+1)
cout << A << B << C << D;
```

This produces

```
[0x0064fd94 -> 0x0064fd78 | 0x0064fd88 | x+1 ]
[0x0064fd78 -> 0x0064fd68 | 0x0040b08c | ln ]
[0x0064fd68 -> 0x0064fd68 | 0x0064fd5c | x*3 ]
[0x0064fd4c -> 0x0064fd4c | 0x0064fd40 | a/x**2 ]
```

The first column contains the hexadecimal addresses in memory of A, B, C, and
D. The second column is what each next entry points to. A.next points to B,
B.next points to C, and C.next points to itself because it is the tail of a list. D
stands alone. The third column is the address of the operative C1 object.

Because of the linkage, A() evaluates 3 ln(x + 1), and A[] evaluates the derivative. This is seen in the definitions of the C1 operators for the Chain class:

```
double Chain::operator () ( double x )
{
   C1 *func;  Chain *now;  now = this;
   for(;;){
      func = now->C1ptr;   x = (*func)(x);
      if( now == now->next ) break;  now = now->next;
   }
   return x;
}
```

The construct for(;;) is an endless loop. The output from each C1 object in the
chain is provided as input to the next. Argument x is an internal copy we are free
to use in this way. The derivative operator includes a recursive update of dx:

```
double Chain::operator [] ( double x )
{
    double dx = 1.0;   C1 *func;   Chain *now;   now = this;
    for(;;){
        func = now->C1ptr;   dx *= (*func)[x];
            x = (*func)(x);
        if( now == now->next ) break;   now = now->next;
    }
    return dx;
}
```

The current example continues and produces output as follows:

```
cout << x(.5) << " | "
        << A(.5) << " | "
        << A[.5] << endl;
cout << x(.5) << " | "
        << D(.5) << " | "
        << D[.5] << endl;
cout << x(.5)        << " | "
        << (A+D)(.5) << " | "
        << (A+D)[.5] << endl;
```

```
0.5 | 1.2164 | 2
0.5 | 4 | -16
0.5 | 5.2164 | -14
```

9.7 MULTIDIMENSIONAL APPLICATIONS

A full and proper treatment of vector functions of multiple variables, as a generalization of the approach employed in this chapter, might begin by defining

```
typedef temp_real_vector (*multivariable) (const
    real_vector&);
```

Working all this out is beyond the scope of this book. However, it is worth knowing that even the comparatively simple treatment at hand is applicable, in a limited sense, to functions of more than one variable.

If function f depends on several variables, x, y, and z, say, the gradient of f is the vector

$$\nabla f \equiv \left[\frac{\partial f}{\partial x} \quad \frac{\partial f}{\partial y} \quad \frac{\partial f}{\partial z} \right]^{\mathrm{T}}$$

This chapter up to now has been devoted to the total differential *df*. If *x*, *y*, and *z* are themselves functions of another variable *t*, then

$$df = \left(\frac{\partial f}{\partial x}\frac{dx}{dt} + \frac{\partial f}{\partial y}\frac{dy}{dt} + \frac{\partial f}{\partial z}\frac{dz}{dt} \right) dt$$

We can set up *x*, *y*, and *z* to be linear in *t*: $[x\ y\ z]^{\mathrm{T}} = \mathbf{v} + \mathbf{u}t$, for example, where $\mathbf{v}$ is constant and $\mathbf{u}^{\mathrm{T}}\mathbf{u} = 1$. Then

$$\frac{df}{dt} = \frac{\partial f}{\partial x}u_1 + \frac{\partial f}{\partial y}u_2 + \frac{\partial f}{\partial z}u_3$$

The sum on the right-hand side fits the definition of a *directional* derivative: $(\mathbf{u}^{\mathrm{T}}\nabla)f$. This is the form in which several multidimensional algorithms employ gradient information, and therefore the present method can be applied despite its lack of separate partial derivatives.

Independent variable *t* is a formality, but it is also literally the distance elapsed along a line in direction $\mathbf{u}$. Our method remains basically one-dimensional, but that one dimension can have any direction in a multidimensional space. Press et al. [25], in describing minimization of functions in multidimensions, display (on p. 425) a *C* function `df1dim()` that returns the scalar product of a gradient and a direction vector. This function is employed in what is usually called *line search*, or *minimization along a ray*. Pierre [24, p. 286] discusses one-dimensional search in *n*-dimensional space, and his presentation requires the scalar product of a direction vector and a gradient.

In simplest terms, line search seeks the point where the directional derivative of a function passes through zero and changes sign. This point is necessarily a local minimum or maximum of the underlying function, and additional logic can guarantee which it is.

9.7.1 Example

Figure 9.1 outlines a minimization problem with which I am familiar [3]. An acoustic source at $\mathbf{s}$ emits a pulse that is scattered (as if) from a point $\mathbf{x}$ on a line and then is detected by a receiver at $\mathbf{r}$. Fermat's principle asserts that the pulse travels from $\mathbf{s}$ to $\mathbf{r}$, via $\mathbf{x}$, on the shortest path possible. Physically, the line containing $\mathbf{x}$ represents the intersection of two planes, like an escarpment. Mathematically, the line is a direction along which we will conduct a line search, positioning $\mathbf{x}$ so as to minimize the total path length from $\mathbf{s}$ to $\mathbf{r}$.

The distance from $\mathbf{s}$ to $\mathbf{r}$ via $\mathbf{x}$ is the sum of two terms: $[(\mathbf{x} - \mathbf{s})^2]^{1/2} + [(\mathbf{x} - \mathbf{r})^2]^{1/2}$, where $\mathbf{x} = \mathbf{v} + \mathbf{u}t$. The setup in terms of our automatic derivative methods is as follows:

```
{
    Variable t;
    Parm x0, y0, z0, xs, ys, xr, yr, cx, cy, cz;
```

```
C1_function x1sq( (x0+cx*t-xs)*(x0+cx*t-xs) );
C1_function y1sq( (y0+cy*t-ys)*(y0+cy*t-ys) );
C1_function z1sq( (z0+cz*t   )*(z0+cz*t   ) );
Chain S( x1sq + y1sq + z1sq , "sumsq");
Chain SSQRT( sqrtf, "sqrt()");
S >> SSQRT;
C1_function x2sq( (x0+cx*t-xr)*(x0+cx*t-xr) );
C1_function y2sq( (y0+cy*t-yr)*(y0+cy*t-yr) );
C1_function z2sq( (z0+cz*t   )*(z0+cz*t   ) );
Chain R( x2sq + y2sq + z2sq , "sumsq");
Chain RSQRT( sqrtf, "sqrt()");
R >> RSQRT;
```

Variable `t` is a placeholder for the argument of `()` and `[]`. Each vector is defined by its three Cartesian components: `(x0 y0 z0)` is **v**; `(xs ys 0)` is **s**; `(xr yr 0)` is **r**; `(cx cy cz)` is **u**. The components of **u** are direction cosines: The sum of their squares is 1. The expression `x1sq + y1sq + z1sq` is $(\mathbf{x} - \mathbf{s})^2$. After being chained to `SSQRT`, S implements $[(\mathbf{x} - \mathbf{s})^2]^{1/2}$. In the same way, R implements $[(\mathbf{x} - \mathbf{r})^2]^{1/2}$. The total function to be minimized is `(S+R)`.

Next we assign values to the fixed parameters:

```
x0 = 0.; y0 = 0.; z0 = 2.; xs = 1.; ys = 0.; xr
   = 2.; yr = 0.;
cx = .6124; cy = .6124; cz = .5;
```

As Fig. 9.1 suggests, vector **u** dips 30 degrees downward in a direction halfway between the horizontal axes. Point **v** lies on the vertical axis 2 units below the plane of the horizontal axes. Points **s** and **r** lie 1 and 2 units from the origin. We print out some function and derivative values:

```
for(double w=-.5; w<=.5; w+=.1)
    cout << t(w) << " | "
         << (S + R)(w) << " | "
         << (S + R)[w] << endl;
```

```
-0.5 | 5.11624 | -0.299973
-0.4 | 5.09014 | -0.222005
-0.3 | 5.07187 | -0.14326
-0.2 | 5.0615  | -0.064116
-0.1 | 5.05905 | 0.0150488
0.0  | 5.0645  | 0.0938612
0.1  | 5.07779 | 0.171963
0.2  | 5.09885 | 0.249018
0.3  | 5.12755 | 0.324719
0.4  | 5.16374 | 0.398791
0.5  | 5.20725 | 0.470997
```

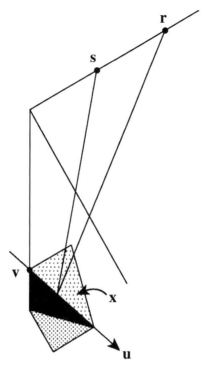

Fig. 9.1   Minimize the path from **s** to **r** via **x**, where **x** = **v** + t**u**, and t is the independent variable.

The list of function values in the second column shows a minimum in the vicinity of t value -0.1. The list of directional derivatives in the third column shows a reversal of sign between t values -0.1 and -0.2. We can pin this down precisely with a simple line search loop. For the sake of demonstration, we start well away from the expected answer:

```
double u, du, w, dw, del, tol = 1.e-12;
u = 1.;   du = (S + R)[u]; del = 0.1;
for(int k=0; k<10; k++){
    cout << t(u) << " | " << (S + R)(u) << " | "
        << du << endl;
    if(fabs(del) < tol) break;
    w = u; dw = du; u += del; du = (S + R)[u];
    del = du*(w-u)/(du-dw);
}
}
```

The tactic of this loop is to find the value of t for which the function is minimum, by finding the t for which the directional derivative is zero. After a couple of gross first steps, convergence is rapid:

```
1 | 5.52705 | 0.798245
1.1 | 5.6098 | 0.856264
-0.375841 | 5.085 | -0.203038
-0.0929646 | 5.05917 | 0.0206094
-0.119032 | 5.0589 | -1.96701e-06
-0.11903 | 5.0589 | 1.02326e-09
-0.11903 | 5.0589 | -1.38778e-17
```

The optimal position of x lies just outside the xz plane, in the direction of $-u$ in Fig. 9.1. Thinking of the distance function $f = [(x - s)^2]^{1/2} + [(x - r)^2]^{1/2}$ in general terms, ∇f is merely perpendicular to u at x, and is not necessarily zero. Algorithms that seek an unconstrained minimum f, at this juncture pick a new direction (away from x) and head out on a new line search.

In regard to automatic differentiation, my notion of acceptable performance differs from that of prior authors, who concentrate their main efforts on machine efficiency. I am content to let the compiler and CPU work overtime on behalf of the user, in order to produce results like this with the greatest convenience for the program writer.

9.8 SUMMARY AND CONCLUSIONS

Pointer to Function. The specific form `ret_type (*func_name) (arg_list);` declares a *function pointer*. The `(* )` is mandatory. The specification is satisfied by the *name* of any function that accepts the stated argument list and yields the declared return type. For example, the declaration `double (*differentiable) (double)` is satisfied by `<math.h>` functions such as `sqrt`, `cos`, and `log`. Further examples defined in the text include `dsqrt`, `negsin`, and `inv`.

Abstract Base Class C1. Every member f derived from C1 returns a `double` value when addressed as `f(double)` and a `double` first derivative when addressed as `f[double]`. Objects of this type are exemplified by

```
dif1 sinf(sin,cos), logf(log,inv), expf(exp,exp);
Variable x;
Parm two(2.), a, tmp(q[j]);   a = 3.;   tmp = q[j];
Prod fifth(sqf,cubf);
C1_function cosec(1./sinf), sin2x(2.*sinf*cosf);
Chain A( 1.0 - 2.0*sinf*sinf, "cos2x");
```

Chain Rule. The chain rule of calculus is implemented *automatically* for arbitrary algebraic combinations of members derived from C1. For example:

```
(1. + logf)[.99];
(1. - 2.*(sinf/cosec))[.5236];
(x * fifth * x)[1.0];
```

```
(sin2x/A)[.3927];
(2.*tanf/((1.-tanf)*(1.+tanf)))[.3927];
```

Functions of Functions. The case in which the argument of a function is another function, $f(g(h(x)))$, is modeled as

```
Chain f, g, h;
h >> g >> f;
double differential = h[3.14];
```

The precedence operator >> determines the order in which the links in the chain are evaluated. The value and derivative of the linked chain are determined by addressing its first (i.e., *innermost*) member.

Functions of More Than One Variable. The methods described in this chapter are sufficient to obtain directional derivatives of the form $(\mathbf{u}^T\nabla)f$, where $\mathbf{u}$ is a unit vector. The methods are merely one-dimensional, but that single dimension can extend in any direction.

10 Constrained Optimization

In this chapter we introduce linear programming and related topics. The methods that we will encounter had their genesis in economics and operations research, where the idea of minimizing a cost function or maximizing a profit measure translates to optimizing the performance of a complicated system, for the benefit of some subset of humankind. The tools that have come forth from this area are simply too good to be ignored in the exact sciences and engineering.

We have touched upon methods of finding the universal minimum or maximum of a function of many variables. The techniques available for solving the least-squares problem, for example, all have counterparts in methods applicable to other forms of objective function. What is sought in *constrained* optimization is not the most extreme value in the range of a function, but rather the extreme value within a restricted domain of the input variables. The subsidiary conditions restricting the input variables are the constraints, and the only form of constraint we need to consider is linear combinations of variables.

Linear programming carries a connotation that its methods are intended for problems whose complexity verges on the incomprehensible and whose size is well into the range of unwieldy. I have found that the latter-day algorithms I will describe are neat and tidy and provide a framework within which perfectly tractable problems can be expressed and solved with less human effort than with conventional approaches.

10.1 LINEAR CONSTRAINTS

If the independent variables in a problem are labeled x_j, and if there are n of these, a linear constraint is a relationship of the form $\sum_{j=1}^{n} a_{ij}x_j$ [op] b_i, where [op] stands for one of the comparisons $\leq$, $=$, or $\geq$. If there are m such constraint relationships, i ranges from 1 to m. In the case that [op] is the equal sign, what we have is the familiar form $\mathbf{Ax} = \mathbf{b}$. $\mathbf{A}$ is an $m \times n$ matrix, vector $\mathbf{x}$ has n components, and vector $\mathbf{b}$ has m.

To head off avoidable confusion, it is wise to set some standards that reduce the number of redundant possibilities. Without limiting the types of problems that can be described, we can insist upon the following conventions:

- All variables x_j shall be nonnegative: $x_j \geq 0$, for all j. In two dimensions, the problem is confined to the first quadrant, in three, the first octant, and so on in higher dimensions.

143

- All constraints shall be expressed as inequalities in the $\leq$ sense. If constraint i is given as $\geq$, convert it by negating b_i and all a_{ij}. If a constraint is given as an equality, restate it as a *pair* of inequalities of opposite senses.
- All inequalities in the $\leq$ sense shall, furthermore, be expressed as *equations* of the form $\sum_{j=1}^{n} a_{ij}x_j + w_i = b_i$, where w_i, an explicit *slack variable*, is nonnegative. The slack variables are to be solved for, as well as the independent variables. A set of constraints according to this convention thus assumes the form $\mathbf{Ax} + \mathbf{w} = \mathbf{b}$.

In these and other aspects of linear programming, I am following the practices set forth in the book by Vanderbei [28]. By comparing other references, the reader will find different choices regarding inequalities and slack variables.

10.1.1 Example

Write matrix $\mathbf{A}$ and the right-hand side, $\mathbf{b}$, for the linear constraints defining the square shown in Fig. 10.1. The square is bounded by lines A, B, C, and D. I prefer to write the equation of a line in the form $x_1/(x_1\text{-intercept}) + x_2/(x_2\text{-intercept}) = 1$,

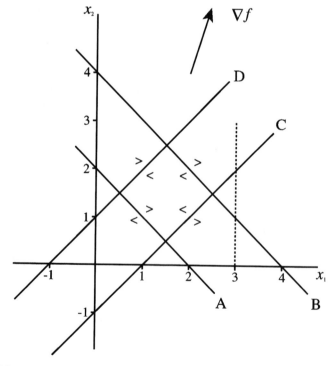

Fig. 10.1 Linear constraints in the first quadrant for the example in Section 10.1.1.

because the axis intercepts can be read directly off a graph. The equations for the four boundary lines are:

$$A: \frac{x_1}{2} + \frac{x_2}{2} = 1; \quad B: \frac{x_1}{4} + \frac{x_2}{4} = 1; \quad C: \frac{x_1}{1} + \frac{x_2}{-1} = 1; \quad D: \frac{x_1}{-1} + \frac{x_2}{1} = 1$$

Relative to line A, the interior of the square is where the left-hand side of the equation is >1. For B, C, and D, the sense of the inequality is $<$. Since we have agreed to write constraints in the form $\mathbf{Ax} + \mathbf{w} = \mathbf{b}$, with nonnegative $\mathbf{w}$, we must negate equation A. Therefore, we have

$$\mathbf{A} = \begin{bmatrix} -0.5 & -0.5 \\ 0.25 & 0.25 \\ 1 & -1 \\ -1 & 1 \end{bmatrix}, \quad \mathbf{b} = \begin{bmatrix} -1 \\ 1 \\ 1 \\ 1 \end{bmatrix}$$

Consider an additional constraint based on the line $x_1 = 3$ (i.e., $x_1/3 + 0 = 1$). If this were to be included as $x_1/3 < 1$, it would be redundant, because every point inside the square already satisfies this condition. If it were to be included as $x_1/3 > 1$, it would be inconsistent with the other constraints, and it would make any problem restricted by these constraints unsolvable.

The right triangle bounded by the x_1 and x_2 axes and the line A would require input of only line A to define it. The two other conditions, $x_1 \geq 0$ and $x_2 \geq 0$, are built into the mathematics and are always enforced.

10.2 LINEAR OBJECTIVE FUNCTION

In this chapter, the function we seek to maximize or minimize is always a linear combination of the independent variables, $\sum_{j=1}^{n} c_j x_j$, or $\mathbf{c}^T \mathbf{x}$. In three-dimensional Cartesian space with two independent variables, such a function is represented by a slanted plane hovering over the (x_1, x_2) plane. In Fig. 10.1, the arrow marked ∇f indicates the direction in which a plane representing $f = x_1 + 3x_2$ is increasing (i.e., its gradient). It is apparent by inspection that f attains its maximum value, consistent with the constraints $\mathbf{Ax} + \mathbf{w} = \mathbf{b}$, at the point where boundaries B and D intersect. It is typical in linear programming that the optimal solution occurs at a vertex where boundaries intersect. An exception is possible when the gradient is exactly perpendicular to a boundary.

Again following Vanderbei, I adopt one additional convention:

• The goal is to *maximize* $\mathbf{c}^T \mathbf{x}$. To solve a minimization problem, negate $\mathbf{c}$.

10.3   DUALITY AND COMPLEMENTARITY

The standard problem we intend to solve is stated:

$$\text{maximize } \mathbf{c}^T\mathbf{x}$$
$$\text{subject to } \mathbf{Ax} + \mathbf{w} = \mathbf{b}$$
$$\mathbf{x}, \mathbf{w} \geq 0$$

This is designated the *primal problem*. In other chapters we have found it useful to incorporate the transpose of a given matrix somehow to generate an expanded but symmetric problem. Symmetry simplified matters more than sufficiently to compensate for greater overall size. The question is: What if any use can be made of $\mathbf{A}^T$ here? The answer is the *dual problem*, stated:

$$\text{minimize } \mathbf{b}^T\mathbf{y}$$
$$\text{subject to } \mathbf{A}^T\mathbf{y} - \mathbf{z} = \mathbf{c}$$
$$\mathbf{y}, \mathbf{z} \geq 0$$

Vector $\mathbf{z}$ is a vector of new slack variables that implement the new constraints $\mathbf{A}^T\mathbf{y} \geq \mathbf{c}$. The historical motivation for formulating the dual problem was that if $\mathbf{A}$ has more rows than columns, then $\mathbf{A}^T$ has fewer rows than columns and is therefore quicker to solve using the simplex method, which was historically, the first reliable method. The *duality theorems* guarantee that the optimal solution of the primal problem is the optimal solution of the dual problem, and vice versa. Moreover, the two objective functions have the same numerical value, at optimality, $\mathbf{c}^T\mathbf{x} = \mathbf{b}^T\mathbf{y}$.

Multiply the primal constraint equation by $\mathbf{y}^T$ and the dual constraint equation by $\mathbf{x}^T$:

$$\mathbf{y}^T(\mathbf{Ax} + \mathbf{w}) = \mathbf{y}^T\mathbf{Ax} + \mathbf{y}^T\mathbf{w} = \mathbf{y}^T\mathbf{b} = \mathbf{b}^T\mathbf{y}$$
$$\mathbf{x}^T(\mathbf{A}^T\mathbf{y} - \mathbf{z}) = \mathbf{x}^T\mathbf{A}^T\mathbf{y} - \mathbf{x}^T\mathbf{z} = \mathbf{x}^T\mathbf{c} = \mathbf{c}^T\mathbf{x}$$

When $\mathbf{x}$ and $\mathbf{y}$ have reached optimal values, *duality*, the expression goes, means that the two equations here are equal. All the terms are scalars, and $\mathbf{y}^T\mathbf{Ax} = \mathbf{x}^T\mathbf{A}^T\mathbf{y}$. So if we subtract the second line from the first, we can conclude that at optimality, $\mathbf{x}^T\mathbf{z} + \mathbf{y}^T\mathbf{w} = 0$.

The reason that $\mathbf{x}^T\mathbf{z} + \mathbf{y}^T\mathbf{w} = 0$ for optimum $\mathbf{x}$ and $\mathbf{y}$ is very powerful. It is not merely as if $\mathbf{x}$ and $\mathbf{z}$ were orthogonal, or as if $\mathbf{x}^T\mathbf{z}$ and $\mathbf{y}^T\mathbf{w}$ were equal but opposed in sign. The reason is that each and every component-by-component product $x_j z_j$ and $y_j w_j$ is individually zero. What's more, x_j is zero if z_j isn't, and vice versa; y_j is zero if w_j isn't, and vice versa. This property is called *complementarity*.

The term for a vector whose components are of the form $x_j z_j$, where x_j and z_j are components of other vectors $\mathbf{x}$ and $\mathbf{z}$, is *Hadamard product*. One way to distinguish this construct is to write it as $\mathbf{Xz}$, where $\mathbf{X} = \mathbf{diag}(x_1, \ldots, x_n)$. In complementarity, it is really the Hadamard products of $\mathbf{x}$ and $\mathbf{z}$, and of $\mathbf{y}$ and $\mathbf{w}$, that vanish.

In linear programming, until the optimum primal and dual solutions are reached, the quantity $\mathbf{b^T y} - \mathbf{c^T x}$ is nonzero, and it is called the *duality gap*. Similarly, until the optimum solution is attained, the quantity $\mathbf{x^T z} + \mathbf{y^T w}$ is nonzero, and it is called the *complementarity gap*.

10.3.1 Example

We continue the example diagrammed in Fig. 10.1. The primal problem is

$$\text{maximize } \mathbf{c^T x}$$
$$\text{subject to } \mathbf{Ax + w = b}$$
$$\mathbf{x, w} \geq 0$$

where

$$\mathbf{A} = \begin{bmatrix} -0.5 & -0.5 \\ 0.25 & 0.25 \\ 1 & -1 \\ -1 & 1 \end{bmatrix}, \quad \mathbf{b} = \begin{bmatrix} -1 \\ 1 \\ 1 \\ 1 \end{bmatrix}, \quad \text{and} \quad \mathbf{c} = \begin{bmatrix} 1 \\ 3 \end{bmatrix}$$

By inspection of Fig. 10.1, we can determine that the value of $\mathbf{x}$ that maximizes $\mathbf{c^T x}$ subject to the constraints is

$$\mathbf{x'} = \begin{bmatrix} 1.5 \\ 2.5 \end{bmatrix}$$

Therefore, optimal

$$\mathbf{w = b - Ax'} = \begin{bmatrix} 1 \\ 0 \\ 2 \\ 0 \end{bmatrix}$$

The second and fourth components of $\mathbf{w}$ are zero because the optimal $\mathbf{x'}$ lies *on* the second and fourth boundaries (lines B and D). The dual problem is

$$\text{minimize } \mathbf{b^T y}$$
$$\text{subject to } \mathbf{A^T y - z = c}$$
$$\mathbf{y, z} \geq 0$$

Since $\mathbf{x}$ and $\mathbf{z}$ are complementary, $\mathbf{z} = 0$. Since $\mathbf{w}$ and $\mathbf{y}$ are complementary,

$$
\mathbf{y} = \begin{bmatrix} 0 \\ y_2 \\ 0 \\ y_4 \end{bmatrix} \quad \text{and} \quad \mathbf{A}^\mathsf{T}\mathbf{y} = \begin{bmatrix} 0.25y_2 - y_4 \\ 0.25y_2 + y_4 \end{bmatrix} = \mathbf{c} = \begin{bmatrix} 1 \\ 3 \end{bmatrix}
$$

Therefore,

$$
\mathbf{y} = \begin{bmatrix} 0 \\ 8 \\ 0 \\ 1 \end{bmatrix}
$$

Finally, the optimal value of f is $\mathbf{c}^\mathsf{T}\mathbf{x} = \mathbf{b}^\mathsf{T}\mathbf{y} = 9$.

10.4 INTERIOR-POINT METHOD

For optimization problems with more than two independent variables, we require a more general approach than simply reading the answer off a graph. The original general optimization method was the simplex method. In one sentence, the simplex method is an orderly procedure for arriving at the optimal solution by crawling along the boundaries of the region defined by the constraints (the *feasible* region). In contrast, interior-point methods were developed more recently. In one sentence, an interior-point method is an orderly procedure for choosing directions and step sizes to iterate from any point in the interior of the feasible region, to the optimal solution on its boundary.

Within the scope of this book, we can implement an interior-point method and demonstrate some of its applications and extensions. A similarly brief presentation of the simplex method would not do it justice. The particular algorithm I will describe is termed a *path-following method* by Vanderbei [28], and what follows is based upon Chapters 17 through 19 of that reference.

Inside the feasible region of a constrained optimization problem, the primal and dual constraint equations are all satisfied, but complementarity is violated. That is, the values of $\mathbf{x}$, $\mathbf{w}$, $\mathbf{y}$, and $\mathbf{z}$ are such that $\mathbf{A}\mathbf{x} + \mathbf{w} = \mathbf{b}$ and $\mathbf{A}^\mathsf{T}\mathbf{y} - \mathbf{z} = \mathbf{c}$, but the Hadamard products $\mathbf{X}\mathbf{z} \neq 0$ and $\mathbf{Y}\mathbf{w} \neq 0$. A theoretical construct called the *central path* is defined by the (remarkable) condition $\mathbf{X}\mathbf{z} = \mu\mathbf{e}$ and $\mathbf{Y}\mathbf{w} = \mu\mathbf{e}$, where $\mathbf{e}$ is a vector containing all ones. In other words, for all components j, $x_j z_j = \mu$ and $y_j w_j = \mu$, and μ is one and the same number. This is a very uniform condition. The strategy of the path-following method is to get onto the central path, and stay there while (average) complementarity error μ is reduced toward zero.

The computation of the path-following method is reminiscent of approaches we have used before in solving multidimensional problems: Iteratively update all the variables at once, based on a computed direction and a reasonable step size. The variables in play are $\mathbf{x}$, $\mathbf{w}$, $\mathbf{y}$, and $\mathbf{z}$, numbering $2n + 2m$ dimensions, and the step directions to be determined are labeled $\Delta\mathbf{x}$, $\Delta\mathbf{w}$, $\Delta\mathbf{y}$, and $\Delta\mathbf{z}$.

The set of equations to be solved, written in partitioned matrix format, is

$$
\left[
\begin{array}{cc|cc}
-\mathbf{XZ}^{-1} & & -\mathbf{I} & \\
& \mathbf{A} & & \mathbf{I} \\
\hline
-\mathbf{I} & \mathbf{A}^{\mathrm{T}} & & \\
\mathbf{I} & & \mathbf{YW}^{-1} &
\end{array}
\right]
\left[
\begin{array}{c}
\Delta\mathbf{z} \\
\Delta\mathbf{y} \\
\hline
\Delta\mathbf{x} \\
\Delta\mathbf{w}
\end{array}
\right]
=
\left[
\begin{array}{c}
-\mu\mathbf{Z}^{-1}\mathbf{e} + \mathbf{x} \\
\mathbf{r} \\
\hline
\mathbf{s} \\
\mu\mathbf{W}^{-1}\mathbf{e} - \mathbf{y}
\end{array}
\right].
$$

In this impressive display, $\mathbf{A}$ is the constraint matrix; $\mathbf{I}$ is the identity matrix; $\mathbf{XZ}^{-1}$ means a diagonal matrix whose jth element is x_j/z_j; $\mathbf{YW}^{-1}$ means a diagonal matrix whose jth element is y_j/w_j; and $\Delta\mathbf{x}$, $\Delta\mathbf{w}$, $\Delta\mathbf{y}$, and $\Delta\mathbf{z}$ are the estimated step directions to be solved for. On the right-hand side, $\mathbf{e}$ means a vector of all ones (of whatever dimension); $\mathbf{x}$ and $\mathbf{y}$ are the current values of the primal and dual variables, respectively; $\mathbf{r}$ is the *primal infeasibility* $\mathbf{b} - \mathbf{Ax} - \mathbf{w}$; and $\mathbf{s}$ is the *dual infeasibility* $\mathbf{c} - \mathbf{A}^{\mathrm{T}}\mathbf{y} + \mathbf{z}$;   Collectively, these equations are called the *Karush–Kuhn–Tucker* (KKT) *system* for this problem.

The (first and fourth row) equations for the slack-variable step directions involve only diagonal matrices and can be dealt with after $\Delta\mathbf{x}$ and $\Delta\mathbf{y}$ are determined:

$$\Delta\mathbf{z} = \mu\mathbf{X}^{-1}\mathbf{e} - \mathbf{z} - \mathbf{X}^{-1}\mathbf{Z}\,\Delta\mathbf{x}$$

$$\Delta\mathbf{w} = \mu\mathbf{Y}^{-1}\mathbf{e} - \mathbf{w} - \mathbf{Y}^{-1}\mathbf{W}\,\Delta\mathbf{y}$$

Substituting these formulas into rows 2 and 3 produces the *reduced* KKT system, which is what we are actually going to work with:

$$
\begin{bmatrix}
-\mathbf{Y}^{-1}\mathbf{W} & \mathbf{A} \\
\mathbf{A}^{\mathrm{T}} & \mathbf{X}^{-1}\mathbf{Z}
\end{bmatrix}
\begin{bmatrix}
\Delta\mathbf{y} \\
\Delta\mathbf{x}
\end{bmatrix}
=
\begin{bmatrix}
\mathbf{b} - \mathbf{Ax} - \mu\mathbf{Y}^{-1}\mathbf{e} \\
\mathbf{c} - \mathbf{A}^{\mathrm{T}}\mathbf{y} + \mu\mathbf{X}^{-1}\mathbf{e}
\end{bmatrix}
$$

The reader will discern that the reduced KKT matrix is symmetric, with $\mathbf{diag}(-w_j/y_j)$ and $\mathbf{diag}(z_j/x_j)$ on the main diagonal and $\mathbf{A}$ and $\mathbf{A}^{\mathrm{T}}$ in the corners. We know that some of the x_j and y_j values in the denominators on the diagonal will tend toward zero as optimality is approached, so we can appreciate that the path-following search must be controlled exquisitely.

The path-following interior-point method is embodied in subroutine `Loop_LP`. This subroutine is more than 60 lines long, and the matrix and vector quantities are defined near the beginning:

```
int Loop_LP (const matrix& A, const real_vector& b,
             const real_vector& c, real_vector& x,
             real_vector& z, real_vector& y, real_vector&
             w, double f)
{//Implements RVDB Fig 17.1, for matrix A, using LDLt_QD().
```

The call list specifies that inputs **A**, **b**, and **c** will not be modified. (There is also a version in which **A** is specified as const sparse&.) The caller allocates and initializes **x**, **z**, **y**, and **w**. Parameter f is a constant that will be added to the objective value in printouts but does not enter into the calculation. The code continues:

```
unsigned i, j, m = A.M(), n = A.N(), nz = m * n;
real_vector rho(m), sigma(n), u(m+n), dw(m), dz(n);
real_vector dy(&u[0],m), dx(&u[m],n), E(m), D(n),
    diag(m+n);
```

The reduced KKT matrix is square with (m+n) rows and columns. It is to be defined implicitly in a call to LDLt_QD(), as in Chapter 8. The primal and dual infeasibility vectors **r** and **s** will be stored in rho and sigma, respectively. Steps Δy and Δx, as dy and dx, occupy the top and bottom, respectively, of a single vector u of dimension m+n. Vectors real_vector E(m), D(n), diag(m+n) will be used in representing the diagonal of the reduced KKT matrix.

The interior-point method does not actually assume that **x** and **y** are necessarily within their respective feasible regions at all times, in order to work. Instead, it accepts whatever the current values of **x** and **y** are, and aims to step from that point to a point on the central path within the feasible region. A central-path target point is selected by proposing a reasonable value of μ, the (average) complementarity gap. A step direction for all $(2m + 2n)$ variables is computed from that assumption. The size of the step actually taken is limited by the (worst-case) criterion that no variable may go negative. The same proportionate step size is applied uniformly to all variables.

The target value of μ is set by multiplying the current actual value of the complementarity gap γ (gamma), normalized to the number of variables, by a "parameter of art" δ (delta). The value of delta is 0.02. The actual worst-case allowable step size θ (theta) is weighted by a safety parameter, r, set to 0.9. So the scalar quantities used in subroutine Loop_LP() include

```
double  gamma, delta = 0.02, mu, theta, r = 0.9;
```

The relentless iteration toward optimality is controlled by a while() loop:

```
    while(1)
    {
//   * Compute infeasibilities.
        rho   = -((A*x) -= b); rho   -= w;
        sigma = -((y*A) -= c); sigma += z;

//   * Compute complementarity gap.
        gamma = z * x + y * w;

//   * Compute central path parameter.
        mu = delta * gamma / (double)(n+m);
```

```
//  * Set up the diagonal of the reduced KKT matrix.
       for(i=1; i<=m; i++) E(i) = w(i)/y(i);
       for(j=1; j<=n; j++) D(j) = z(j)/x(j);
//     Store -E and D into the Quasidefinite diagonal
       for(i=1; i<=m; i++) // upper left diagonal [-E]
           diag(i)   = -max( E(i), EPSDIAG);
       for(j=1; j<=n; j++) // lower right diagonal [D]
           diag(j+m) =  max( D(j), EPSDIAG);
```

Cholesky subroutine LDLt_QD() (Chapter 8) requires the caller to initialize the diagonal. The code above puts $-\mathbf{Y}^{-1}\mathbf{W}$ and $\mathbf{X}^{-1}\mathbf{Z}$ into place on the KKT diagonal, with safeguards against too-small values. Parameter EPSDIAG equals 1.0e-14.

```
//  * Define L and decompose
       sparse L(m+n, m+n, nz*MULT);
       L.LDLt_QD( A, diag);
```

```
//  * Construct the rhs and backsolve
       for(i=1; i<=m; i++) dy(i) = rho(i)    + w(i)
           - mu/y(i);
       for(j=1; j<=n; j++) dx(j) = sigma(j) - z(j)
           + mu/x(j);
       u.Lsolve(L).Dsolve(diag).TLsolve(L);
```

```
//  * The rest of the solution
       for(i=1; i<=m; i++) dw(i) = mu/y(i) - w(i)
           - E(i)*dy(i);
       for(j=1; j<=n; j++) dz(j) = mu/x(j) - z(j)
           - D(j)*dx(j);
```

At this point the subroutine has computed a step *direction* defined by $\Delta\mathbf{x}$, $\Delta\mathbf{w}$, $\Delta\mathbf{y}$, and $\Delta\mathbf{z}$. The next task is to find a step *size* such that no variable is made negative when the step is applied:

```
//  * Ratio test to find step length.
       theta = r;
       for(j=1; j<=n; j++){
           if (theta < -dx(j)/x(j)) { theta = -dx(j)/x(j); }
           if (theta < -dz(j)/z(j)) { theta = -dz(j)/z(j); }
       }
       for(i=1; i<=m; i++){
           if (theta < -dy(i)/y(i)) { theta = -dy(i)/y(i); }
           if (theta < -dw(i)/w(i)) { theta = -dw(i)/w(i); }
       }
       theta = r/theta;
```

Finally, **x**, **w**, **y**, and **z** are incremented, and computation reverts to the top of the loop:

```
//   * Step to new point
      dx *= theta;   dz *= theta;   dy *= theta;
         dw *= theta;
      x   += dx;        z += dz;        y += dy;
         w += dw;
   }//Bottom of Loop
```

The normal exit from the iterative loop occurs when three quantities are all found to be less than a certain value (10^{-6}): the complementarity gap gamma, the Euclidean norm of the primal infeasibility normr, and the Euclidean norm of the dual infeasibility norms. An abnormal exit is taken if and when theta is found to be less than 10^{-5} or if the number of iterations exceeds an outrageous maximum number (200).

10.5   SOLVING LP PROBLEMS

The greatest challenge in a typical linear programming problem is to set up the matrix **A** and the right-hand-side vector **b** that express the constraints. Once that is accomplished, the vector **c** defining the objective function is usually obvious, and the solution from there forward is produced mechanically. To help standardize the solution process, the interior-point method Loop_LP() can be called through the interface routine INT_PT():

```
int INT_PT(const matrix& A, const real_vector& b,
      const real_vector& c, real_vector& x, real_vector&
      y, double f)
{//Sets up Loop_LP(), for matrix A.
   unsigned m, n, i, j;
   if((m = A.M()) != b.N() || (n = A.N()) != c.N())
      exit(1);
   real_vector w(m), z(n);
   int status;
   for(j=0; j<n; j++){ x[j] = 10.0; z[j] = 10.0; }
   for(i=0; i<m; i++){ y[i] = 10.0; w[i] = 10.0; }
   status = Loop_LP( A, b, c, x, z, y, w, f);
   cout << 'w'; w.dumpall();
   cout << 'z'; z.dumpall();
   w.zap(); z.zap();
   cout << "Return status = " << status << endl;
   return status;
}
```

Subroutine `INT_PT()` allocates slack vectors **w** and **z**, and it initializes all four vectors **x**, **z**, **y**, and **w**. The initialization value is not critical; it can be many orders of magnitude away from the final answer.

The example in Section 10.3.1 is no great challenge to `INT_PT()` and `Loop_LP()`, considering that the optimal values can be read directly from Fig. 10.1, but it provides a demonstration of how `Loop_LP()` typically behaves. Within the process loop of that subroutine I inserted the following print statements:

```
printf("%3d %14.7e %8.1e %14.7e %8.1e %8.1e",
       iter, primal_obj, normr, dual_obj, norms,
       gamma);
printf(" %8.5f\n", theta);
```

The following printout was obtained as `Loop_LP()` processed the example of Section 10.3.1:

```
A:  |-0.5|-0.5
    |0.25|0.25
    |   1|  -1
    |  -1|   1

b:  |-1|1|1|1
c:  |1|3
```

iter	primal_obj	normr	dual_obj	norms	gamma	theta
0	4.0000000e+01	1.9e+01	2.0000000e+01	2.1e+01	6.0e+02	0.65363
1	3.9054749e+01	6.6e+00	2.6998883e+01	7.1e+00	2.1e+02	0.47962
2	2.7604191e+01	3.4e+00	3.1226956e+01	3.7e+00	1.1e+02	0.81489
3	1.1819253e+01	6.3e-01	3.1373739e+01	6.9e-01	3.7e+01	1.00000
4	8.1288457e+00	2.3e-17	1.6206121e+01	4.7e-14	8.1e+00	0.74585
5	8.3503342e+00	2.5e-16	1.0523646e+01	1.3e-14	2.2e+00	0.67829
6	8.7322846e+00	2.6e-16	9.4609339e+00	3.8e-15	7.3e-01	0.87452
7	8.9658309e+00	5.4e-16	9.0700075e+00	1.4e-15	1.0e-01	0.90351
8	8.9962218e+00	3.3e-16	9.0081564e+00	2.3e-15	1.2e-02	0.90940
9	8.9995862e+00	5.0e-16	9.0008846e+00	1.4e-15	1.3e-03	0.90959
10	8.9999547e+00	2.5e-16	9.0000957e+00	2.4e-16	1.4e-04	0.91036
11	8.9999951e+00	5.1e-16	9.0000103e+00	9.4e-16	1.5e-05	0.91117
12	8.9999995e+00	3.4e-16	9.0000011e+00	1.3e-15	1.6e-06	0.91197
13	8.9999999e+00	2.6e-16	9.0000001e+00	1.0e-15	1.7e-07	

```
Return status = 0
w:  |1|2.95761e-09|2|3.28046e-08
z:  |2.75582e-08|9.83557e-09
x:  |1.5|2.5
y:  |3.02058e-08|8|1.02022e-08|1
```

As initialized (`iter` 0), the variables are well outside the feasible region, with `normr` = 19 and `norms` = 21. By step 4, however, both the primal and dual infeasibility parameters `normr` and `norms` have been reduced to the level of round-off error, meaning that all constraints are satisfied. The remaining nine steps are devoted to reducing the complementarity gap γ (`gamma`). It shrinks by about an order of magnitude per step. At the same time, the last six or seven steps affect the primal and dual objective values farther and farther to the right of the decimal point.

The values of `theta` shown in this iteration range from 1.0 down to about 0.5, and this behavior is typical. One of the ways for the iteration to terminate abnormally is for `theta` to become very small (<0.00001). This means that the iteration is stuck on a point from which it cannot move away. In my experience, this is symptomatic that the constraints are inconsistent or that the initial values are inadequate.

The final answers are essentially the same as those we obtained by hand, but the "zeros" retain a residual value around 10^{-8}. We approach the optimal solution but remain a carefully controlled distance away. Notice that $\mathbf{y}^T\mathbf{w} \approx (3.02 + 2.38 + 2.02 + 3.28) \times 10^{-8}$ and that $\mathbf{x}^T\mathbf{z} \approx (4.14 + 2.46) \times 10^{-8}$. Each of the summands contributing to the complementarity gap `gamma` is roughly equal.

The reader can verify that when `normr` and `norms` are small, `gamma` is about the same as the difference of `dual_obj` and `primal_obj`. This reflects a general theoretical truism, namely, that the complementarity gap and the duality gap should be equal.

This example required 13 iterations for a problem with 12 variables, including duals and slacks. I have observed with the present algorithm that the iteration count grows roughly in proportion to the number of variables. Advanced forms of step-size determination (e.g., predictor–corrector [28]) aim to improve upon this.

Often, it happens that we are confronted with solving a sequence of problems where each new problem is only marginally different from the preceding one. Typically, each solution, when found, makes a good point from which to start the next series of iterations. With interior-point methods, *this does not work*. Each solution obtained is too close to the boundary to leave room to maneuver.

10.6   LP APPLICATIONS

In scientific and engineering computation, maximizing or minimizing a linear combination of variables is seldom a task of interest in itself. However, since the tools to accomplish this are so effective, it is often worthwhile to make the effort to express an interesting problem in the required standard form. Considerable theoretical preparation may be required to recast an engineering problem in a form to which linear programming is applicable. Good examples are to be found in control theory, network theory, circuit design, structural design, and differential equations [24,28].

A modest problem of interest to me is the following: In two or three dimensions, the feasible region for an LP problem amounts to a polygon or polyhedron bounded by lines or planes, respectively. The lines and planes are rather easy to specify merely by stating the axis intercepts. Polygons and polyhedrons are comparatively difficult to describe, because they are defined by vertex points that must be precisely positioned, and in a particular order. We can define geometry simply in terms of lines and planes, and then exploit the LP software to determine the corresponding vertex description.

The lines and planes circumscribing a feasible region in an LP problem are given as **A** and **b**, the constraint matrix and right-hand-side vector. In two dimensions, a linear objective function as simple as $x_1 \cos \phi + x_2 \sin \phi$ is sufficient. As angle ϕ sweeps through the full circle (in small steps), each vertex in turn inevitably becomes the point that maximizes the objective. This strategy is implemented in the following subroutine:

```
int polygon_vertices(const matrix& A, const real_vector&
    b, matrix& V)
{//Polygon implied by A*x < b; maximize x(1)*cos(ang)
 //    + x(2)*sin(ang)
   unsigned m = b.N(), n = A.N();
   real_vector c(n), x(n), y(m);   c.init();
   int status, k=0, mv = V.M();
   double angrad=.01, dangrad= -.315, f=0.;

   for(int lk=0; lk<20; lk++)
   {
      c(1) = cos(angrad); c(2) = sin(angrad);
      if((status = INT_PT( A, b, c, x, y, f)) != 0 )
         break;
      if(k == 0 || euc( x - V[k-1] ) > .01)
      {  V[k] = x; k++;
         cout << "k: " << k << " x"; x.dumpall();
      }
      if(k >= mv) break;
      angrad += dangrad;
   }//bottom lk-loop
   c.zap(); x.zap(); y.zap();
   return k;
}
```

The `for` loop calls `INT_PT()` 20 times. On each successive call, the gradient of the objective function rotates clockwise by about 18 degrees. The location of the optimal point is returned from `INT_PT()` in `x`, and it is necessarily one of the polygon vertices. Point `x` is stored in the kth row of `matrix V` if and only if `x` is different from the previous vertex.

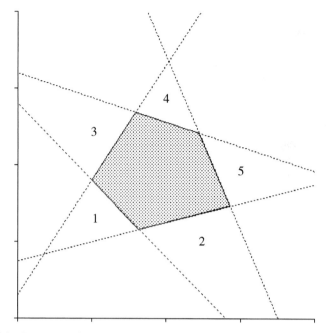

Fig. 10.2   Polygon defined by linear constraints in the example in Section 10.6.1.

10.6.1   Example

Figure 10.2 shows five lines that intersect to form an irregular pentagon. The **A** matrix and **b** vector that define the corresponding constraints are

```
A:
1|-0.357143|-0.357143
2| 0.333333|-1.33333
3| 5       | 3.33333
4| 0.1     | 0.3125
5| 0.285714| 0.125
```

```
b:  |-1|-1|1|1|1
```

Recall that if b_i is negative, the ith constraint has the $>$ sense, and the ith row of **A** has also been negated. Apart from that, a_{i1} and a_{i2} are the inverses of the x_1 and x_2 axis intercepts of line i, respectively. This **A** and **b** were input to polygon_vertices() and the following printout resulted:

```
    w|0.544266|5.1547e-08|10.4131|0.256338|4.49343e-09
k: 1 x|2.85915|1.46479
```

```
      w|2.27399e-08|3.73889e-08|5.33333|0.4735|0.386429
k:  2 x|1.64|1.16

      w|2.5373e-08|1.06667|4.0002e-06|0.3375|0.489286
k:  3 x|1|1.8

      w|0.529827|2.05568|1.99538e-07|4.78847e-07|0.208478
k:  4 x|1.59341|2.69011

      w|0.73588|1.41085|5.14727|5.24905e-09|7.33491e-07
k:  5 x|2.44186|2.41861

      w|0.544266|3.31443e-07|10.4131|0.256338|7.19772e-09
k:  6 x|2.85915|1.46479
```

The six x values are the five vertices of the pentagon that is shaded in Fig. 10.2, in order clockwise. (Of course, the sixth point is the same as the first.) The w slack vector that accompanies each x indicates which two lines intersect at each vertex (i.e., which two primal constraints are equalities there: 1: $5 \cap 2$, 2: $2 \cap 1$, 3: $1 \cap 3$, 4: $3 \cap 4$, 5: $4 \cap 5$). Any two lines intersect somewhere, and there are two intersections visible in Fig. 10.2 that are not part of the pentagon. The pentagon is where all five inequalities are satisfied concurrently.

Consider the result if we converted line 5, say, to an equality by appending an inequality in the opposite sense. This is not inconsistent with inequalities 1 through 4, but it reduces the feasible region of the problem to line 5 itself, between lines 2 and 4.

10.6.2 Example

Subroutine `polygon_vertices` just as it stands is useful in three dimensions to find the polygonal faces of polyhedral surfaces (as long as such a face is not purely perpendicular to the plane containing x_1 and x_2). Consider the following matrix:

```
1|0.0647048|0.241481 |0.125
2|0.176777 |0.176777 |0.125
3|0.241481 |0.0647048|0.125
4|0.0323524|0.120741 |0.25
5|0.0883883|0.0883883|0.25
6|0.120741 |0.0323524|0.25
7|0.0161762|0.0603704|0.285714
8|0.0441942|0.0441942|0.285714
9|0.0603704|0.0161762|0.285714
```

Each row represents the inverse (x, y, z) intercepts of a plane in three dimensions. These numbers were generated automatically by a simple set of loops. The **b** vector that goes with this **A** matrix is all positive ones, so we are dealing with < inequal-ities. The question is what the implied surface looks like.

Each row of matrix **A** defines the plane of one face of a polyhedron. The strat-egy is to convert *one* planar constraint to an equality, so that only solutions that lie in that particular plane can be found. Subroutine `polygon_vertices` then finds the vertices of the polygon that constitutes the feasible region within that particular plane. Then we do the same thing for the other constraints in turn. Specifically, as-suming that **A** and **b** are dimensioned to accommodate an extra constraint:

```
matrix V(8,3);   b(10) = -1.;
for(int i=0;  i<9;  i++){
    A[9] = A[i];   -A[9];
    nverts = polygon_vertices( A, b, V );
    DRAWING_SUBROUTINE( V, nverts );
}
```

Figure 10.3 is an isometric drawing of the polyhedral surface defined by the matrix above, produced using this method.

To make this work whatever the orientation, note that the three row entries for each face are also the components of a vector normal to that face. Use Gram–Schmidt

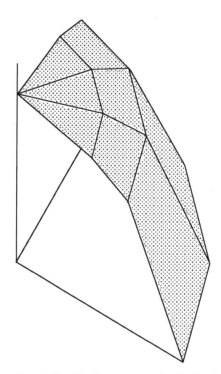

Fig. 10.3 Polyhedral surface defined by linear constraints in the first octant, of the exam-ple in Section 10.6.2.

to define a pair of vectors **u** and **v** orthogonal to the normal and therefore *within* the plane. Then set c = u*cos(angrad) + v*sin(angrad);.

10.7 THEORETICAL ADDENDUM

Pierre [24] discourses at length about classical optimization theory and its reliance upon a concept called *Lagrange multipliers.* Vanderbei [28] presents an analysis like the following that relates our work with primal–dual linear programming to the classical optimization theory.

Consider this very symmetrical Lagrangian function of variables **x** and **y**:

$$\pi(x_1, \ldots, x_n; y_1, \ldots, y_m) \equiv \sum_j c_j x_j - \sum_i \sum_j y_i a_{ij} x_j + \sum_i b_i y_i$$

Complementarity supplants the simple criterion that the partial derivatives of π must vanish at an extremum. This allows us simultaneously to maximize the primal objective, minimize the dual objective, and satisfy the constraints! The expression for π can be rearranged to emphasize its primal aspect or dual aspect, as follows:

$$\pi = \sum_j c_j x_j + \underbrace{\sum_i y_i \left(b_i - \sum_j a_{ij} x_j\right)}_{= \partial\pi/\partial y_i \equiv w_i} = \underbrace{\sum_j \left(c_j - \sum_i y_i a_{ij}\right) x_j}_{\equiv -z_j = \partial\pi/\partial x_j} + \sum_i b_i y_i$$

Bear in mind that all components of **x**, **y**, **w**, and **z** are nonnegative, and that the primal problem is to maximize, while the dual problem is to minimize. On the primal side, $\sum_i y_i w_i \geq 0$, and on the dual side, $-\sum_j x_j z_j \leq 0$. Therefore, $\sum_j c_j x_j \leq \pi \leq \sum_i b_i y_i$, *whatever* **x** and **y** are. When complementarity is attained, so that all $x_j z_j$ and all $y_i w_i$ are zero, π attains its maximum minimum value and its minimum maximum value, which are equal and are also the primal and dual optimal values.

From the primal viewpoint, the y_i are Lagrange multipliers of the primal constraints. If $y_i > 0$, the ith primal constraint must be satisfied as an equality. From the dual viewpoint, the x_j are Lagrange multipliers of the dual constraints, and if $x_j > 0$, the jth dual constraint must be satisfied as an equality.

10.8 SUMMARY AND CONCLUSIONS

Linear Programming. The standard form of linear optimization problem in this book is stated:

primal:

  maximize $\mathbf{c}^T \mathbf{x}$
  subject to $\mathbf{Ax} + \mathbf{w} = \mathbf{b}$
      $\mathbf{x}, \mathbf{w} \geq 0$

dual:

minimize $\mathbf{b}^T\mathbf{y}$
subject to $\mathbf{A}^T\mathbf{y} - \mathbf{z} = \mathbf{c}$
$\mathbf{y}, \mathbf{z} \geq 0$

All variables are nonnegative. Vector $\mathbf{w}$ is a slack variable employed to enforce primal constraints of the form $\mathbf{Ax} \leq \mathbf{b}$. Vector $\mathbf{z}$ is a slack variable employed to enforce dual constraints of the form $\mathbf{A}^T\mathbf{y} \geq \mathbf{c}$. As optimal values of all variables are found, the following quantities become zero:

$$\text{duality gap: } \mathbf{b}^T\mathbf{y} - \mathbf{c}^T\mathbf{x} \qquad \text{complementarity gap: } \mathbf{x}^T\mathbf{z} + \mathbf{y}^T\mathbf{w}$$

Moreover, complementarity implies that x_j is zero if z_j isn't, and vice versa; and that y_i is zero if w_i isn't, and vice versa.

Interior-Point Solution. Optimization is achieved by iteratively solving the reduced Karush–Kuhn–Tucker system

$$\begin{bmatrix} -\mathbf{Y}^{-1}\mathbf{W} & \mathbf{A} \\ \mathbf{A}^T & \mathbf{X}^{-1}\mathbf{Z} \end{bmatrix} \begin{bmatrix} \Delta\mathbf{y} \\ \Delta\mathbf{x} \end{bmatrix} = \begin{bmatrix} \mathbf{b} - \mathbf{Ax} - \mu\mathbf{Y}^{-1}\mathbf{e} \\ \mathbf{c} - \mathbf{A}^T\mathbf{y} + \mu\mathbf{X}^{-1}\mathbf{e} \end{bmatrix}$$

$$\Delta\mathbf{z} = \mu\mathbf{X}^{-1}\mathbf{e} - \mathbf{z} - \mathbf{X}^{-1}\mathbf{Z}\,\Delta\mathbf{x}$$

$$\Delta\mathbf{w} = \mu\mathbf{Y}^{-1}\mathbf{e} - \mathbf{w} - \mathbf{Y}^{-1}\mathbf{W}\,\Delta\mathbf{y}$$

Here $\Delta\mathbf{x}$, $\Delta\mathbf{y}$, $\Delta\mathbf{w}$, and $\Delta\mathbf{z}$ are update directions for all the variables, and μ is proportional to the current value of the complementarity gap.

Subroutine Loop_LP(A, b, c, x, z, y, w, f) embodies a path-following interior-point solution method that relies upon the Cholesky factorization subroutine LDLt_QD() (Chapter 8). Arguments A, b, and c are not changed by the computation.

LP Problem Setup

All variables x_j shall be nonnegative: $x_j \geq 0$, for all j. In two dimensions, the problem is confined to the first quadrant; in three, the first octant.

All primal constraints shall be expressed as inequalities in the $\leq$ sense. If constraint i is given as $\geq$, convert it by negating b_i and all a_{ij}. If a constraint is given as an *equality*, restate it as a *pair* of inequalities of opposite sense.

To solve a *minimization* problem, negate its objective function.

The subset of the domain of the objective function $\mathbf{c}^T\mathbf{x}$ that satisfies the primal constraints is termed the primal *feasible* region.

Subroutine INT_PT(A, b, c, x, y, f) computes an interior-point solution to any linear optimization problem posed in this manner.

11 Interior-Point Extensions

In this chapter we present some variations on interior-point optimization that provide significant new capabilities at the cost of little additional effort. We will see how to use curve-fitting criteria besides least squares, and how to work with nonlinear objective functions.

11.1 L^1 REGRESSION AS A LINEAR PROGRAMMING PROBLEM

In Chapter 4, the residual vector $\mathbf{r} = \mathbf{b} - \mathbf{A}\mathbf{x}$ was identified as the (negative) gradient of a particular quadratic scalar function. Minimizing that function was tantamount to solving $\mathbf{A}\mathbf{x} = \mathbf{b}$ exactly. In Chapter 6, $\mathbf{A}\mathbf{x} = \mathbf{b}$ was solved approximately, in the sense of minimizing $[(\mathbf{b} - \mathbf{A}\mathbf{x})^{\mathrm{T}}(\mathbf{b} - \mathbf{A}\mathbf{x})]^{1/2}$. This, the Euclidean length or L^2 norm of the residual, is sometimes written $\|\mathbf{b} - \mathbf{A}\mathbf{x}\|_2$. In the present section we consider minimizing $\|\mathbf{b} - \mathbf{A}\mathbf{x}\|_1$, the L^1 *norm*, defined as $\|\mathbf{r}\|_1 = \sum |r_i|$, the sum of the absolute values of the components of a vector.

An excellent use of L^1 minimization is L^1 *regression*, finding a straight line or other curve that best fits a scatter plot of data points. Compared to the L^2 criterion, L^1 regression produces a more sensible result for data containing outliers—a few points radically different from the others. Outliers exert undue leverage on the least-squares method.

The manner in which L^1 minimization is formulated as a linear programming problem can be fairly described as a trick. Corresponding to each row of the coefficient matrix $\mathbf{A}$, we define a new variable, $t_i \equiv |b_i - \sum_j a_{ij}x_j|$. Then we seek to minimize $\sum_i t_i$ as the objective function. The trick is how the definition of t_i is implemented as a pair of *inequalities*: $-t_i \le b_i - \sum_j a_{ij}x_j \le t_i$. Try this. For any number η, $-|\eta| \le \eta \le |\eta|$, because either η is positive and $-|\eta| < \eta = |\eta|$, or η is negative and $-|\eta| = \eta < |\eta|$.

The x_j do not participate in the objective function. Instead, we seek to *maximize* $-\sum_i t_i$ while observing two inequality constraints per variable t_i: $-t_i \le b_i - \sum_j a_{ij}x_j$, written as $\sum_j a_{ij}x_j - t_i \le b_i$, and $b_i - \sum_j a_{ij}x_j \le t_i$, written as $-\sum_j a_{ij}x_j - t_i \le -b_i$, in our standard form.

In partitioned-matrix notation, we have

$$\left[\begin{array}{c|c} \mathbf{A} & -\mathbf{I} \\ \hline -\mathbf{A} & -\mathbf{I} \end{array}\right]\left[\begin{array}{c} \mathbf{x} \\ \mathbf{t} \end{array}\right] \le \left[\begin{array}{c} \mathbf{b} \\ -\mathbf{b} \end{array}\right], \quad \text{and} \quad \mathbf{c} = \left[\begin{array}{c} \mathbf{0} \\ -\mathbf{e} \end{array}\right], \mathbf{e} \text{ being a vector of ones}$$

All variables in our present formulation of interior-point optimization are always nonnegative. The software is incapable of returning a negative value for an optimized variable. This condition is well suited to the absolute-value variables t_i. However, in regression problems, the parameters we are fitting to the data can potentially have either sign. We must determine in advance which sign we expect. If x_j, say, wants to be negative, we can compensate for that by negating all a_{ij} in column j of $\mathbf{A}$.

In either least-squares or L^1 regression, there is a risk of confusion due to the fact that the data points are often denoted as (x,y) and that the answer required is often the parameters of a straight line, conventionally a and b. These uses conflict with how we are employing these symbols here. The matrix $\mathbf{A}$ contains the data points in its first and second columns, and the unknown vector $\mathbf{x}$ returns the inverse axis intercepts in its first two entries. To make this concrete, let us rework a previous example as an L^1 problem.

As in the example of Section 6.3.1, we put the data points directly into the first and second columns of matrix A.

```
{   double data[20] = {-5., 2.,-1., 4., 2., 6., 3., 7.,10.,
                        11.,9.,11., 1., 5., 1., 6., 7.,
                        9.,4., 8.};
    matrix A(data,10,2);
```

The large partitioned matrix for the L^1 version of the problem is defined as

```
    sparse S(20,12,60);
    for(int i=1; i<=10; i++){
        S(i,1)    = -A(i,1);   S(i,2)    =  A(i,2);
        S(i+10,1) =  A(i,1);   S(i+10,2) = -A(i,2);
        S(i, i+2) = -1.;       S(i+10,i+2) = -1.;    }
    print_matrix( S );
```

This produces

```
|   5|   2|-1|  0|0|0|0|0|0|0|0|0|
|   1|   4| 0|-1|0|0|0|0|0|0|0|0|
|  -2|   6| 0| 0|-1|0|0|0|0|0|0|0|
|  -3|   7| 0| 0|0|-1|0|0|0|0|0|0|
| -10|  11| 0| 0|0|0|-1|0|0|0|0|0|
|  -9|  11| 0| 0|0|0|0|-1|0|0|0|0|
|  -1|   5| 0| 0|0|0|0|0|-1|0|0|0|
|  -1|   6| 0| 0|0|0|0|0|0|-1|0|0|
|  -7|   9| 0| 0|0|0|0|0|0|0|-1|0|
|  -4|   8| 0| 0|0|0|0|0|0|0|0|-1|
|  -5|  -2|-1|  0|0|0|0|0|0|0|0|0|
|  -1|  -4| 0|-1|0|0|0|0|0|0|0|0|
```

```
|  2| -6|  0|0|-1|0|0|0|0|0|0|0|
|  3| -7|  0|0|0|-1|0|0|0|0|0|0|
| 10|-11|  0|0|0|0|-1|0|0|0|0|0|
|  9|-11|  0|0|0|0|0|-1|0|0|0|0|
|  1| -5|  0|0|0|0|0|0|-1|0|0|0|
|  1| -6|  0|0|0|0|0|0|0|-1|0|0|
|  7| -9|  0|0|0|0|0|0|0|0|-1|0|
|  4| -8|  0|0|0|0|0|0|0|0|0|-1|
```

I have negated the first column of **A** because I expect the x_1 axis intercept to be negative. I have positioned **A** in the upper-left partition of S and $-$**A** in the lower-left partition. The upper-right and lower-right partitions of S each contain $-$**I**. I defined **b**, **c**, **x**, and **y**, as required, and then ran INT_PT() :

```
real_vector b(20);
for(int i=1; i<=10; i++){ b(i)= 1.; b(i+10) = -1.; }
real_vector c(12);  c.init() += (-1.);  c(1) = c(2) = 0.;
real_vector x(12), y(20);

INT_PT( S, b, c, x, y, 0.);
x.dumpall();
}
```

The composite x (i.e., $[\mathbf{x}\ \mathbf{t}]^T$) was returned as

```
|0.12|0.2|
1.41783e-08|0.08|0.04|0.04|2.86135e-08|0.12|0.12|0.08|
    0.04|0.12
```

The first line here implies that the axis intercepts are -8.333 and 5.0, respectively. Least-squares previously found -7.988 and 4.99. The second line gives the 10 t_i values for the 10 data points. Note that t_1 and t_5 are essentially zero. One should not generalize from this fact, but this L^1 line (in Fig. 6.1) does fit directly through these leftmost and rightmost data points. Half the remaining points are above the line, and half are below.

11.2 L^∞ REGRESSION

The notation $\|\mathbf{r}\|_\infty$ means $\max_i |r_i|$, the maximum absolute value of any of the components of **r**, and it is called the L^∞ *norm*. As applied to regression, the L^∞ norm is useful to minimize the worst-case misfit, defined as $\max_i |b_i - \sum_j a_{ij}x_j|$. Fitting a line to some points by minimizing the L^∞ norm can be accomplished as a linear programming problem through a slight modification of the previous setup.

Consider a single unsubscripted variable t and the inequalities $-t \le r_i \le t$. For any r_i, if r_i is negative, $-t$ is more negative. If r_i is positive, t is more positive. In other words, $t \ge \max_i |r_i|$. The L^∞ norm is minimized by maximizing the lone variable $-t$, observing the inequality constraints $-t \le b_i - \sum_j a_{ij} x_j$, written as $\sum_j a_{ij} x_j - t \le b_i$, and $b_i - \sum_j a_{ij} x_j \le t$, written as $-\sum_j a_{ij} x_j - t \le -b_i$, in standard form. In partitioned-matrix notation, we have

$$\left[\begin{array}{c|c} \mathbf{A} & -\mathbf{e} \\ \hline -\mathbf{A} & -\mathbf{e} \end{array}\right] \left[\begin{array}{c} \mathbf{x} \\ \hline t \end{array}\right] \le \left[\begin{array}{c} \mathbf{b} \\ \hline -\mathbf{b} \end{array}\right], \quad \text{and} \quad \mathbf{c} = \left[\begin{array}{c} \mathbf{0} \\ \hline -1 \end{array}\right]$$

By $\mathbf{e}$, I mean a vector of all ones. The built-up matrix has just one more column than $\mathbf{A}$, and all the entries in the added column are -1.

I modified the L^1 line-fitting code so that S, b, c, x, and y were dimensioned and defined suitably for the L^∞ objective and constraints. I submitted these to INT_PT(), and it returned the composite x (i.e., $[\mathbf{x}\ t]^\mathrm{T}$) as

```
|0.137931|0.206897|0.103448
```

The first two entries imply that the axis intercepts for the fitted line are -7.25 and 4.833. The third entry is the worst-case misfit actually achieved, 0.103448. To check this assertion, I printed out the residual $\mathbf{r}$ yielded by this fit:

```
r|-0.103448|0.0344828|0.0344828|-0.0344828|0.103448|
 |-0.0344829|0.103448|-0.103448|0.103448|-0.103448
```

Indeed, the largest absolute value here is 0.103448, and there are several such instances. It is fair to compare these 10 numbers to the 10 t_i values printed out at the end of the L^1 demonstration. The misfits there are both larger and smaller than the present ones.

11.2.1 Example

As a *tour de force* finale to our investigation of regression methods, consider the data points scattered about in Fig. 11.1. Denoting the horizontal and vertical coordinates as h and v, respectively, I propose to fit the data by three straight-line segments according to the following parameterization scheme:

$$v = \begin{cases} x_1 + x_2 h, & 0 \le h \le 6 \\ x_3, & 6 \le h \le 14 \\ x_4 + x_5 h, & 14 \le h \end{cases}$$

The data points at h values 6 and 14 are each common to two adjoining segments. There are five unknown parameters to be solved for: x_2 and x_5 are slopes; x_1, x_3, x_4 are v-intercepts.

The basic $\mathbf{A}$ matrix in this problem therefore has 24 rows and 5 columns. Right-hand-side vector $\mathbf{b}$ has 24 components:

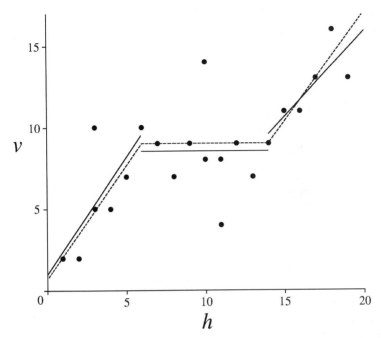

Fig. 11.1 Twenty-two data points with straight-line segments fit by different regression criteria. Solid lines, L^2; dashed lines, L^1 and L^∞ with continuity conditions (Section 11.2.1).

```
{  double data[22][2] = {{1.,2.},{2.,2.},{3.,5.},
                         {3.,10.},{4.,5.},{5.,7.},
                         {6.,10.},{7.,9.},{8.,7.},
                         {9.,9.},{10.,8.},{10.,14.},
                         {11.,4.},{11.,8.},{12.,9.},
                         {13.,7.},{14.,9.},{15.,11.},
                         {16.,11.},{17.,13.},{18.,16.},
                         {19.,13.}};

matrix A(24,5);  real_vector b(24);
for(int i=1;  i<=7;  i++){
    A(i,1) = 1.; A(i,2) = data[i-1][0]; b(i) = data
       [i-1][1];}
for(int i=8;  i<=18; i++){
    A(i,3) = 1.;                        b(i) = data
       [i-2][1];}
for(int i=19; i<=24; i++){
    A(i,4) = 1.; A(i,5) = data[i-3][0]; b(i) = data
       [i-3][1];}
```

We are representing $\mathbf{Ax} = \mathbf{b}$, where $\mathbf{x}$ is the vector of unknown parameters and $\mathbf{b}$ is a vector of v values. Columns 1, 3, and 4 of $\mathbf{A}$, corresponding to the v-intercept unknowns, contain only ones, if not zero. Columns 2 and 5 contain appropriate h values.

First, let's see how the L^2 or least-squares regression criterion handles this case. We employ the method of Chapter 6 (summarized in Section 6.6), in which QR factorization of the design matrix $\mathbf{A}$ combined with backsolve applied to $\mathbf{b}$ produces $\mathbf{x}$:

```
A.HouseholderQR();
printf(" Rank %u\n", A.col_rank( 1.e-12 ));
b.Qsolve(A).Usolve(A);
real_vector x( &(b(1)), 5);
x.dumpall();
```

The result is

```
Rank 5
x|0.935484|1.43548|8.54545|-5.27619|1.05714
```

The second line contains the five x_i values. These values were used to generate the three solid lines in Fig. 11.1. Apart from the discontinuities, this is not a bad fit.

For comparison, I propose to rework the problem using the L^1 criterion to fit the two sloping lines while using the L^{∞} criterion to fit the x_3 parameter. We use a sparse S to store $\mathbf{A}$ in its upper left partition and $-\mathbf{A}$ in its lower left partition. Similarly, $\mathbf{b}$ is enlarged to contain a negative copy of itself in the lower half. We reverse the sign of column 4 of $\mathbf{A}$, because we expect that x_4 is intrinsically negative.

```
int l = 25;
for(int i=1; i<=24; i++){ b(i+l)= -b(i);   A(i,4)
   = -A(i,4);}

sparse S(50, 19, 128);
for(int i=1;  i<=7;  i++){
   S(i+1,1)  = -A(i,1); S(i,1)  = A(i,1);
   S(i+1,2)  = -A(i,2); S(i,2)  = A(i,2);
   S(i,i+5)  = S(i+1,i+5) = -1.;          }
for(int i=8;  i<=18; i++){
   S(i+1,3)  = -A(i,3); S(i,3)  = A(i,3);
   S(i,13)   = S(i+1,13) = -1.;           }
for(int i=19; i<=24; i++){
   S(i+1,4)  = -A(i,4); S(i,4)  = A(i,4);
   S(i+1,5)  = -A(i,5); S(i,5)  = A(i,5);
   S(i,i-5)  = S(i+1,i-5) = -1.;          }
```

Sparse matrix S has 14 more columns than A. The first seven and last six extra columns contain elements of $-\mathbf{I}$ as prescribed for the L^1 method. The eighth extra column (the thirteenth) contains a piece of $-\mathbf{e}$ vector as required for the L^∞ method.

One advantage of treating the three separate line segments as a single unified problem is that we can enforce specific relationships among the three segments. For example, we can require that the first two segments have the same v value (whatever it may be) where $h = 6$: $x_1 + 6\,x_2 = x_3$. We encode this *continuity* condition as a pair of inequalities of opposite sense:

```
S(25,1) =   1.; S(25,2) =   6.;  S(25,3) = -1; b(25) = 0;
S(50,1) =  -1.; S(50,2) =  -6.;  S(50,3) =  1; b(50) = 0;
```

Vector $\mathbf{c}$ reflects that we seek to minimize the sum of 14 absolute values. Vectors $\mathbf{y}$ and $\mathbf{x}$ are dimensioned for a 50 by 19 problem, and INT_PT() is called:

```
real_vector c(19), x(19), y(50);  c.init();
for(int i=6; i<=19; i++) c(i) = -1.;

INT_PT( S, b, c, x, y, 0.);
x.dumpall();  }
```

The composite x (i.e., $[\mathbf{x}\ \mathbf{t}]^{\mathrm{T}}$) is returned as

|0.6|1.4|9|9.66667|1.33333|, i.e., $x_1, x_2, x_3, -x_4, x_5$;

|3.09855e-08|1.4|0.2|5.2|1.2|0.6|1|, the seven t_i for the left segment;

|5|, the worst-case t for the center segment;

|1.00965e-07|0.666667|0.666667|9.42303e-08 |1.66667|2.66667|, the last six t_i.

The x_i values were used to generate the dashed lines in Fig. 11.1. Continuity is enforced at the point (6, 9), where the left and center segments have the same value. Continuity is obtained fortuitously at the point (14, 9), where the center and right segments have the same value. A total of six points lie exactly on one segment or another.

11.3 QUADRATIC PROGRAMMING

The next step up from linear programming is a class of constrained optimization problems in which the constraints remain linear but the objective function becomes quadratic. By extension, this is called *quadratic programming*, and the interior-point method we have implemented can readily be extended to handle this case.

According to Vanderbei's presentation of the subject [28], it is common to define the standard QP problem with the roles of the primal and dual forms essentially reversed from LP practice. The standard *primal* QP problem we intend to solve is stated:

$$\text{minimize } \mathbf{c}^T\mathbf{x} + \tfrac{1}{2}\mathbf{x}^T\mathbf{Q}\mathbf{x}$$

$$\text{subject to } \mathbf{Ax} \geq \mathbf{b} \text{ (i.e., } \mathbf{Ax} - \mathbf{w} = \mathbf{b})$$

$$\mathbf{x}, \mathbf{w} \geq 0$$

The corresponding *dual* QP problem is stated:

$$\text{maximize } \mathbf{b}^T\mathbf{y} - \tfrac{1}{2}\mathbf{x}^T\mathbf{Q}\mathbf{x}$$

$$\text{subject to } \mathbf{A}^T\mathbf{y} + \mathbf{z} - \mathbf{Q}\mathbf{x} = \mathbf{c}$$

$$\mathbf{y}, \mathbf{z} \geq 0$$

We can require that matrix $\mathbf{Q}$ be diagonal. Vanderbei shows how any QP problem can be reformulated to make $\mathbf{Q}$ diagonal, if necessary. It is more important that $\mathbf{Q}$ be positive semidefinite (i.e., there must exist no vector $\boldsymbol{\xi}$ for which $\boldsymbol{\xi}^T\mathbf{Q}\boldsymbol{\xi} < 0$). If this condition is met, the problem is termed *convex*, and the solution is straightforward. Another point of difference between LP and QP is that $\mathbf{x}$ appears in both the primal and dual problems. The problem must be convex for the same value of $\mathbf{x}$ to be both primal and dual optimal.

The path-following interior-point method encoded in `Loop_LP()` can be modified to solve the convex QP problem. The reduced Karush–Kuhn–Tucker equations upon which the solution method is based become modified to read

$$\begin{bmatrix} -(\mathbf{X}^{-1}\mathbf{Z} + \mathbf{Q}) & \mathbf{A}^T \\ \mathbf{A} & \mathbf{Y}^{-1}\mathbf{W} \end{bmatrix} \begin{bmatrix} \Delta\mathbf{x} \\ \Delta\mathbf{y} \end{bmatrix} = \begin{bmatrix} \mathbf{c} - \mathbf{A}^T\mathbf{y} - \mu\mathbf{X}^{-1}\mathbf{e} + \mathbf{Q}\mathbf{x} \\ \mathbf{b} - \mathbf{Ax} + \mu\mathbf{Y}^{-1}\mathbf{e} \end{bmatrix}$$

Compared to the reduced KKT system for the linear case, $\mathbf{Q}$ appears as an addition to the diagonal of the matrix and $\mathbf{Qx}$ is added to the dual infeasibility. The subsidiary equations for $\Delta\mathbf{w}$ and $\Delta\mathbf{z}$ remain the same as in the case of a linear objective:

$$\Delta\mathbf{w} = \mu\mathbf{Y}^{-1}\mathbf{e} - \mathbf{w} - \mathbf{Y}^{-1}\mathbf{W}\,\Delta\mathbf{y}$$

$$\Delta\mathbf{z} = \mu\mathbf{X}^{-1}\mathbf{e} - \mathbf{z} - \mathbf{X}^{-1}\mathbf{Z}\,\Delta\mathbf{x}$$

The most exemplary quadratic objective function, in my view, is the squared distance between two points: $|\mathbf{x} - \mathbf{x}_0|^2 \equiv (\mathbf{x} - \mathbf{x}_0)^T(\mathbf{x} - \mathbf{x}_0) = 2(-\mathbf{x}_0^T\mathbf{x} + \tfrac{1}{2}\mathbf{x}^T\mathbf{I}\mathbf{x} + \tfrac{1}{2}\mathbf{x}_0^T\mathbf{x}_0)$. Here I mean that $\mathbf{x}_0$ is a fixed point and that $\mathbf{x}$ is to be solved for. In terms of the QP standard form, it is apparent that $\mathbf{c} = -\mathbf{x}_0$ and $\mathbf{Q} = \mathbf{I}$. The constant $\tfrac{1}{2}\mathbf{x}_0^T\mathbf{x}_0$ is not involved in the optimization but is added into the optimized value.

When I modified `Loop_LP()` to use this modified KKT system, I assumed that **Q** is **I**, which means that it need not be passed through the call list:

```
int Loop_QPI (const matrix& A, const real_vector& b,
              const real_vector& c, real_vector& x,
              real_vector& z,real_vector& y,
              real_vector& w, double f)
{//RVDB Fig 23.3, for case that Q is the identity, A is
 //matrix.
```

The points of difference from `Loop_LP()` include the signs of the slack variables and the term added to the dual infeasibility:

```
//   * Compute infeasibilities.
     rho = -((A*x) -= b); rho += w;    //sign w
     sigma = -((y*A) -= c); sigma -= z; sigma += x;
        //sign z, +Qx
     normr = euc( rho );        norms = euc( sigma );
```

Perhaps the major difference is that `LDLt_QDt()` is called instead of `LDLt_QD()` to perform the Cholesky decomposition:

```
//     Store -(D+Q) and E into the Quasidefinite diagonal
       for(i=1; i<=m; i++) // now lower right diagonal [+E]
           diag(i+n) = max( E(i), EPSDIAG);
       for(j=1; j<=n; j++) // now upper left diagonal
           diag(j)   = -max( D(j) + 1., EPSDIAG);
//   * Define L and decompose
       sparse L(m+n, m+n, nz*MULT);
       L.LDLt_QDt( A, diag);
```

A convenient interface to `Loop_QPI()` is provided through subroutine `INT_PTQ()`.

11.3.1   Example

Figure 11.2 displays a convex three-dimensional polyhedral surface, the interior of which is the feasible set defined implicitly by a certain system of linear constraints. I propose to demonstrate `INT_PTQ()` by computing the minimum squared distance between this surface and an arbitrary point external to the surface. (The reader

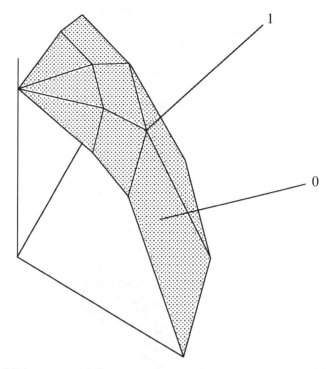

Fig. 11.2   Minimum squared distance to each of two points exterior to a polyhedral surface defined by linear constraints, from that surface (Section 11.3.1).

may contemplate the result if an origin point is chosen internal to the surface.)

The same A(9,3) is defined as in Section 10.6.2. Then A and b are both negated, because the QP primal constraints are defined in the opposite sense from LP constraints:

```
b.init() += (-1.);                    //-1 for QP
for(int i=0; i<9; i++)  -A[i];
```

I selected two different origin points in this exercise, for reasons that will soon be made apparent. They, and the respective calls to INT_PTQ(), are shown in

```
// Minimize (1/2)x*Q*x + c*x s.t. A*x > b and x > 0
//     taking Q = I .
   real_vector x0(3), x1(3);

   x0(1) = 6.15; x0(2) = 1.65; x0(3) = 3.2;  -x0;
   INT_PTQ( A, b, x0, x, y, .5*(x0*x0));

   x1(1) = 4.5;  x1(2) = 2.6;  x1(3) = 4.85; -x1;
   INT_PTQ( A, b, x1, x, y, .5*(x1*x1));
```

The printout obtained as these problems were solved included

```
x0|-6.15|-1.65|-3.2
x |3.08416|0.828509|1.613
w |0.398746|0.106707|9.31252e-10|0.396935|
  |0.250916|0.197562|0.439235|0.366225|0.339549

x1|-4.5|-2.6|-4.85
x |2.39087|1.38037|2.66667
w |0.178633|8.33012e-09|8.82012e-09|0.0893164|
  |1.12777e-08|1.15227e-08|0.116087|0.0714286|0.0714286
```

Figure 11.2 repeats the isometric drawing of the polyhedral surface defined by the A matrix and shown in Fig. 10.3. Each of the two minimum-squared-distance results is also shown as a straight line connecting each point of origin to its respective solution point. The reader will note that the line from x0 intersects a face of the polyhedron well away from any edge, whereas the line from x1 connects to a vertex where four faces intersect. The line from x0 is in fact perpendicular to the face. Examination of the slack vector **w** for the x0 case reveals that w(3) ≈0, so that the intersected face corresponds to row 3 of A. For the x1 case, the slack variables for four rows of the constraint matrix vanish: 2, 3, 5, 6. These correspond to the four faces that meet at the vertex in question.

11.4   SUCCESSIVE QUADRATIC PROGRAMMING

The broad category of convex programming encompasses optimization methods in which the constraints as well as the objective are general nonlinear functions of the variables. The objective function must be *convex* (to be defined below). The particular approach to convex objectives presented here depends on a strategy of successive quadratic approximations. A sequence of Taylor series is substituted for the actual function. Under favorable conditions, the approximate function converges to the exact one concurrently with the determination of the optimum constrained value.

In this section I propose to adapt the path-following interior-point quadratic programming method of Section 11.3 for use with a nonlinear nonquadratic form of objective function, while continuing to allow only linear constraints. What I am presenting is a simplified version of the discussion in Vanderbei's Chapter 24 [28]. The heart of the matter is that a Taylor series representation of a general function *looks* like a quadratic objective function. If $f(\mathbf{x})$ is a scalar function of vector $\mathbf{x}$, the value $f(\mathbf{x} + \Delta\mathbf{x})$ at a point $\mathbf{x} + \Delta\mathbf{x}$ a short distance away is given by the Taylor series

$$f(\mathbf{x} + \Delta\mathbf{x}) = f(\mathbf{x}) + \nabla f(\mathbf{x})^{\mathrm{T}} \Delta\mathbf{x} + \tfrac{1}{2}\Delta\mathbf{x}^{\mathrm{T}} \mathbf{H}f(\mathbf{x}) \Delta\mathbf{x} + \text{remainder}$$

The remainder can be shown to vanish faster than $|\Delta \mathbf{x}|^2$, as $\Delta \mathbf{x}$ approaches zero. The gradient of f is a vector

$$\nabla f(\mathbf{x}) \equiv [\partial f(\mathbf{x})/\partial x_1 \quad \partial f(\mathbf{x})/\partial x_2 \quad \partial f(\mathbf{x})/\partial x_3]^{\mathrm{T}}$$

if we are thinking in three dimensions. The symbol $\mathbf{H}f(\mathbf{x})$ denotes a matrix called the *Hessian* of f, which is an array of second derivatives; its ijth element $h_{ij} \equiv \partial^2 f(\mathbf{x})/\partial x_i \partial x_j$. Putting aside the remainder and comparing the quadratic form defined previously, (i.e., $\mathbf{c}^{\mathrm{T}}\mathbf{x} + \frac{1}{2}\mathbf{x}^{\mathrm{T}}\mathbf{Q}\mathbf{x}$), we can identify that the Taylor series above makes a perfectly good quadratic objective function, with $\Delta \mathbf{x}$ taking the role of optimization variable, $\mathbf{c} = \nabla f(\mathbf{x})$, $\mathbf{Q} = \mathbf{H}f(\mathbf{x})$, and $f(\mathbf{x})$ here merely a constant.

To construct a quadratic approximation, what we need to know about function $f(\mathbf{x})$ is its gradient vector and its Hessian matrix. In Section 11.3 it was required that matrix $\mathbf{Q}$ be positive semidefinite. Hence, it is also required that the Hessian $\mathbf{H}f(\mathbf{x})$ be positive semidefinite. A function $f(\mathbf{x})$ of which this is true is termed *convex*.

11.4.1 Distance Function

The most instructive convex objective function, in my view, is the distance between two points: $|\mathbf{x} - \mathbf{x}_0| \equiv [(\mathbf{x} - \mathbf{x}_0)^{\mathrm{T}}(\mathbf{x} - \mathbf{x}_0)]^{1/2}$. Nothing is simpler, and our results can be visualized geometrically. Here I intend that $\mathbf{x}_0$ is a fixed point and that $\mathbf{x}$ is variable. The sum of two distance functions is also convex, but the same cannot be said for the difference, as the Hessian can go negative.

For simplicity in coding, I have implemented `dist_func` as a special-purpose struct:

```
struct dist_func
{
    double d, o[3], x[3];
    dist_func( double=0., double=0., double=0.);
    double val( const real_vector& );
    real_vector& grad( real_vector& );
    matrix& hessian( matrix& );
    void origin( const real_vector& );
};
```

Each instance of `dist_func` contains two small arrays o and x, which correspond to $\mathbf{x}_0$ and $\mathbf{x}$, respectively. Scalar d holds the present value of the distance between $\mathbf{x}_0$ and $\mathbf{x}$. Member function `val` sets x and computes d, and returns that value to the caller; `grad` computes the gradient and stores it in a `real_vector` supplied by the caller; `hessian` computes the Hessian and stores it in a caller-supplied `matrix`. The latter two functions assume the most recent values of o, x, and d. Callers can use `origin` to reset o. The implementation of `dist_func` and its member functions can be found in the source files. It works in two or three dimensions.

If distance $d = [(\mathbf{x} - \mathbf{x}_0)^T(\mathbf{x} - \mathbf{x}_0)]^{1/2}$, then $\nabla d = (\mathbf{x} - \mathbf{x}_0)/d$, as it is easy to verify. We recognize that $(\mathbf{x} - \mathbf{x}_0)/d$ is also $\mathbf{n}$, a vector of unit length pointing from $\mathbf{x}_0$ to $\mathbf{x}$. The Hessian of d is therefore an array of derivatives of $\mathbf{n}$, of which there are two types: $(\partial/\partial x_i)n_i = (1 - n_i^2)/d$ and $(\partial/\partial x_i)n_j = -(n_i n_j)/d$. These results can be neatly summarized in the conclusion $\mathbf{H} = (\mathbf{I} - \mathbf{n}\mathbf{n}^T)/d$, where $\mathbf{I}$ is the identity matrix and $\mathbf{n}\mathbf{n}^T$ is the dyadic product of the gradient with itself.

Hessian $\mathbf{H}$ of the distance function is almost positive definite. The question is: For what $\mathbf{q}$ is $\mathbf{q}^T\mathbf{H}\mathbf{q} = 0$? By the preceding definition, $\mathbf{q}^T\mathbf{H}\mathbf{q} = \mathbf{q}^T(\mathbf{I} - \mathbf{n}\mathbf{n}^T)\mathbf{q}/d = (\mathbf{q}^T\mathbf{q} - (\mathbf{q}^T\mathbf{n})^2)/d = |\mathbf{q}|^2(1 - (\mathbf{q}^T\mathbf{n})^2/|\mathbf{q}|^2)/d = |\mathbf{q}|^2(1 - \cos^2\theta)/d$, where θ is the angle between $\mathbf{q}$ and $\mathbf{n}$. In words, $\mathbf{q}^T\mathbf{H}\mathbf{q}$ vanishes if $\mathbf{q}$ is collinear with $\mathbf{n}$ (i.e., an add-on in the same direction). This is no problem. It means that the first two terms of the Taylor series yield an exact result in this case.

Let's test the Taylor series for the distance function, numerically. Consider the following code:

```
double taylor, val0;
dist_func exact, comparison;
real_vector x(3), dx(3), g(3); dx.init();
matrix H(3,3);
x(1) = x(2) = x(3) = 1.;
printf("d = %f\n", (val0 = exact.val(x)) );
exact.grad(g);   g.dumpall();
exact.hessian(H);   H.dumpall();

for(int i=1; i<=3; i++){
    dx(3) += 0.1;   dx(2) += 0.1; dx.dumpall();
    taylor = val0 + g*dx + .5*(dx*(H*dx));
    printf("Taylor %f", taylor );
    x(3) += 0.1;      x(2) += 0.1;
    printf(", exact %f\n", comparison.val(x) );
}
```

The result (with some annotation added) is

```
d = 1.732051
grad:  |0.57735|0.57735|0.57735
hessian: |  0.3849|-0.19245|-0.19245
         |-0.19245|  0.3849|-0.19245
         |-0.19245|-0.19245|0.3849

dx|0|0.1|0.1: Taylor 1.849445, exact 1.849324
dx|0|0.2|0.2: Taylor 1.970689, exact 1.969772
dx|0|0.3|0.3: Taylor 2.095781, exact 2.092845
```

With the magnitude of $\Delta\mathbf{x}$ between 8 and 24% of d, the Taylor series error occurs in the fifth to fourth significant figure. If we were to set all three components of dx to the same number, in this test, the second-order term `.5*(dx*(H*dx))` would vanish, and the Taylor series value would be exact for all step sizes.

The statement of the successive quadratic programming problem is a little different from what we have seen up to now. Our standard SQP problem is stated:

$$\text{minimize } c(\mathbf{x})$$

$$\text{subject to } \mathbf{Ax} \geq \mathbf{b} \text{ (i.e., } \mathbf{Ax} - \mathbf{w} = \mathbf{b})$$

$$\mathbf{w} \geq 0$$

There is no explicit dual problem, and no dual slack vector $\mathbf{z}$. It is not required that $\mathbf{x}$ is nonnegative. The objective $c(\mathbf{x})$ must be convex and must possess a well-behaved gradient and Hessian. The constraints remain linear.

If $c(\mathbf{x})$ is approximated by a Taylor series expanded about a given point $\bar{\mathbf{x}}$, and if we set $\Delta \mathbf{x} = \mathbf{x} - \bar{\mathbf{x}}$, the quadratic reduced KKT system that determines the step directions $\Delta \mathbf{x}$ and $\Delta \mathbf{y}$ becomes, after some algebra,

$$\begin{bmatrix} \mathbf{Y}^{-1}\mathbf{W} & \mathbf{A} \\ \mathbf{A}^{\mathrm{T}} & -\mathbf{H} \end{bmatrix} \begin{bmatrix} \Delta \mathbf{y} \\ \Delta \mathbf{x} \end{bmatrix} = \begin{bmatrix} \mathbf{b} - \mathbf{Ax} + \mu \mathbf{Y}^{-1}\mathbf{e} \\ \nabla c - \mathbf{A}^{\mathrm{T}}\mathbf{y} \end{bmatrix}$$

In this equation, $\mathbf{H}$ and ∇c, respectively, indicate the Hessian and gradient of c, evaluated at $\bar{\mathbf{x}}$. The subsidiary equation for $\Delta \mathbf{w}$ remains as before:

$$\Delta \mathbf{w} = \mu \mathbf{Y}^{-1}\mathbf{e} - \mathbf{w} - \mathbf{Y}^{-1}\mathbf{W} \, \Delta \mathbf{y}$$

Although $\mathbf{x}$ can now become zero (or negative), this causes no problem, because we no longer divide by $\mathbf{x}$ ($\mathbf{X}^{-1}$ terms in the comparable QP equations).

The algebra leading to the KKT equations includes some fortuitous cancellations that remove $\mathbf{Q}$ (i.e., $\mathbf{H}$) from the system except for the lower-right partition of the KKT matrix. This is not entirely a simplification, for it means that the KKT matrix is no longer purely diagonal. Instead of the special Cholesky decomposition `LDLt_QD()`, we will use the general `LDLt()` routine.

The SQP algorithm for the distance function is demonstrated in

```
void SQP_alg( const matrix& A, const real_vector& b,
    dist_func& dist,
                        real_vector& x, real_vector& w)
{
    unsigned m, n, i, j;
    if((m = A.M()) != b.N() || (n = A.N()) != x.N()) exit(1);
    sparse C(m+n, m+n, m + n + m*n + n*(n-1)/2);
    matrix H(n,n);
    real_vector y(m), c(n);
    (more...)
```

As usual, A is the constraint matrix, b is the right-hand-side vector, x is the vector of variables, and w is a vector to store the slack variables. Lowercase m is the number of constraints, and n is the number of dimensions (2 or 3). SQP_alg() allocates sparse C to contain the KKT matrix and (not shown) copies the transpose of A into the lower-left partition. It is not necessary to initialize C above its diagonal, because LDLt() assumes symmetry. The matrix H is provided to contain the Hessian of dist, and real_vector c is provided to contain the gradient.

The first thing that happens in each pass through the SQP loop is to obtain the current values of dist, its gradient, and its Hessian:

```
    while(1)
    {
//   * Current values
        obj_val = dist.val(x);
        dist.grad(c);
        dist.hessian(H);
//   * Infeasibilities
        rho = -((A*x) -= b);   rho += w;
        sigma = -((y*A) -= c);
        normr = euc( rho );    norms = euc( sigma );
//   * Complementarity gap & central path parameter
        gamma = y * w;
        mu = delta * gamma / (double)m;
//   * Print current values.
        if(prolix){
            printf("%3d %14.7e %8.1e %8.1e %8.1e",
                iter, obj_val, normr, norms, gamma ); }
      (more...)
```

The code defining the working parameters thus is generally similar to what we have already seen in LP and QP subroutines. The Cholesky decomposition is accomplished by LDLt():

```
//      Define L and decompose
        sparse L(m+n, m+n, C.NZ()*MULT );
        L.LDLt( C, diag);
//      Construct the rhs and backsolve
        for(i=1; i<=m; i++) dy(i) = rho(i) - w(i) + mu/y(i);
        for(j=1; j<=n; j++) dx(j) = sigma(j);
        u.Lsolve(L).Dsolve(diag).TLsolve(L);
//      The rest of the solution
        for(i=1; i<=m; i++) dw(i) = mu/y(i) - w(i)
            - E(i)*dy(i);
      (more...)
```

At the bottom of the SQP loop, x is updated, affecting both the accuracy of the quadratic approximation and the search for the optimum value:

```
//  * Step to new point
    dx *= theta;  dy *= theta;  dw *= theta;
    x  += dx;      y += dy;      w += dw;
    if( ++iter > max_iter){ status = iter; break;}
  }// Bottom of Loop
```

11.4.2 Example: Ray Tracing

In optics and acoustics, and related disciplines where the physics is governed by a second-order wave equation, accurate solutions of geometrical time–distance problems can be found by tracing rays. In Section 11.3.1 the minimum squared distance between each of two points and a three-dimensional polyhedral surface was determined by INT_PTQ(). The same result can be obtained by using SQP_alg() to minimize dist_func distances. This corresponds to a type of ray tracing in which the positions of an emitter and a detector coincide, and the returning ray path retraces the outgoing ray path.

It is more interesting to trace rays where the outgoing and returning ray paths are different. SQP_alg() serves this purpose admirably if we simply replace the dist_func& in the argument list with a ray_func&. The argument type ray_func is essentially the sum of two dist_func objects having different origins but a common endpoint. Its gradient is the vector sum of their two gradients, and its Hessian is the sum of their two positive semidefinite Hessians.

In Fig. 11.3, points 0 and 1 are the same as in Fig. 11.2, and point S is midway between them. A black dot marks the spot where the ray from point 0 reflected in Fig. 11.2. In Fig. 11.3, I intend that S represents a source of acoustic energy. A ray from S reflects from facet 3 of the surface and returns to point 0. A second ray *diffracts* from the point where facets 2, 3, 5, and 6 join, then goes on to point 1. (Recall that each "facet" is described by the like-numbered row of A.) These results were obtained by employing SQP_alg() to minimize two appropriate ray_func objectives.

Physically, diffraction is caused by the discontinuity in slope where the different facets meet. Geometrically, the time–distance relationship behaves as if that single point scatters rays in all directions. More information can be found in Berryhill [3].

I can demonstrate that the ray path from S to 0 via reflection at facet 3 obeys Snell's equal-angle law of reflection. Points S and 0 and the reflection point **x** are

```
xS|5.325|2.125|4.025
x0|6.15|1.65|3.2
 x|2.76206|1.10209|2.09363
```

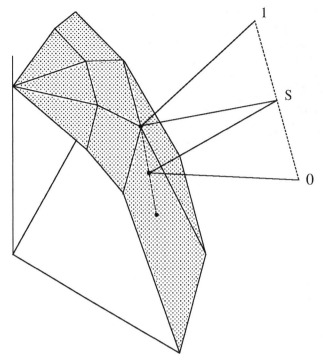

Fig. 11.3 Minimum path length from point S, by way of the polyhedral surface, to each of the two points of Fig. 11.2 (Section 11.4.2).

A vector perpendicular to face 3 is constructed as

```
real_vector normal; normal = A[2]*(1./euc(A[2]));
```

A dist_func originating at x is

```
dist_func oneway; oneway.origin( x );
```

For the leg of the triangle from x to xS:

```
cout << "val " << oneway.val( xS );  oneway.grad( p );
cout << "xS*normal " << (p*normal) << endl;
```

val 3.36827 xS*normal -0.984123

For the leg of the ray path from x to x0:

```
cout << "val " << oneway.val( x0 );  oneway.grad( p );
cout << "x0*normal " << (p*normal) << endl;
```

val 3.60589 x0*normal -0.984123

The outgoing and returning legs of the reflection ray path are of different lengths, but their dot products with the normal to the reflecting surface are the same, -0.984123. This is the (negative) cosine of 10.2235 degrees. (The isometric projection employed in Fig. 11.3 exaggerates the size of this angle.)

To someone who is familiar with ray-tracing methods, a remarkable feature of the SQP minimization approach is that the algorithm inherently determines and reports *which* face of a polyhedron is the actual reflector, in each instance. The reader who has taken to heart the lessons of Chapter 9 will appreciate that what suggests itself for the argument list of `SQP_alg()` is an abstract base class of objects that possess `val`, `grad`, and `hessian` members.

11.5   SUMMARY AND CONCLUSIONS

L^2 Regression. The L^2 norm $\|\mathbf{b} - \mathbf{A}\mathbf{x}\|_2 = [(\mathbf{b} - \mathbf{A}\mathbf{x})^\mathrm{T}(\mathbf{b} - \mathbf{A}\mathbf{x})]^{1/2}$ is minimized by the QR solution of the overdetermined system $\mathbf{A}\mathbf{x} = \mathbf{b}$ (see Chapter 6).

L^1 Regression. The L^1 norm $\|\mathbf{b} - \mathbf{A}\mathbf{x}\|_1 = \Sigma |(\mathbf{b} - \mathbf{A}\mathbf{x})_i|$ is minimized by minimizing the objective function $\Sigma_i t_i$, subject to the linear constraints

$$\left[\begin{array}{c|c} \mathbf{A} & -\mathbf{I} \\ \hline -\mathbf{A} & -\mathbf{I} \end{array}\right] \left[\begin{array}{c} \mathbf{x} \\ \hline \mathbf{t} \end{array}\right] \leq \left[\begin{array}{c} \mathbf{b} \\ \hline -\mathbf{b} \end{array}\right]$$

Implicitly, $t_i = |b_i - \Sigma_j a_{ij} x_j|$.

L^∞ Regression. The L^∞ norm $\|\mathbf{b} - \mathbf{A}\mathbf{x}\|_\infty = \max_i |b_i - \Sigma_j a_{ij} x_j|$ is minimized by maximizing the auxiliary unknown t, subject to the linear constraints

$$\left[\begin{array}{c|c} \mathbf{A} & -\mathbf{e} \\ \hline -\mathbf{A} & -\mathbf{e} \end{array}\right] \left[\begin{array}{c} \mathbf{x} \\ \hline t \end{array}\right] \leq \left[\begin{array}{c} \mathbf{b} \\ \hline -\mathbf{b} \end{array}\right]$$

Vector $\mathbf{e}$ contains all ones.

Quadratic Programming. The standard form of quadratic optimization problem in this book is stated:

primal:

minimize $\mathbf{c}^\mathrm{T}\mathbf{x} + \frac{1}{2}\mathbf{x}^\mathrm{T}\mathbf{Q}\mathbf{x}$

subject to $\mathbf{A}\mathbf{x} \geq \mathbf{b}$ (i.e., $\mathbf{A}\mathbf{x} - \mathbf{w} = \mathbf{b}$)

$\mathbf{x}, \mathbf{w} \geq 0$

dual:

maximize $\mathbf{b}^\mathrm{T}\mathbf{y} - \frac{1}{2}\mathbf{x}^\mathrm{T}\mathbf{Q}\mathbf{x}$

$$\text{subject to } \mathbf{A}^T\mathbf{y} + \mathbf{z} - \mathbf{Q}\mathbf{x} = \mathbf{c}$$

$$\mathbf{y}, \mathbf{z} \geq 0$$

It is required that matrix $\mathbf{Q}$ be diagonal and positive semidefinite. The reduced KKT equations become modified to read

$$\begin{bmatrix} -(\mathbf{X}^{-1}\mathbf{Z} + \mathbf{Q}) & \mathbf{A}^T \\ \mathbf{A} & \mathbf{Y}^{-1}\mathbf{W} \end{bmatrix} \begin{bmatrix} \Delta\mathbf{x} \\ \Delta\mathbf{y} \end{bmatrix} = \begin{bmatrix} \mathbf{c} - \mathbf{A}^T\mathbf{y} - \mu\mathbf{X}^{-1}\mathbf{e} + \mathbf{Q}\mathbf{x} \\ \mathbf{b} - \mathbf{A}\mathbf{x} + \mu\mathbf{Y}^{-1}\mathbf{e} \end{bmatrix}$$

Subroutine `Loop_QPI( A, b, c, x, z, y, w, f )` embodies a path-following interior-point solution method that relies on the Cholesky factorization subroutine `LDLt_QDt()` (Chapter 8). Subroutine `Loop_QPI()` is limited to the special case that $\mathbf{Q}$ is $\mathbf{I}$, the identity matrix.

Quadratic objective functions that fall within this limitation include the squared distance function $|\mathbf{x} - \mathbf{x}_0|^2 \equiv (\mathbf{x} - \mathbf{x}_0)^T(\mathbf{x} - \mathbf{x}_0) = 2(-\mathbf{x}_0^T\mathbf{x} + \frac{1}{2}\mathbf{x}^T\mathbf{I}\mathbf{x} + \frac{1}{2}\mathbf{x}_0^T\mathbf{x}_0)$. For this case, `Loop_QPI()` is called through `INT_PTQ()` with `c` set to $-\mathbf{x}_0$ and `f` set to the constant $\frac{1}{2}\mathbf{x}_0^T\mathbf{x}_0$.

Successive Quadratic Programming. The standard form of SQP problem in this book is stated:

$$\text{minimize } c(\mathbf{x})$$

$$\text{subject to } \mathbf{A}\mathbf{x} \geq \mathbf{b} \text{ (i.e., } \mathbf{A}\mathbf{x} - \mathbf{w} = \mathbf{b}\text{)}$$

$$\mathbf{w} \geq 0$$

There is no explicit dual problem and no dual slack vector $\mathbf{z}$. It is not required that $\mathbf{x}$ be nonnegative. The objective $c(\mathbf{x})$ must possess a well-behaved gradient ∇c and Hessian $\mathbf{H}$. $\mathbf{H}$ must be nonnegative definite. The reduced KKT system that applies is

$$\begin{bmatrix} \mathbf{Y}^{-1}\mathbf{W} & \mathbf{A} \\ \mathbf{A}^T & -\mathbf{H} \end{bmatrix} \begin{bmatrix} \Delta\mathbf{y} \\ \Delta\mathbf{x} \end{bmatrix} = \begin{bmatrix} \mathbf{b} - \mathbf{A}\mathbf{x} + \mu\mathbf{Y}^{-1}\mathbf{e} \\ \nabla c - \mathbf{A}^T\mathbf{y} \end{bmatrix}$$

$$\Delta\mathbf{w} = \mu\mathbf{Y}^{-1}\mathbf{e} - \mathbf{w} - \mathbf{Y}^{-1}\mathbf{W}\,\Delta\mathbf{y}$$

Subroutine `SQP_alg( A, b, c, x, w )` demonstrates a path-following interior-point solution for the case that c is the sum of two distances $|\mathbf{x} - \mathbf{x}_0| + |\mathbf{x} - \mathbf{x}_1|$. Hessian $\mathbf{H}$ is not diagonal, and the solution method relies on the Cholesky factorization subroutine `LDLt()` (Chapter 8).

12 LU Factorization

In this chapter we present a method for factoring a general matrix into the product of a lower-triangular matrix and an upper-triangular matrix. When you have no alternative—when you can find no way to reformulate your application so that the matrix in question is symmetric, let alone positive definite—the last resort available to you is the factorization $\mathbf{A} = \mathbf{LU}$. It is not that this method is any more complicated or obscure than others we have seen. The trouble is that the matrix in question, by definition, lacks the properties required to guarantee the satisfactory performance inherent in the other methods.

The basis of LU factorization is Gaussian elimination. Several algorithms are available that differ as to the order in which they perform the arithmetic, but they all produce the same algebraic result. The Doolittle variant is quite similar to what we employed in Cholesky decomposition, if you take away the symmetry. It works its way through a matrix row by row. The Crout variant is its column-by-column counterpart.

12.1 CROUT LU ALGORITHM

This is the simplest and briefest form of LU factorization. As a specific example of how this iterative method works, assume that $\mathbf{A}$ is 6×6 and that we have computed the first three columns of $\mathbf{L}$ (and $\mathbf{U}$, of course). If we imagine multiplying the part of $\mathbf{L}$ that we know by the unknown *fourth* column of $\mathbf{U}$, we obtain the following display:

$$
\begin{bmatrix}
1 & & & \\
l_{21} & 1 & & \\
l_{31} & l_{32} & 1 & \\
l_{41} & l_{42} & l_{43} & 1 \\
l_{51} & l_{52} & l_{53} & (l_{54}) \\
l_{61} & l_{62} & l_{63} & (l_{64})
\end{bmatrix}
\begin{bmatrix}
u_{14} \\
u_{24} \\
u_{34} \\
u_{44} \\
\\
\end{bmatrix}
=
\begin{bmatrix}
a_{14} \\
a_{24} \\
a_{34} \\
a_{44} \\
a_{54} \\
a_{64}
\end{bmatrix}
=
\begin{bmatrix}
u_{14} \\
l_{21}u_{14} + u_{24} \\
l_{31}u_{14} + l_{32}u_{24} + u_{34} \\
l_{41}u_{14} + l_{42}u_{24} + l_{43}u_{34} + u_{44} \\
l_{51}u_{14} + l_{52}u_{24} + l_{53}u_{34} + (l_{54})u_{44} \\
l_{61}u_{14} + l_{62}u_{24} + l_{63}u_{34} + (l_{64})u_{44}
\end{bmatrix}
$$

I have appended a fourth column to $\mathbf{L}$, which contains the *unknowns* l_{54} and l_{64}, which I have enclosed in parentheses to indicate their different status. To be perfectly clear, the unknown quantities here are u_{14}, u_{24}, u_{34}, u_{44}, l_{54}, and l_{64}. On the far right-hand side, where the matrix multiplication is shown carried out, we recognize that the solution is obvious. This is the classic forward substitution problem seen in Section 5.2. The top four rows give us

$$u_{14} = a_{14}$$

$$u_{24} = a_{24} - l_{21}u_{14}$$

$$u_{34} = a_{34} - l_{31}u_{14} - l_{32}u_{24}$$

$$u_{44} = a_{44} - l_{41}u_{14} - l_{42}u_{24} - l_{43}u_{34}$$

and with u_{44} in hand, the last two rows yield

$$l_{54} = \frac{a_{54} - l_{51}u_{14} - l_{52}u_{24} - l_{53}u_{34}}{u_{44}}$$

$$l_{64} = \frac{a_{64} - l_{61}u_{14} - l_{62}u_{24} - l_{63}u_{34}}{u_{44}}$$

The pattern is clear. If we proceed from top to bottom within each new column, each unknown element of $\mathbf{U}$ and $\mathbf{L}$ in that column can be solved for in terms of elements already determined. The general formulas for any column j are

$$u_{ij} = a_{ij} - \sum_{k<i} l_{ik}u_{kj}, \qquad i \le j$$

$$l_{ij} = \frac{a_{ij} - \sum_{k<j} l_{ik}u_{kj}}{u_{jj}}, \qquad i > j$$

These formulas do not access elements of $\mathbf{A}$ to the right of column j.

12.1.1 Partial Pivoting

The last three rows of the matrix display above are interchangeable. That is, if we remove the specific connotation of each unknown, what we really have is

$$q_4 = a_{44} - l_{41}u_{14} - l_{42}u_{24} - l_{43}u_{34}$$

$$q_5 = a_{54} - l_{51}u_{14} - l_{52}u_{24} - l_{53}u_{34}$$

$$q_6 = a_{64} - l_{61}u_{14} - l_{62}u_{24} - l_{63}u_{34}$$

We are free to choose any of the q_i to assume the role of u_{44}.

In the absence of special matrix properties such as symmetry and positive definiteness, Gaussian elimination is not completely trustworthy. The "answers" it produces may contain errors introduced by the process and not present in the data. References such as Chapter 4 of Duff et al. [9] contain practical discussions of this problem. As a rule of thumb, the LU decomposition should be reliable if the elements $|l_{ij}|$ of the **L** matrix are *all* ≤ 1. Fortunately, we are exactly in a position to ensure this.

In the example above, we would select whichever of q_4, q_5, and q_6 is largest and designate that to be u_{44}. Then the other two would become l_{54} and l_{64} after division by u_{44}. By construction, therefore, we have ensured that our two new $|l_{ij}| \leq 1$. The cost is that we must actually reorder the rows within the matrix and keep track of what we have done. This strategy is called *partial pivoting* because it reorders only rows, not columns.

12.2   DENSE MATRIX CROUT LU SUBROUTINE

The following subroutine implements LU factorization for `matrix` objects by means of the Crout algorithm. In this initial listing, I have omitted the code that carries out partial pivoting:

```
unsigned Crout_LU( matrix& A, pivot& P )
{//Crout elimination column by column
    unsigned i,j,k,p;   double Ujj, Ukj;

    for (j=1; j<=A.N(); j++)   //col-by-col
//      computation of L\U                                       //5
    {
//      Recursion on the first j-1 entries of col j    //7
        for(k=1; k<j; k++){
            if( (Ukj = A(k,j)) == 0.) continue;
//          prior column k of L:
            for(i=k+1; i<=A.M(); i++) A(i,j) -= A(i,k)*Ukj;
        }
        Ujj = A(j,j);   if( Ujj == 0.) return j-1;      //13
//      Finalize
        for(i=j+1; i<=A.M(); i++){
            if (A(i,j) == 0.) continue;
            A(i,j) /= Ujj;                              //Lij
        }
    }//bottom of j-loop
    return j-1;
}
```

This subroutine overwrites the **L**\U factors into the same storage as **A**. The loop beginning in line 5 converts each column j of **A**, in order, into a column of **L**\U. The loop beginning in line 7 executes the summations $(a_{ij} - \sum l_{ik}u_{kj})$ for all rows i and all leftward columns k. The entries of A above the diagonal thus become entries of **U**; A(j,j) is the pivot u_{jj}; and entries of A below the diagonal become entries of **L**.

It is instructive to apply this subroutine to a matrix that *is* symmetric, namely, one that served to illustrate Cholesky subroutine LDLt() in Chapter 8. There, matrix **A** was defined as

```
1|1|5|8|0|
2|5|2|6|9|
3|8|6|3|7|
4|0|9|7|4|
```

Factors **L** and **D** (as in $\mathbf{A} = \mathbf{LDL}^T$) were found to be

```
1|0|0|0|0|
2|5|0|0|0|
3|8|1.47826|0|0|
4|0|-0.391304|0.587045|0|

d|1|-23|-10.7391|11.2227
```

When I ran Crout_LU() without pivoting on the same input, I obtained the following L\U decomposition:

```
1|1|5|8|0
2|5|-23|-34|9
3|8|1.47826|-10.7391|-6.30435
4|0|-0.391304|0.587045|11.2227
```

This result can be separated into **L**:

```
1|0|0|0|0
2|5|0|0|0
3|8|1.47826|0|0
4|0|-0.391304|0.587045|0
```

and **U**:

```
1|1|5|8|0
2|0|-23|-34|9
3|0|0|-10.7391|-6.30435
4|0|0|0|11.2227
```

Clearly, **L** is the same for both Cholesky and Crout. The main diagonal of **U** is the same as that of **D**, as displayed in d. Less obviously, above the diagonal, the reader can verify that $u_{ij} = u_{ii}l_{ji}$, that is, $\mathbf{U} = \mathbf{DL}^T$. The stipulation that **L** shall have all ones on its main diagonal defines **L** uniquely, so if $\mathbf{LU} = \mathbf{A} = \mathbf{LDL}^T$ for matrix **A**, it is necessary, in retrospect, that $\mathbf{U} = \mathbf{DL}^T$.

The next step is to insert the code that carries out partial pivoting. Replace line 13 of the foregoing listing of `Crout_LU()` with

```
//     Find the pivot
       Ujj = A(j,j);  p = j;
       for(i=j+1; i<=A.M(); i++){
          if(fabs(A(i,j)) <= fabs(Ujj)) continue;
          Ujj = A(i,j);  p = i;
       }
       if( Ujj == 0.) break;
//     Swap rows
       if(p != j){ A.swaprows(j,p);  P.swaprows(j,p); }
```

The loop finds the element in column j with the greatest magnitude, and its row number, p. Then rows p and j are swapped. The `matrix` member function `swaprows()` merely switches pointers and does not move data. Swapping the indices in the `pivot` structure P reports the change to the caller. Partial pivoting yields the following modified result:

```
1|8|6|3|7
2|0|9|7|4
3|0.625|-0.194444|5.48611|5.40278
4|0.125|0.472222|0.787342|-7.01772
```

As we hoped, all the $|l_{ij}|$ are now less than 1. If we print out the content of the P structure, we find

```
|3|4|2|1[R]
|1|2|3|4[C]
```

The formerly third row is now first, the fourth is second, and so on. The columns remain in original order.

12.3   SPARSE MATRIX CROUT LU SUBROUTINE

When we apply any process to a sparse matrix, a principal concern is to minimize the creation of additional nonzero elements. Pivoting comes into play as a means toward this end in LU factorization, just as it did in LDL^T factorization in Section 8.1. In the LU case, however, pivoting to minimize fill-in comes into conflict with pivoting to ensure numerical reliability. Later in this chapter we will see a method that strikes a balance between these conflicting goals. In the present section we describe a `sparse` version of Crout LU that emphasizes numerical stability without compromise.

The `sparse` counterpart of the `matrix` subroutine `Crout_LU()` is a member function that begins

```
unsigned sparse::Crout_LU( pivot& P )
{
    unsigned i,j,k,l,p;  double Ujj, Ukj;   element *elem;
    real_vector tmp(mrows);   tmp.init();
    (more...)
```

This subroutine uses a work vector `tmp` to contain the column of the matrix that is currently being worked on. A sufficient reason for this is that the algorithm processes each column from top to bottom, but we have no prior knowledge of the order in which `sparse` elements are stored. Therefore, the first step is a linked-list traversal that copies one column of the input data into `tmp`:

```
    for (j=1; j<=ncols; j++)   //col-by-col computation
//     of L\U
    {
//     Dump col j into tmp:
        elem = col[j-1];
        while((l = elem->mext) != 0){ elem = e+l;
                i = elem->row;   tmp(i) = elem->value; }

//     Recursion on the first j-1 entries of tmp
        for(k=1; k<j; k++){
            if((Ukj = tmp(k)) == 0.) continue;
//         prior column k of L:
            elem = col[k-1];
            while((l = elem->mext) != 0){ elem = e+l;
                if((i = elem->row) <= k) continue;
                    //since it's Uik
                tmp(i) -= (elem->value)*Ukj;     }
        }
    (more...)
```

The `tmp` vector thus accumulates the summations $(a_{ij} - \sum l_{ik} u_{kj})$. If a_{ij} was zero to begin with, this is the point at which a new nonzero may be spawned. Data must be copied back to the matrix if either `tmp(i)` or the input a_{ij} is nonzero:

```
//     Finalize col j from top to j-1:
        for(i=1; i<j; i++){
            if( tmp(i) == 0. && getval(i,j) == 0.) continue;
            (*this)(i,j) = tmp(i); tmp(i) = 0.;         //Uij
        }
    (more...)
```

As in the `matrix` subroutine, any element on or below the diagonal may be selected as pivot, and the rows may be swapped:

```
//      Find the pivot
        Ujj = tmp(j);   p = j;
        for(i=j+1; i<=mrows; i++){
            if(fabs(tmp(i)) <= fabs(Ujj)) continue;
            Ujj = tmp(i);   p = i;
        }
        if( Ujj == 0.) break;
//      Swap rows
        if(p != j){
            swaprows(j,p);  P.swaprows(j,p);
            Ukj = tmp(j);   tmp(j) = tmp(p);   tmp(p) = Ukj;
        }
    (more...)
```

A subtlety here is that entries p and j of `tmp` must be swapped, along with the corresponding entries of `P.R` and corresponding rows of `(*this)`. The processing of each column concludes:

```
//      Finalize col j from j to bottom:
        (*this)(j,j) = Ujj;   tmp(j) = 0.;
        for(i=j+1; i<=mrows; i++){
            if( tmp(i) == 0. && getval(i,j) == 0.) continue;
            (*this)(i,j) = tmp(i)/Ujj;   tmp(i) = 0.;   //Lij
        }
    }Bottom j loop
    tmp.zap();
    return j-1;
}
```

This subroutine includes no features to reduce fill-in. The caller may find it profitable to run `Min_Deg_Pivot()` on the input matrix. This will move the dense columns toward the right and the dense rows toward the bottom of the matrix before `Crout_LU()` works on it. Of course, selecting the largest element in each column may then swap some dense row right back to the top. This effect might be mitigated by prescaling the matrix so that all rows contain the same initial maximum value (i.e., 1).

12.4 GAUSS LU ALGORITHM

Fully fledged Gauss LU factorization proceeds through a matrix by rows and by columns simultaneously. It selects pivot elements as it proceeds, and it reorders both rows and columns. It provides a trade-off between the incompatible goals of minimum fill-in and numerical reliability. An enlightening treatment of the underlying theory is given in Golub and Van Loan [14, Sec. 3.2].

In analogy with the Householder transformation, Golub and Van Loan define a Gauss transformation that takes the form of a special matrix, $\mathbf{M}_k = \mathbf{I} - \boldsymbol{\tau}\,\mathbf{e}_k^{\mathrm{T}}$. Here $\mathbf{e}_k$ is a vector of n zeros except for its kth component $e_k = 1$, and $\boldsymbol{\tau}$ is called a *Gauss vector*. Its first k entries are zero. The effect of $\mathbf{M}_k$ upon column k of a square matrix $\mathbf{A}$ is to zero everything below the main diagonal:

$$
\begin{bmatrix}
1 & \cdots & 0 & 0 & \cdots & 0 \\
\vdots & \ddots & \vdots & \vdots & & \vdots \\
0 & & 1 & 0 & & 0 \\
0 & & -\tau_{k+1} & 1 & & 0 \\
\vdots & & \vdots & \vdots & \ddots & \vdots \\
0 & \cdots & -\tau_n & 0 & \cdots & 1
\end{bmatrix}
\begin{bmatrix}
a_{1k} \\
\vdots \\
a_{kk} \\
a_{k+1,k} \\
\vdots \\
a_{nk}
\end{bmatrix}
=
\begin{bmatrix}
a_{1k} \\
\vdots \\
a_{kk} \\
a_{k+1,k} - \tau_{k+1}\,a_{kk} \\
\vdots \\
a_{nk} - \tau_n a_{kk}
\end{bmatrix}
=
\begin{bmatrix}
a_{1k} \\
\vdots \\
a_{kk} \\
0 \\
\vdots \\
0
\end{bmatrix}
$$

It is clear from the last few rows that the nonzero components of $\boldsymbol{\tau}$ must be $\tau_i = a_{ik}/a_{kk}, i > k$. This is essentially what we have been computing for the elements l_{ik} of the lower-triangular factor $\mathbf{L}$.

The reader can verify the useful fact that if $\mathbf{A}$ is an $n \times n$ matrix, then $\mathbf{A}\mathbf{e}_k$ is the kth column of $\mathbf{A}$ and $\mathbf{e}_k^{\mathrm{T}}\mathbf{A}$ is the kth row. Thus the total effect of the Gauss transformation $\mathbf{M}_k$ on matrix $\mathbf{A}$ is $\mathbf{M}_k\mathbf{A} = (\mathbf{I} - \boldsymbol{\tau}\,\mathbf{e}_k^{\mathrm{T}})\mathbf{A} = \mathbf{A} - \boldsymbol{\tau}\,(\mathbf{e}_k^{\mathrm{T}}\mathbf{A})$. In words, this is a rank-one update of $\mathbf{A}$ by the outer product of the Gauss vector $(-\boldsymbol{\tau})$ and row k of $\mathbf{A}$ itself $(\mathbf{e}_k^{\mathrm{T}}\mathbf{A})$. This includes zeroing all elements of column k below the main diagonal.

Therefore, a succession of Gauss transformations applied to $\mathbf{A}$ makes $\mathbf{A}$ upper-triangular: $\mathbf{M}_{n-1}\mathbf{M}_{n-2}\cdots\mathbf{M}_2\mathbf{M}_1\mathbf{A} = \mathbf{U}$. The inverse of $(\mathbf{I} - \boldsymbol{\tau}\,\mathbf{e}_k^{\mathrm{T}})$ is $(\mathbf{I} + \boldsymbol{\tau}\,\mathbf{e}_k^{\mathrm{T}})$; it adds back what was subtracted out. If $\mathbf{LU} = \mathbf{L}(\mathbf{M}_{n-1}\mathbf{M}_{n-2}\cdots\mathbf{M}_2\mathbf{M}_1)\mathbf{A} = \mathbf{A}$, then $\mathbf{L} = \mathbf{M}_1^{-1}\mathbf{M}_2^{-1}\cdots\mathbf{M}_{n-2}^{-1}\mathbf{M}_{n-1}^{-1} = \mathbf{I} + \sum \boldsymbol{\tau}^{(k)}\mathbf{e}_k^{\mathrm{T}}$, where $\boldsymbol{\tau}^{(k)}$ denotes the Gauss vector appropriate to column k. This expression is identical to the $\mathbf{L}$ that we have been computing all along.

We will apply the outer-product update form of LU factorization to any matrix beginning with its leading row and column and progressing step by step down its main diagonal. The $\mathbf{L}$ and $\mathbf{U}$ factors will be overwritten into the same storage space occupied by the input. Refer to Fig. 12.1 for clarification. At any stage r, the pivot element is a_{rr}, common to row r and column r. Factor $\mathbf{U}$ (so far) is housed on and above the main diagonal in rows 1 through $r - 1$, and factor $\mathbf{L}$ (so far) is contained below the main diagonal in columns 1 through $r - 1$. Factor $\mathbf{L}$ is assumed to possess a unit diagonal that is not stored anywhere. The remaining partition of $\mathbf{A}$ is referred to as the *reduced matrix*.

12.4.1 Gauss LU Subroutine

The following subroutine implements Gauss LU factorization for `sparse` matrices without provision for pivoting.

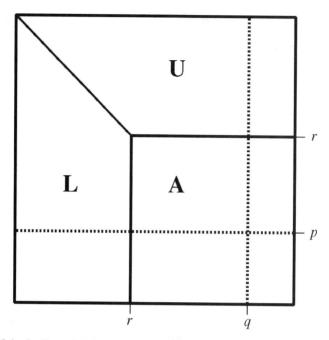

Fig. 12.1   In Gauss LU factorization with threshold pivoting, L\U overwrites **A**.

```
unsigned sparse::Gauss_LU()
{
    element* elem;   unsigned i,j,k,l,r,rank;
    element* cand;   double Lir, Urr;

    for( r=1; r<mrows; r++){                                //5
        if( (Urr = (*this)(r,r)) == 0.) break;             //6

        elem = col[r-1];
        while( (k = elem->mext) != 0){ elem = e+k;         //8
            if( (i = elem->row ) <= r) continue;           //9
            Lir = (elem->value) /= Urr;

            cand = row[r-1];
            while( (l = cand->next) != 0){ cand = e+l;     //12
                if( (j = cand->col) <= r) continue;        //13
                (*this)(i,j) -= Lir * cand->value;         //Urj
        } }   //bottom outer-product update
    } //bottom r loop
    if(r == mrows && getval(r,r) != 0.) rank = mrows;
    else rank = r-1;
    return rank;
}
```

Line 5 is the top of the loop that steps down the main diagonal. Line 6 selects the rth diagonal element of **A** to be the pivot and terminates if it is zero. Line 8 drives a traversal of column r, and line 9 ensures that elements in rows belonging to **U** are bypassed. Each accepted value is divided by the pivot: $l_{ir} = a_{ir}/u_{rr}$. Line 12 drives a traversal of row r, and line 13 ensures that elements in columns belonging to **L** are bypassed. Each accepted value u_{rj} is multiplied by l_{ir} and subtracted from a_{ij}. At the conclusion of processing, the subroutine returns the number of rows and columns that were handled successfully. This subroutine is useful if pivoting is not needed or has been performed in advance, by `Min_Deg_Pivot()`, for example.

12.5   THRESHOLD PIVOTING

One purpose of pivoting is to ensure numerical stability, by selecting the largest element remaining in the reduced matrix to serve as u_{rr}. A second purpose is to minimize the number of products computed in each outer-product update. These goals are inconsistent. The best numerical pivot candidate may well occur at the intersection of a row and a column each containing a large number of remaining elements.

A tactic for striking a balance between these two objectives is known as *threshold pivoting*. Instead of insisting that the pivot element have the greatest magnitude of any in its column, we require only that it have some fraction of the greatest magnitude. Duff et al. [9] suggest a threshold fraction of around 0.1, and in Chapter 7 of their book, they report some empirical results showing how the threshold parameter affects both fill-in and numerical error. The choice of threshold value did not vary the amount of fill-in by as much as two to one, but there was consistently some reduction of fill-in as threshold values decreased from 1.0 to 0.1.

Recall that in Section 3.2.5 I outlined my system for maintaining a count of the number of elements in each row and each column of a `sparse` matrix. In terms of the `sparse` member functions defined there, the number of products computed by the Gauss outer-product update is `(colcount(q)-1) * (rowcount(p)-1)` if the pivot element occurs in row p and column q.

A threshold pivoting strategy is embodied in the `sparse` member function `Pivot()`. It is called from within `Gauss_LU` using the current value of `r`. The subroutine returns the value of some element a_{pq} that it has selected as the current pivot. Before returning, it obligingly swaps row p with row r, and column q with column r.

```
double sparse::Pivot( const unsigned r)
{
    element* elem;   unsigned i,k,p;
    unsigned count, cost;   double v,val,Urr;   p = r;

// Ensure good starting column
    while ((count = colcount(p)) == 0 && p < ncols) p++;
    if ((cost = count) == 0) return 0.;
```

```
// Find first column with least colcount
   for(k=p+1; k<=ncols; k++){
      if ( cost  == 1) break;  //(preemptive)
      if ((count = colcount(k)) < 1 ) continue;
      if ( count >= cost ) continue;
      p = k; cost = count;
   }
   if (p != r ) swapcols(r,p);
   (more...)
```

The lines above make use of the sparse::colcount() utility to determine the first reduced column containing the current minimum number of nonzero elements. Then, generally, that column is swapped into position r. The biggest element in that column is next identified:

```
// Find max pivot value in this column
   elem = col[r-1];  val = 0.;  cost = ncols+1;  p = r;
   while ((k = elem->mext) != 0){ elem = e+k;
      if ((i = elem->row) < r) continue;    //Assert
//        i >= r !
      if ((v = fabs(elem->value)) <= val ) continue;
      val = v;  p = i;  Urr = elem->value;
         cost = rowcount(i); }
   (more...)
```

This p and Urr define the pivot *unless* another entry in this column is associated with a rowcount() less than cost and has an acceptably large absolute value:

```
// Find row with acceptable value and least rowcount
   elem = col[r-1]; val *= THRESHOLD;
   while ((k = elem->mext) != 0){ elem = e+k;
      if ((i = elem->row) < r) continue;
      if ((count = rowcount(i)) >= cost || count < 1)
         continue;
      if ( fabs(elem->value) < val ) continue;
      p = i;  cost = count;  Urr = elem->value;
   }
   if (p != r) swaprows(r,p);
   return Urr;
}
```

The designated pivot row is swapped into position r, and the subroutine returns the pivot value.

12.5.1 Complications

Figure 12.1 reminds us that doing all this in place, with **L** and **U** overwriting **A**, is tricky. The first $r - 1$ rows of column q belong to **U**, and the first $r - 1$ columns of row p belong to **L**. In the basic Gauss_LU() subroutine above, this bookkeeping issue is addressed by the tests

```
if( (i = elem->row ) <= r) continue;         //9
```

for columns, and

```
if( (j = cand->col)  <= r) continue;         //13
```

for rows. These tests make sure that elements of **L** and **U** do not enter into further computations.

This is not sufficient for Pivot(r) to work as designed. Elements belonging to **L** and **U** also need to be eliminated from rowcount(r) and colcount(r). The solution I have settled on is embodied in the following convention: At the conclusion of successful, full-rank, LU factorization,

- Access to **U** shall be via row traversals and shall include the diagonal.
- Access to **L** shall be via column traversals and shall exclude the diagonal.

In other words, after LU factorization with threshold pivoting, a linked-list traversal of a row will only find elements on and above the main diagonal, and a linked-list traversal of a column will only find elements below the main diagonal. Solvers Lsolve, TLsolve, Usolve, and TUsolve conform to this convention already.

In Section 3.2.6 I described a sparse utility unlink(i,j) that would uncouple an element from the both the row and column linked lists of a matrix so that the element, in effect, disappears. What we need now is the ability to uncouple an element from just its row or just its column. These capabilities are provided by

```
void sparse::row_unlink( const unsigned i, const
    unsigned j)
{  element* seek;  unsigned k, r;
    seek = row[i-1];  r = seek->row;  //original row number
    while( (k = seek->next) != 0){ if( e[k].col == j){
        seek->next = e[k].next;  e[k].next = 0;
        e[k].row = r;  rowcount(i)--;  break; } seek = e+k; }
}


void sparse::col_unlink( const unsigned i, const unsigned j)
{  element* seek;  unsigned k, c;
```

```
        seek = col[j-1];   c = seek->col;   //original col number
        while( (k = seek->mext) != 0){ if( e[k].row == i){
          seek->mext = e[k].mext;   e[k].mext = 0;
          e[k].col = c;   colcount(j)--;   break; } seek = e+k; }
}
```

Each of these contains half the code of `unlink` and works as described in
Section 3.2.6. Both subroutines decrement the appropriate `colcount` or `rowcount`.

The pointer `seek = col[j-1]` is the address of the header `element` for
column `j`, as detailed in Section 3.2. I use the `row` entry in that `element` to maintain the `colcount`. In the present case I also use the `col` entry of the column
header `element` to store the original column number of this column, defined as
the number assigned to this column at the onset of processing, before any columns
are swapped by pivoting. Then, when any `element` is unlinked from its column,
it is assigned its original column number. Of course, original row numbers are handled similarly.

Despite performing a great deal of row and column swapping, `Pivot` does not
make use of a `pivot` structure. That aspect of the bookkeeping is handled by the
calling routine.

12.6   GAUSS LU SUBROUTINE WITH
THRESHOLD PIVOTING

Expanding `Gauss_LU()` to incorporate calls to `Pivot()` leads to the following
subroutine:

```
unsigned sparse::Gauss_LU( pivot& P )
{
    element* elem;   unsigned i,j,k,l,r,rank,*idx,n;
    double Lir,Urr;
    real_vector Urj(ncols);   idx = P.R;

    for (i=0; i<mrows; i++) (row[i])->row = P.R[i];      //5
    for (j=0; j<ncols; j++) (col[j])->col = P.C[j];      //6
    (more...)
```

This subroutine takes a `pivot` argument that specifies the initial row and
column order and reports the final order. Two work arrays are used, `Urj` and
`idx`. The first is specified as a `real_vector`, and the second overwrites
`P.R`. In lines 5 and 6, the original row and column numbers are stored where
`row_unlink` and `col_unlink` expect to find them. The main processing loop
begins

```
for( r=1; r<mrows; r++)
{
   if ((Urr = Pivot( r ) ) == 0.) break;

   elem = row[r-1];   n = 0;   Urr = 0.;
      //copy pivot row
   while( (k = elem->next) != 0){ elem = e+k;
      if( (j = elem->col)  <  r) continue;
         //includes diag
      Urj[n] = elem->value;  idx[n] = j;   n++;
         if(j == r){ n--;  Urr = Urj[n]; }
            //the diagonal
      col_unlink(r,j);
   }                               //Row r of U now complete
(more...)
```

Subroutine Pivot(r) is called to put the best pivot row and column in position r. Then each element of the pivot row is copied into array Urj[], while the corresponding column number is stored in idx[]. Each element is unlinked from its column and becomes an element of **U**. The pivot element Urr is handled in this loop (redundantly) just for the sake of unlinking. Continuing,

```
   if( Urr == 0.) break;

   elem = col[r-1];                //work pivot column
   while( (k = elem->mext) != 0){ elem = e+k;
      if( (i = elem->row ) <= r) continue;
      Lir = (elem->value) /= Urr;
      row_unlink(i,r);

      for(l=0; l<n; l++){          //outer product
         j = idx[l];   (*this)(i,j) -= Lir * Urj[l]; }

   }                               //col r of L complete
}//bottom r-loop
col_unlink( mrows, mrows);
(more...)
```

Each element of the pivot column r is accessed, divided by Urr, unlinked from its row, and thus transformed into purely an element of **L**. The outer products $l_{ir}u_{rj}$ are computed and subtracted for each of the n values of j. The last col_unlink statement reflects the subtlety that the last diagonal element is never examined in the main loop and therefore would not otherwise get unlinked from the last column of **L**.

After the LU factorization has been completed, the subroutine take steps to report the effect of all the pivoting, before returning. First, the P.R[] and P.C[] arrays are used to store the *final* row and column numbers as functions of the *original* row and column numbers. Subroutine reset(P) then updates the row number of each element of **L** and the column number of each element of **U** from their original to their final values:

```
for (i=0; i<mrows; i++) {k = (row[i])->row; P.R[k-1]
   = i + 1;}
for (j=0; j<ncols; j++) {k = (col[j])->col; P.C[k-1]
   = j + 1;}
reset(P); //update row and col numbers
(more...)
```

Finally, the P.R[] and P.C[] arrays are set to the values they will return to the caller, namely, the original row and column numbers as functions of the final row and column numbers. This is the same result as if the pivot array entries had been swapped synchronously with the actual rows and columns:

```
for (i=0; i<mrows; i++) {k = (row[i])->row;
   P.R[i] = k;}
for (j=0; j<ncols; j++) {k = (col[j])->col;
   P.C[j] = k;}
Urj.zap();
if(r == mrows && getval(r,r) != 0.) rank = mrows;
else rank = r-1;
return rank;
}
```

12.6.1 Review Question

In the row and column linked-list traversals, the tests

```
if( (i = elem->row ) <= r) continue;        //9
if( (j = cand->col)  <= r) continue;        //13
```

have been brought forward from basic Gauss_LU() into Pivot(r) and Gauss_LU(P). Are they really functional in the latter two subroutines?

12.7 COMPARISON AND CONTRAST

It will be instructive to examine the behavior of different factorization methods working on the same data. We will use a symmetric matrix so that we can include **LDL**^{T} in the comparison. Recall that in interior-point optimization (Section 10.4), the matrix in question takes the form

$$\begin{bmatrix} -\mathbf{I} & \mathbf{A} \\ \mathbf{A}^{\mathrm{T}} & \mathbf{I} \end{bmatrix}$$

in the initial pass through the iterative loop. Any factorization method needs to be able to handle this. The code to set this up is

```
sparse S(m+n, m+n, (nz*2+m+n)*MULT);   element a;
   for(i=1; i<=m; i++) S.stash(i,i)      = -1.;
   for(j=1; j<=n; j++) S.stash(j+m,j+m) =  1.;
   for(k=0; k<nz; k++){
        a = A.nonz(k);   if((value = a.value) == 0.)
          continue;
        i = a.row;   j = a.col;
        S.stash(i,m+j) = value;
        S.stash(m+j,i) = value;  }
```

This assumes that sparse A is m by n with nz nonzeros.

Figure 12.2*a* displays the pattern of nonzeros in a test matrix set up by means of this plan. The **A** matrix comes from the Netlib [23] linear-programming problem ADLITTLE.MPS. After the inclusion of slack variables, the dimensions of **A** are 71 rows by 97 columns, with 556 nonzero elements. Therefore, the overall dimensions of the S test matrix are 168 by 168, with a total of 1280 nonzeros.

Because S is symmetric, it is a suitable subject for $\mathbf{LDL}^{\mathrm{T}}$ factorization. This is carried out as in

```
sparse L(m+n, m+n, (nz*2+m+n)*MULT);
real_vector d(m+n);
L.LDLt(S,d);
```

The result is displayed in Fig. 12.2*b*. Output L is lower triangular, and the absent main diagonal is contained in vector d, not shown. Recall that for a matrix S of this configuration, no action is required for the first m diagonal elements. (Cholesky subroutine LDLt_QD is specialized to exploit this fact.) Therefore, the image of $\mathbf{A}^{\mathrm{T}}$ itself remains as input, in the lower-left partition of L. The computed output is all in the lower-right partition, and the number of new nonzero elements inserted there is 1524.

The code for carrying out Crout **LU** factorization is

```
pivot P(m+n,m+n);
S.Crout_LU( P );
```

Figure 12.2*c* displays the result from Crout_LU. This algorithm proceeds from left to right, selecting the largest element in each column as pivot, and swapping

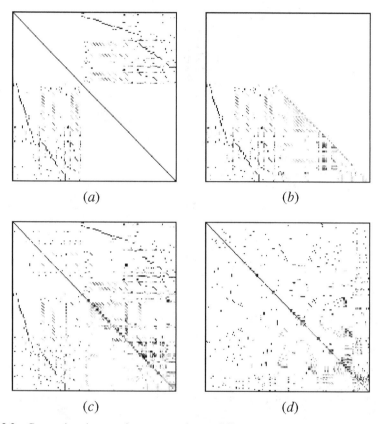

Fig. 12.2   Comparing the sparsity patterns due to different matrix factorizations: (*a*) Input matrix S; (*b*) L output from LDLt(); (*c*) S overwritten by output from Crout_LU() with partial pivoting; (*d*) S overwritten by output from Gauss_LU() with threshold pivoting.

that row up to the diagonal. The evidence of Fig. 12.2*c* is that among the first m rows and columns, the diagonal most often contains the element of largest magnitude (−1): Enough of $\mathbf{A}^T$ remains in place to be recognizable. The most new elements appear in the lower-right partition. The total number of fill-in elements is 4792.

The code to run Gauss **LU** factorization is

```
pivot P(m+n,m+n);
S.Gauss_LU( P );
```

Figure 12.2*d* displays the result from Gauss_LU. This algorithm proceeds down the main diagonal, swapping both rows and columns, disregarding symmetry, with a view to minimizing fill-in. Indeed, the total fill-in for this case is 936. No trace of the original **A** structure is apparent.

The factored results of these methods are, of course, intended to solve equations. The solution takes the form

```
u.Lsolve(L).Dsolve(d).TLsolve(L);
```

in the $\mathbf{LDL}^T$ approach, and

```
u.Map(P.R).Lsolve(S).Usolve(S).Pam(P.C);
```

for the Crout and Gauss methods. I verified that all three techniques produced the same u.

The execution times for these methods and these data on a Pentium PC are measured in milliseconds. The times for LDLt : Gauss_LU : Crout_LU were in ratio 1:1.2:12. The ratios for fill-in cited above amount to 1.6:1:5.1.

12.8 SUMMARY AND CONCLUSIONS

LU Factorization. If $\mathbf{A}$ is $n \times n$, the factorization $\mathbf{A} = \mathbf{LU}$ may be computed such that $\mathbf{L}$ is lower triangular and $\mathbf{U}$ is upper triangular. The reliability of the result depends on ensuring $|l_{ij}| \leq 1$ as the computation proceeds.

Crout Algorithm. Subroutine Crout_LU(A, P) overwrites an $\mathbf{L\backslash U}$ decomposition onto matrix A. The notation $\mathbf{L\backslash U}$ indicates that $\mathbf{L}$ is stored below the main diagonal of A, and $\mathbf{U}$ is stored on and above the main diagonal. Partial pivoting (row interchange) enforces $|l_{ij}| \leq 1$ and is reported via pivot P.

If A is sparse, A.Crout_LU(P) overwrites an $\mathbf{L\backslash U}$ decomposition onto A using partial pivoting and reports the row interchanges via pivot P.

Gauss Algorithm. If A is sparse, A.Gauss_LU() overwrites an $\mathbf{L\backslash U}$ decomposition onto A and performs no internal pivoting. A.Gauss_LU(P) overwrites an $\mathbf{L\backslash U}$ decomposition onto A and employs threshold pivoting, which it reports via pivot P. Threshold pivoting interchanges rows and columns, so as to reduce the creation of additional nonzero entries while enforcing the more permissive rule $|l_{ij}| \leq T, T > 1$.

L\U Solutions. Once the LU factorization has been computed, with $\mathbf{L\backslash U}$ overwriting $\mathbf{A}$, the code to solve $\mathbf{Ax} = \mathbf{b}$ is

```
b.Map(P.R).Lsolve(A).Usolve(A).Pam(P.C);
```

If pivoting is omitted, the Map() and Pam() calls may be deleted.

13 Complex Arrays

In Chapter 1 I noted that C does not provide a standardized, intrinsic, complex arithmetic. It is left to users to define their own. The approach taken by Press et al. [25] is typical. One starts by defining a data structure to represent a complex number:

```
typedef struct { float r, i; } fcomplex;
```

Then the name `fcomplex` can be used like `float` or `double` to declare variables, as in `fcomplex c`. The real and imaginary parts of c are addressed as `c.r` and `c.i`, respectively. Functions can accept `fcomplex` arguments and return values of type `fcomplex`:

```
fcomplex Csqrt( fcomplex );
```

Traditional C does not allow arithmetic operators to be overloaded, however, so the only way to provide complex arithmetic is through explicit functions such as

```
fcomplex Cadd( fcomplex a, fcomplex b)
{
    fcomplex c;  c.r = a.r + b.r;  c.i = a.i + b.i;
      return c;
}
```

On the other hand, most C++ compilers come with at least one implementation of complex arithmetic, including overloaded operators and standard math functions. The Turbo C++ 3.0 compiler [5], for example, came with a header file `complex.h` that declared (in part)

```
class complex
{
private:
   double re, im;

public:
   complex( double re_val, double im_val=0)
      { re = re_val;  im = im_val; }
```

```
complex& operator+= (complex& z)
   { re += z.re;  im += z.im;  return *this; }

friend double real( complex& z){ return z.re; }
friend double imag( complex& z){ return z.im; }
friend complex conj( complex& z){ return complex
   (z.re, -z.im); }
friend complex operator+ (complex& z1, complex& z2)
   { return complex( z1.re + z2.re, z1.im + z2.im); }
};
```

I have edited this listing extensively, just to show typical constructors, operators, and functions. Altogether, this implementation provided a fully functional complex type that could be used as flexibly as float or double:

```
complex a(1.,.5), b(2.), c;  c = conj( a + b );
```

More recent compilers such as Borland C++ 5.0 [6] provide an alternative complex implementation based on the use of templates. The first few lines of this newer version read, in part (edited):

```
template <class T>
class complex
{
private:
   T re, im;

public:
   complex( const T& re_arg = 0, const T& im_arg = 0)
      { re = re_arg; im = im_arg; }

    T imag () const { return im; }
    T real () const { return re; }
};

template <class T>
complex<T> conj (const complex<T>& a){
   return complex<T>(a.real(), -a.imag()); }

template <class T>
complex<T> operator+ (const complex<T>& lhs, const
   complex<T>& rhs){
   complex<T> tmp = lhs; return tmp += rhs; }
```

The syntax template <class T> means that in the code that follows, T is a placeholder to be replaced by a type name such as float or long double. The user invokes the corresponding specific class by coding, for example:

```
complex<double> a(1.,.5), b(2.), c;  c = conj( a + b );
```

In theory, the `template` feature would enable the authors of the compiler to provide users like you and me with several flavors (i.e., degrees of precision) of complex variables by writing a single implementation. In fact, I note that the `<complex>` file in question contains a separate complete implementation for each type of floating-point variable, as a backup, in case the `template` approach doesn't work.

13.1 COMPLEX ARRAY TEMPLATES

Obviously, we could develop complex array classes paralleling `real_vector`, `matrix`, and `sparse`. We would begin by duplicating our existing classes and substituting `complex` or `complex<double>` for `double` in all the declarations of variable types. That is not how we shall proceed, however. Complex arrays support a set of algorithms substantially different from those involving real vectors and matrices. We shall direct our efforts to developing only what the algorithms actually require.

The principal applications in which complex arrays appear involve Fourier transforms, the subject of Chapter 14. A one-dimensional Fourier transform can be stored as a complex vector, and a two-dimensional Fourier transform can be contained in a complex matrix. The result of an inverse Fourier transform is correspondingly a real vector or matrix.

At a very basic level, we can regard a *complex* object as an ordered pair of ordinary objects, the first of which we label *real*, and the second of which we label *imaginary*. We can employ ordinary arithmetic to perform complex algorithms if we can arrange to handle the real and imaginary parts separately. Rather than proliferate full-blown complex classes, I prefer to do the minimum necessary to model complex arrays and to use `real_vector` and `matrix` methods to perform the actual computations.

In Section 9.2 we designed an abstract base class to unite a disparate group of objects that had only one thing in common, namely, that parentheses and brackets were defined to return `double` values for `double` arguments. The syntax was

```
class C1
{  public:
   virtual double operator() (double x) = 0;
   virtual double operator[] (double x) = 0;
};
```

Each class derived from C1 then implemented its particular method to return a function value via `operator()` and a derivative via `operator[]`. What we need now is to do something similar for `real()` and `imag()`, the attributes that define the essence of complex objects. An abstract base class analogous to C1 won't work, however, because the pure virtual functions it contains assume fixed argument types and return types. Instead, we can use a `template`:

```
template<class T> struct cplxfy
{
    T *re, *im;
    cplxfy (T& a, T& b){ re = &a; im = &b; }
};

template<class T> inline T& real( const cplxfy<T>& x)
    { return *(x.re); }
template<class T> inline T& imag( const cplxfy<T>& x)
    { return *(x.im); }
```

When we subsequently write `"cplxfy<real_vector>"`; for example, the compiler copies the definitions above, substituting `"real_vector"` for `"T."` With nothing more than this, we can generate executable code in which we "complexify" scalars, vectors, and matrices:

```
void test(void)
{
    double x=1., y=2.;
    cplxfy<double> num(x,y);
    printf("Re = %g Im = %g\n", real(num), imag(num) );
    (more...)
```

This code creates an object num of type `cplxfy<double>` that is initialized with the *addresses* of x and y. Then it uses `real()` and `imag()` to print out the values stored at those addresses:

```
Re = 1 Im = 2
```

A difference between this approach and `complex<double>` is that our `real()` and `imag()` are bidirectional and can be used on both sides of the assignment operator: `imag(num) = 5.; double z = real(num);`. Our num is basically an alias for the ordered pair (x,y). The trade-off is that we cannot safely write `cplxfy<double> dumb(3.,4.);`, for example, because the constants 3. and 4. have no permanent address. Continuing,

```
double data[10] = { 0., 1., 2., 3., 4., 5., 6., 7.,
                    8., 9.};
real_vector a(data,5,2), b(data+1,5,2);              //2
cplxfy<real_vector> vec(a,b);                        //3
```

```
    cout << "Re"; real(vec).dumpall();
    cout << "Im"; imag(vec).dumpall();
    (more...)
```

Line 2 creates 2 real_vectors a and b by copying the even and odd entries of data, respectively. Then line 3 creates a cplxfy<real_vector> variable named vec that is initialized with the addresses of a and b. The last two lines print the contents of vec:

```
Re|0|2|4|6|8
Im|1|3|5|7|9
```

The printout of vec invokes real_vector::dumpall(), an existing member function. Finally, in the complex matrix case,

```
    double arry[18] = { 1., 0., 0., 0., 2., 0., 0., 0., 3.,
                        4., 0., 0., 0., 5., 0., 0., 0., 6.};
    matrix A(arry,3,3), B(arry+9,3,3);                          //3
    cplxfy<matrix> mat(A,B);                                    //4
    cout << "Re:\n"; real(mat).dumpall();
    cout << "Im:\n"; imag(mat).dumpall();
    return;
}
```

prints out

```
Re:
1|1|0|0
2|0|2|0
3|0|0|3
Im:
1|4|0|0
2|0|5|0
3|0|0|6
```

Array arry is viewed as a complex matrix mat whose real part coincides with the first nine entries of arry and whose imaginary part coincides with the last nine. It is not unprecedented for the real and imaginary parts of a complex matrix to be stored as distinct matrices. This was the arrangement preferred in the Cray-2 [4]. No matter what the storage arrangement, separate access to the real and imaginary parts of the data is the essence of what we require.

If the form cplxfy<matrix> seems ungainly for a variable type, there is an easy remedy:

```
typedef cplxfy<matrix> complex_matrix;
complex_matrix mat(A,B);
```

13.2 SPECIALIZATION

The full definition of the `cplxfy` `template` contains statements in addition to the fundamental ones shown above:

```
template<class T> struct cplxfy
{
    T *re, *im;
    cplxfy (T& a, T& b){ re = &a; im = &b; }
    cplxfy (unsigned);

    cplxfy<T>& operator=  (const cplxfy<T>& );
    cplxfy<T>& operator+= (const cplxfy<T>& );
    cplxfy<T>& operator-= (const cplxfy<T>& );
    cplxfy<T>& operator*= (const double& );
    cplxfy<T>& operator*= (const cplxfy<double>& );
};

template<class T> inline T& real( const cplxfy<T>& x)
    { return *(x.re); }
template<class T> inline T& imag( const cplxfy<T>& x)
    { return *(x.im); }
template<class T> inline void swap( cplxfy<T>& x1,
    cplxfy<T>& x2)
{
    T *t;   t = x1.re;  x1.re = x2.re;  x2.re = t;
            t = x1.im;  x1.im = x2.im;  x2.im = t;
                return;
}
```

The definition of swap illustrates a point. When we write a general `template` definition, C++ presumes that the thing defined is workable no matter what is substituted for T. To execute the swap code is always feasible, because it only manipulates pointers, and pointer types `double`, `real_vector`, and `matrix` all exist. On the other hand, the `cplxfy(unsigned)` constructor makes sense only in the `real_vector` case:

```
inline cplxfy<real_vector>::cplxfy (unsigned n)
{
    re = new real_vector(n);   im = new real_vector(n);
}
```

As always with `real_vectors` allocated dynamically, the caller is expected to handle deallocation:

```
    cplxfy<real_vector> cv(500);
    ...
    real(cv).zap(); imag(cv).zap();
```

Even though constructor cplxfy(unsigned) is *declared* for all T, it is *defined* only for real_vector. This is called *specialization*. This distinction extends to other cplxfy<class T> member functions. For example, the assignment operator is defined only for real_vector and double:

```
inline cplxfy<double>&
cplxfy<double>::operator= (const cplxfy<double>& rhs)
{
    *re = *rhs.re; *im = *rhs.im;   return *this;
}

inline cplxfy<real_vector>&
cplxfy<real_vector>::operator= (const
    cplxfy<real_vector>& rhs)
{
    *re = *rhs.re; *im = *rhs.im;   return *this;
}
```

In the second case, real_vector::operator= is invoked, which copies data from the right-hand-side real and imaginary vectors as described in Chapter 2.

The combined assignment operator += is defined only for cplxfy<double> and cplxfy<real_vector> variables:

```
inline cplxfy<double>&
cplxfy<double>::operator+= (const cplxfy<double>& rhs)
{
    *re += *rhs.re; *im += *rhs.im; return *this;
}

inline cplxfy<real_vector>&
cplxfy<real_vector>::operator+= (const
    cplxfy<real_vector>& rhs)
{
    *re += *rhs.re; *im += *rhs.im; return *this;
}
```

These implementations simply hand off the work to the corresponding double and real_vector operators. The implementations of operator-= are similar. The combined assignment operator *= is defined for both real and complex right-hand sides, but only for cplxfy<double> and cplxfy<real_vector> variables:

```
inline cplxfy<double>&
cplxfy<double>::operator*= (const double& c)
{
    *re *= c; *im *= c; return *this;
}
```

```
inline cplxfy<real_vector>&
cplxfy<real_vector>::operator*= (const double& c)
{
    *re *= c; *im *= c; return *this;
}
```

We see that the definitions for +=, -=, and *= are identical for double and real_vector. They cannot be coded as templates, however, because matrix::operator+=, sparse::operator+=, and so on, do not exist. Moreover, the case of a complex multiplier definitely requires specialized definitions:

```
inline cplxfy<double>&
cplxfy<double>::operator*= (const cplxfy<double>& c)
{
    double tmp;  tmp = (*re)*(*c.re) - (*im)*(*c.im);
    *im = (*re)*(*c.im) + (*im)*(*c.re);   *re = tmp;
    return *this;
}
```

```
cplxfy<real_vector>&
cplxfy<real_vector>::operator*= (const cplxfy<double>& c)
{
    real_vector tmp;
    tmp = (*re)*(*c.re) - (*im)*(*c.im);
    *im = (*re)*(*c.im) + (*im)*(*c.re); *re = tmp;
        tmp.zap();
    return *this;
}
```

These perform $(a + ib)(c + id) = (ac - bd) + i(ad + bc) \rightarrow (a + ib)$. To replace the input with the result like this requires temporary storage. The compiler manages temporary scalars automatically, but we must handle temporary vectors ourselves. Storage is assigned to real_vector tmp by the first operator= (see Section 2.1.4). Then tmp.zap(); releases that storage.

A member function with only one version can, of course, be declared in only that specialized form. In the next chapter, for instance, we must add to the member-function declarations for cplxfy,

```
    cplxfy<real_vector>& fft (const real_vector&);
```

Any nonmember function can be defined as a template without objection from the compiler. No problem arises unless and until we attempt to *use* the function where the underlying T functions do not exist. For example:

```
template<class T> double abs( const cplxfy<T>& a)
{
```

```
      double x = sqrt( real(a)*real(a) + imag(a)*imag(a) );
      return x;
}
```

In the example of Section 13.1 we can include

```
      printf("abs(num) = %g\n", abs(num));
      printf("abs(vec) = %g\n", abs(vec));
```

which yields

```
abs(num) = 2.23607
abs(vec) = 16.8819
```

However, if we attempt to use abs(mat);, we receive a compiler message to the effect that abs(const cplxfy<T>&) calls for an *illegal structure operation* because the scalar product (*) is not defined for matrix variables.

In summary, C++ distinguishes member functions from nonmember functions and definitions from mere declarations. Caution is advised whenever we express a definition as a template<class T>. If the definition relies on features of class T that do not exist for some choice of T, an error occurs. If the thing defined is a member function, the compiler senses the error immediately. If the thing defined is a nonmember function, the error is detected when we attempt to use the function. This fact limits the usefulness of applying templates to classes more complicated than scalars.

13.2.1 Example

The following code exercises the scalar and vector cplxfy functions defined up to this point. I have interspersed the results *in italics* at the appropriate points:

```
void test(void)
{   double w=1., x=2., y=3., z=4.;
    cplxfy<double> p(w,x), q(y,z);
    printf("Re = %g Im = %g\n", real(p), imag(p) );
    printf("Re = %g Im = %g\n", real(q), imag(q) );
            Re = 1 Im = 2
            Re = 3 Im = 4
    p *= 2.0;
    printf("Re = %g Im = %g\n", real(p), imag(p) );
            Re = 2 Im = 4
    p *= q;
    q -= p;
    printf("Re = %g Im = %g\n", real(p), imag(p) );
    printf("Re = %g Im = %g\n", real(q), imag(q) );
```

```
        Re = -10 Im = 20
        Re = 13 Im = -16
double data[10] = { 0., 1., 2., 3., 4., 5., 6., 7.,
                    8., 9.};
real_vector a(data,5,2), b(data+1,5,2);
cplxfy<real_vector> C(a,b);
cout << "Re"; real(C).dumpall(); cout << "Im";
   imag(C).dumpall();
        Re|0|2|4|6|8    Im|1|3|5|7|9
cplxfy<real_vector> D(5), E(5), F(5), G(5), H(5);
H = G = F = E = D = C;
cout << "Re"; real(H).dumpall(); cout << "Im";
   imag(H).dumpall();
        Re|0|2|4|6|8    Im|1|3|5|7|9
D *= 2.;
E *= q;
cout << "Re"; real(D).dumpall(); cout << "Im";
   imag(D).dumpall();
cout << "Re"; real(E).dumpall(); cout << "Im";
   imag(E).dumpall();
        Re|0|4|8|12|16    Im|2|6|10|14|18
        Re|16|74|132|190|248    Im|13|7|1|-5|-11
F += H;
G -= (H*=.5);
cout << "Re"; real(F).dumpall(); cout << "Im";
   imag(F).dumpall();
cout << "Re"; real(G).dumpall(); cout << "Im";
   imag(G).dumpall();
        Re|0|4|8|12|16    Im|2|6|10|14|18
        Re|0|1|2|3|4    Im|0.5|1.5|2.5|3.5|4.5
swap(F,G);
cout << "Re"; real(F).dumpall(); cout << "Im";
   imag(F).dumpall();
cout << "Re"; real(G).dumpall(); cout << "Im";
   imag(G).dumpall();
        Re|0|1|2|3|4    Im|0.5|1.5|2.5|3.5|4.5
        Re|0|4|8|12|16    Im|2|6|10|14|18
}
```

13.3   VECTOR SUMS AND DIFFERENCES

In Chapter 9, where we used an abstract base class in computing derivatives automatically for a variety of functions, we employed derived classes Sum and Dif to implement the chain rule for sums and differences. We shall do something analogous for complex vectors so that our existing `temp_real_vector` class suffices to manage dynamic storage. We begin by defining an appropriate structure:

```
struct Csum
{
    cplxfy<real_vector> *v1, *v2;

    Csum( cplxfy<real_vector>& a,
          cplxfy<real_vector>& b){ v1 = &a; v2 = &b; }
};
```

A Csum structure contains simply the addresses of two complex vectors (i.e., objects of type `cplxfy<real_vector>`). This is a subterfuge that allows us to postpone actually computing the sum until we have a place to put the result. A Csum is created when we undertake to add two complex vectors:

```
Csum operator+( cplxfy<real_vector>& a,
                cplxfy<real_vector>& b){ return Csum
                    (a, b); }
```

In other words, (a+b) is a Csum. The actual summation is carried out when we code `c = a + b;`, for example, thereby invoking a special assignment operator:

```
cplxfy<real_vector>& cplxfy<real_vector>::
    operator=( const Csum& rhs)
{
    *re = *(rhs.v1->re) + *(rhs.v2->re); //3
    *im = *(rhs.v1->im) + *(rhs.v2->im); //4
    return *this;
}
```

Line 3 adds the two `real_vectors` that are the real parts of a and b. The `real_vector::operator+` function is called to do this, and it returns the result in a `temp_real_vector`. The `real_vector::operator=` function then copies the data to the real part of c. The temporary vector is deallocated. Line 4 performs the same steps for the imaginary parts.

The other way to cause Csum (a+b) actually to be evaluated is by taking its real or imaginary parts:

```
temp_real_vector real( Csum& S)
{
    if (S.v1->re->N() != S.v2->re->N()) exit(1);
    real_vector s (S.v1->re->N());
    s.sum( real(*(S.v1)), real(*(S.v2)));
    return temp_real_vector(s);
}
```

```
temp_real_vector imag( Csum& S)
{
   if (S.v1->im->N() != S.v2->im->N()) exit(1);
   real_vector s (S.v1->im->N());
   s.sum( imag(*(S.v1)), imag(*(S.v2)));
   return temp_real_vector(s);
}
```

These functions invoke the `real_vector::sum` function (compare Section 2.1.5). The compiler I use did not object that the constructor `temp_real_vector(s)`, which is `private`, was called in this context. If your compiler objects, the remedy is to declare each of these functions a `friend` of `temp_real_vector`. The code for class `Cdif` to compute complex vector differences is analogous to `Csum`.

13.3.1   Example

The following code exercises the `Csum` and `Cdif` functions and demonstrates addition and subtraction of `cplxfy<real_vector>` variables. I have interspersed the results *in italics* at the appropriate points:

```
void test(void)
{   double data[10] = { 0., 1., 2., 3., 4., 5., 6., 7.,
                        8., 9.};
    real_vector a(data,5,2), b(data+1,5,2);
    cplxfy<real_vector> C(a,b), D(5), E(5), F(5), G(5),
       H(5);
    D = C;
    cout << "Re"; real(D).dumpall(); cout << "Im";
       imag(D).dumpall();
                 Re|0|2|4|6|8    Im|1|3|5|7|9
    Csum S(C,D);
    real(E) = real(S); imag(E) = imag(S);  //using
       //imag(Csum&) etc.
    cout << "Re"; real(E).dumpall(); cout << "Im";
       imag(E).dumpall();
                 Re|0|4|8|12|16    Im|2|6|10|14|18
    Cdif T(C,D);
    F = T;            // using cplxfy<real_vector>::
       //operator=( Cdif& )
    cout << "Re"; real(F).dumpall(); cout << "Im";
       imag(F).dumpall();
                 Re|0|0|0|0|0    Im|0|0|0|0|0|0
    real(G) = real(E+C); imag(G) = imag(E+C);
       //imag(Csum(E,C)) etc.
```

```
cout << "Re"; real(G).dumpall(); cout << "Im";
    imag(G).dumpall();
        Re|0|6|12|18|24    Im|3|9|15|21|27
H = E + C;  //using Csum& operator+( E, C) etc.
cout << "Re"; real(H).dumpall(); cout << "Im";
    imag(H).dumpall();
        Re|0|6|12|18|24    Im|3|9|15|21|27
}
```

13.4 COMPLEX MATRICES

The interesting properties of complex matrices have special names. For clarity, assume that the complex matrix $\mathbf{C} = \mathbf{A} + i\mathbf{B}$, where $\mathbf{A}$ and $\mathbf{B}$ are ordinary real matrices and i is the imaginary unit $\sqrt{-1}$. Instead of the transpose of $\mathbf{A}$, we concentrate on its *Hermitian conjugate*, defined as $\mathbf{C}^H = \mathbf{A}^T - i\mathbf{B}^T$. If $\mathbf{C}^H = \mathbf{C}$, the matrix $\mathbf{C}$ is said not to be symmetric, but *Hermitian*. If the Hermitian conjugate of $\mathbf{C}$ is also its inverse (i.e., if $\mathbf{C}^H\mathbf{C} = \mathbf{C}\mathbf{C}^H = \mathbf{I}$), matrix $\mathbf{C}$ is said not to be orthogonal, but *unitary*. The scalar product of two complex vectors $\mathbf{p}$ and $\mathbf{q}$ is not $\mathbf{p}^T\mathbf{q}$, but rather $\mathbf{p}^H\mathbf{q}$.

If $\mathbf{C}$, $\mathbf{c}$, and $\mathbf{z}$ are complex, with $\mathbf{C} = \mathbf{A} + i\mathbf{B}$, $\mathbf{c} = \mathbf{a} + i\mathbf{b}$, and $\mathbf{z} = \mathbf{x} + i\mathbf{y}$, the equation $\mathbf{Cz} = \mathbf{c}$ separates into two independent equations for the real and imaginary parts: $\mathbf{Ax} - \mathbf{By} = \mathbf{a}$, and $i(\mathbf{Bx} + \mathbf{Ay}) = i\mathbf{b}$, or $\mathbf{Bx} + \mathbf{Ay} = \mathbf{b}$. In turn, these equations can be written as a single partitioned matrix equation:

$$\begin{bmatrix} \mathbf{A} & -\mathbf{B} \\ \mathbf{B} & \mathbf{A} \end{bmatrix} \begin{bmatrix} \mathbf{x} \\ \mathbf{y} \end{bmatrix} = \begin{bmatrix} \mathbf{a} \\ \mathbf{b} \end{bmatrix}$$

This is a system of real equations whose top and bottom rows correspond to the real and imaginary parts, respectively, of the original complex equation. To this system we can apply our previous methods for **LU** factorization and back-solution, such as `Gauss_LU()`, `Lsolve()`, and `Usolve()`.

Even better, if $\mathbf{C}$ is Hermitian, so that $\mathbf{C}^H = \mathbf{A}^T - i\mathbf{B}^T = \mathbf{C} = \mathbf{A} + i\mathbf{B}$, it follows that $-\mathbf{B} = \mathbf{B}^T$ and that the partitioned real matrix is symmetric:

$$\begin{bmatrix} \mathbf{A} & \mathbf{B}^T \\ \mathbf{B} & \mathbf{A} \end{bmatrix} \begin{bmatrix} \mathbf{x} \\ \mathbf{y} \end{bmatrix} = \begin{bmatrix} \mathbf{a} \\ \mathbf{b} \end{bmatrix}, \qquad \text{if } \mathbf{C}^H = \mathbf{C}.$$

To this system, we can apply our previous methods that rely upon symmetry, including `LDLt()` and `Sym_Indef_Bicon_Grad()`.

Furthermore, if $\mathbf{C}$ is Hermitian, the complex eigenvalue problem $\mathbf{Cw} = \lambda\mathbf{w}$ boils down to a partitioned symmetric real eigenvalue problem:

$$\begin{bmatrix} \mathbf{A} & \mathbf{B}^T \\ \mathbf{B} & \mathbf{A} \end{bmatrix} \begin{bmatrix} \mathbf{u} \\ \mathbf{v} \end{bmatrix} = \lambda \begin{bmatrix} \mathbf{u} \\ \mathbf{v} \end{bmatrix}, \qquad \text{if } \mathbf{C}^H = \mathbf{C}, \text{ and } \mathbf{u} + i\mathbf{v} = \mathbf{w}.$$

To this system we can apply our previous methods for the symmetric eigenvalue problem, including `HouseTridiag()`, `LanczosTridiag()`, and `alg_823()`, from Chapters 6 and 7.

Because the problem solvers we have developed for real matrices are so generally applicable for complex matrices, I see no great urgency to develop and test equivalent code specifically for the complex case. Most of my use of complex matrices occurs in connection with Fourier transforms.

13.4.1 Example

In Chapter 14 it is stated that the discrete Fourier transform is equivalent to the multiplication of a complex vector by a complex matrix **W**, where element $w_{ij} = e^{(-2\pi\sqrt{-1}/n)ij}$ and n is the length of the data. This is not the *fast* Fourier transform, of course, but then the FFT trick doesn't apply if n is prime (e.g., 7):

```
matrix U(7,7), V(7,7);
cplxfy<matrix> W(U,V);

double arg, d = 8.* atan(1.) / 7.;
for(int i=0; i<7; i++)
    for(int j=0; j<7; j++){
        arg = d*(double)i*(double)j;
        real(W)[i][j] =  cos(arg);
        imag(W)[i][j] = -sin(arg); }
(more...)
```

Recall that `real(W)` is a `matrix` and that `real(W)[i]` is a row of that matrix. Indices run from 0 to $n-1$ in DFT applications. The fundamental frequency $2\pi/n$ is d.

```
cout << "Re:\n"; real(W).dumpall();
cout << "Im:\n"; imag(W).dumpall();
```

```
Re:
1|1|1|1|1|1|1|1
2|1|0.62349|-0.222521|-0.900969|-0.900969|-0.222521|
   0.62349
3|1|-0.222521|-0.900969|0.62349|0.62349|-0.900969|
   -0.222521
4|1|-0.900969|0.62349|-0.222521|-0.222521|0.62349|
   -0.900969
5|1|-0.900969|0.62349|-0.222521|-0.222521|0.62349|
   -0.900969
6|1|-0.222521|-0.900969|0.62349|0.62349|-0.900969|
   -0.222521
7|1|0.62349|-0.222521|-0.900969|-0.900969|-0.222521|
   0.62349
```

```
Im:
1| 0| 0| 0| 0| 0| 0| 0
2| 0| -0.781831| -0.974928| -0.433884| 0.433884| 0.974928|
    0.781831
3| 0| -0.974928| 0.433884| 0.781831| -0.781831| -0.433884|
    0.974928
4| 0| -0.433884| 0.781831| -0.974928| 0.974928| -0.781831|
    0.433884
5| 0| 0.433884| -0.781831| 0.974928| -0.974928| 0.781831|
    -0.433884
6| 0| 0.974928| -0.433884| -0.781831| 0.781831| 0.433884|
    -0.974928
7| 0| 0.781831| 0.974928| 0.433884| -0.433884| -0.974928|
    -0.781831
```

Matrix **W** is symmetric rather than Hermitian. The product of this matrix and a complex vector is the DFT of the vector. If we initialize the vector as a pure cosine wave, the DFT result will be predictable:

```
real_vector x(7), y(7);
cplxfy<real_vector> z(x,y);
for(int j=0; j<7; j++){
    arg = d*(double)j;  real(z)[j] = cos(arg); }
imag(z).init();
cout << "Re"; real(z).dumpall();  cout << "Im";
    imag(z).dumpall();
    Re|1|0.62349|-0.222521|-0.900969|-0.900969|
        -0.222521|0.62349
    Im|0|0|0|0|0|0|0
```

When we apply a forward DFT, we must also divide the result by n:

```
z *= W;  z *= (1./7.);
cout << "Re"; real(z).dumpall();  cout << "Im";
    imag(z).dumpall();
    Re|0|0.5|0|0|0|0|0.5
    Im|0|0|0|0|0|0|0
```

I have edited round-off error (e-17) to zero in the printout. In DFT terms, if the frequency attributable to z[j] is f, the frequency attributable to z[n-j] is $-f$. Since a pure cosine is $\cos(f) = [\exp(if) + \exp(-if)]/2$, a value 0.5 for z[1] and z[6] is what we expect. The inverse DFT is a multiplication by the complex conjugate of **W**:

```
for(int i=0; i<7; i++)  -imag(W)[i];
z *= W;
```

```
cout << "Re"; real(z).dumpall();  cout << "Im";
   imag(z).dumpall();
Re|1|0.62349|-0.222521|-0.900969|-0.900969|
   -0.222521|0.62349
Im|0|0|0|0|0|0|0
```

We recover our original complex vector z (again ignoring round-off).

13.5 QUATERNIONS

Complex numbers are useful in representing phenomena in two dimensions. A complex number $z = x + iy$ represents a point in a plane if we define the horizontal coordinate as real and the vertical coordinate as imaginary. There is no three-dimensional equivalent of complex numbers, but the mathematical physicist Hamilton invented a *four*-dimensional generalization called *quaternions* [22]. These are not much used today, but they make a nontrivial C++ class demonstration.

To the real and imaginary parts of the familiar complex numbers, quaternions add two new flavors of imaginary, which we'll call j and k. The squares of all three imaginary units are -1, and the product of any two is the third:

$$i^2 = j^2 = k^2 = -1$$

$$ij = k, jk = i, ki = j$$

$$ji = -ij, kj = -jk, ik = -ki$$

The third line defines the novel and interesting property that multiplication among the three imaginary units *anti*commutes.

Just as a complex number is represented by an ordered pair of real numbers, so a quaternion can be represented by an ordered pair of complex numbers:

$$q = a + bi + cj + dk = (a + bi) + (c + di)j$$

This expression exploits $ij = k$, and it's important to keep the factors in the order shown. By themselves, $(a + bi)$ and $(c + di)$ are plain complex numbers, and the relationship between them is the same as that between the real and imaginary parts of a two-dimensional complex number. Therefore, the concise way to write a quaternion class is to build on a complex foundation. To begin,

```
#include <complex.h>
class quatern
{
```

```
private:

   complex re, im;

public:

   quatern( complex re_val, complex im_val){
      re = re_val;   im = im_val; }

   quatern( double a, double b, double c, double d){
      re = complex (a, b);   im = complex (c, d); }

   quatern( const quatern& q) { re = q.re;   im = q.im; }

   quatern(){ re = im = complex(0.); }

   ~quatern();
   (more...)
```

The private members of quatern are two complex numbers re and im. This will not be as confusing as it seems, because C++ is so rigorous in regard to scope and type. The first constructor takes two complex arguments, and the second takes four of type double. In a class like this, where dynamic allocation is not an issue, I include a copy constructor quatern(quatern&). The default constructor quatern() initializes everything to zero (if complex works as expected). The listing continues:

```
   friend double real(quatern&);
   friend double imag(quatern&);
   friend double jmag(quatern&);
   friend double kmag(quatern&);
   friend double norm(quatern&);   // (squared)
   (more...)
```

Each of these nonmember functions is implemented by way of a complex function. For example:

```
inline double jmag( quatern& q){ return real( q.im ); }

inline double norm( quatern& q){ return norm( q.re )
   + norm( q.im ); }
```

Remember, q.re and q.im are complex. Function norm is the sum of squared values. The class definition continues:

```
quatern& operator=(const quatern&);
quatern& operator+=(quatern&);
quatern& operator-=(quatern&);
quatern& operator*=(quatern&);
quatern& operator*=(double);
quatern& operator/=(double);
```

These member functions are also implemented by calling `complex` functions. For example:

```
inline quatern& quatern::operator-=( quatern& q2){
   re -= q2.re;  im -= q2.im;  return *this; }

inline quatern& quatern::operator*=( double x){
   re *= x;  im *= x;  return *this; }

quatern& quatern::operator*=( quatern& q)
{
   quatern tmp(*this);
   re = tmp.re*q.re - tmp.im*conj(q.im);
   im = tmp.re*q.im + tmp.im*conj(q.re);
   return *this;
}
```

The last of these is the most interesting. It uses the copy constructor to create a temporary quaternion `tmp`. The computational statements correspond to Morse and Feshbach's equation (1.6.30) [22]. The roles of `tmp` and `q` are not symmetric, and the result of exchanging them would be more than just a reversal of sign.

The `quatern` class definition includes the usual complement of `friend` two-argument arithmetic operators `+`, `-`, `*`, and `/`. Several important functions are neither members nor friends:

```
quatern conj( quatern& q){
   return quatern( real(q), -imag(q), -jmag(q),
      -kmag(q)); }

quatern inv( quatern& q){
   return conj(q) / norm(q); }

inline double arg( quatern& q){
   return acos( real(q) / sqrt( norm(q) ) ); }
```

The first of these is an obvious generalization of complex conjugation, but the last two require some explanation. For complex variables, we define the complex exponential $e^{i\theta} = \cos\theta + i\sin\theta$. The corresponding definition for quaternions is $e^{(i\alpha+j\beta+k\gamma)\theta} = \cos\theta + (i\alpha + j\beta + k\gamma)\sin\theta$, with the proviso that $\alpha^2 + \beta^2 + \gamma^2 = 1$. Any quaternion q can be written in the form $q = |q|e^{(i\alpha+j\beta+k\gamma)\theta}$, where $|q|^2 = \mathrm{norm}(q)$. Since $\mathrm{conj}(q) = |q|e^{-(i\alpha+j\beta+k\gamma)\theta}$, it follows that $q\,\mathrm{conj}(q) = |q|^2 = \mathrm{norm}(q)$. Therefore, the inverse of q is $\mathrm{conj}(q)/\mathrm{norm}(q)$ and the argument of the exponential, θ, is the inverse cosine of $\mathrm{real}(q)/|q|$.

Quaternions model four-vectors, as in a space–time continuum. The three spatial Cartesian coordinates x, y, and z correspond to i, j, and k. If $q = |q|e^{(i\alpha+j\beta+k\gamma)\theta}$, the spatial part of q has direction cosines α, β, and γ. The exponential $e^{(i\mu+jv+k\lambda)\varphi/2}$ is a spatial rotation operator such that $e^{(i\mu+jv+k\lambda)\varphi/2}\,q\,e^{-(i\mu+jv+k\lambda)\varphi/2}$ rotates the spatial part of q through an angle φ about an axis whose direction cosines are μ, v, and λ. More about this can be found in Korn and Korn [20, Sec. 14.10] and Morse and Feshbach [22, Sec. 1.6].

13.5.1 Example

The following code exercises some functions of the `quatern` class. I have interjected the results *in italics* at appropriate points:

```
main(){
    complex a (1., 0.); complex b (0., 1.);
    quatern A (a, b); quatern B (1., 1., 0., 0.);
    quatern C (a, a); quatern D (b, b);
    cout << A << B << C << D;
        (1, 0, 0, 1) (1, 1, 0, 0) (1, 0, 1, 0) (0, 1, 0, 1)
    quatern X, Y;  X = D * C;  Y = C * D;
    cout << X << Y;   //multiplication does not commute
    printf("%g %g %g %g\n", norm(X), arg(X), norm(Y),
        arg(Y));
        (0, 0, 0, 2) (0, 2, 0, 0)  4 1.5708 4 1.5708
    double deg = 45./atan(1.); double ang = 53.13 *
        0.5;// rotate
    quatern zrot( cos(ang/deg), 0., 0., sin(ang/deg));
        // clockwise
    A = conj(zrot)*=A*=zrot;
    B = conj(zrot)*=B*=zrot;
    C = conj(zrot)*=C*=zrot;
    D = conj(zrot)*=D*=zrot;
    cout << A << B << C << D << arg(zrot)*deg << "\n";
        (1, 0, 0, 1)
        (1, 0.600001, -0.799999, 0)
        (1, 0.799999, 0.600001, 0)
        (0, 0.600001, -0.799999, 1)
        26.565
```

```
A *= inv(A); B *= inv(B); C *= inv(C); D *= inv(D);
cout << A << B << C << D;
   (1, 0, 0, 0) (1, 0, 0, 0) (1, 0, 0, 0) (1, 0, 0, 0)
}
```

The quaternion `zrot` is intended to rotate others about the z axis clockwise through an angle of 53.13 degrees. (This angle has tangent 8/6.) Quaternion A is not affected by the rotation, because it has zero i and j (i.e., x and y) components.

13.6 SUMMARY AND CONCLUSIONS

The syntax `template <class T> struct cplxfy{...};` declares an ordered pair of `double`, `real_vector`, or `matrix` objects to be the real and imaginary parts of a complex object C. They can then be accessed as `real(C)` and `imag(C)`, so that our existing vector and matrix methods can be extended to work with complex arrays.

Constructors

```
double a, b, d, e;  cplxfy<double> c(a,b), f(d,e);
real_vector u, v, x, y;
cplxfy<real_vector> w(u,v), z(x,y), t(n);
matrix X(m,n), Y(m,n);  cplxfy<matrix> Z(X,Y);
```

Access and Assignment

```
f = c;  imag(c) = 1.;  d = real(c);
z = w;  imag(z) = v;   v = real(z);
d = real(z)(1);      imag(t)[n-1] = d;
d = real(Z)(m,n);    imag(Z)(1,1) = 0.;
t = real(Z)[m-1];    imag(Z)[0] = t;
```

Arithmetic

```
c += f; c -= f; f *= 3.14; f *= c;
z += w; z -= w; w *= 2.72; w *= c;
z *= v; and z *= w; (element-by-element), t *= Z; (t = Zt)
a = abs(f);  b = abs(z);
z = w + t; x = real(w + t); y = imag(w + t);
z = w - t; x = real(w - t); y = imag(w - t);
```

Complex Matrices. The Hermitian conjugate of a complex vector $\mathbf{c} = \mathbf{a} + i\mathbf{b}$ is $\mathbf{c}^H = \mathbf{a}^T - i\mathbf{b}^T$. The scalar product of two complex vectors $\mathbf{p}$ and $\mathbf{q}$ is $\mathbf{p}^H\mathbf{q}$.

The Hermitian conjugate of a complex matrix $C = A + iB$ is $C^H = A^T - iB^T$. C is unitary if $C^H C = I$. C is Hermitian if $C^H = C$, in which case, $B^T = -B$.

If C, c, and z are complex, with $C = A + iB$, $c = a + ib$, and $z = x + iy$, the equation $Cz = c$ is equivalent to the partitioned matrix equation

$$\begin{bmatrix} A & -B \\ B & A \end{bmatrix} \begin{bmatrix} x \\ y \end{bmatrix} = \begin{bmatrix} a \\ b \end{bmatrix}$$

Moreover, if C is Hermitian, the equivalent system is symmetric:

$$\begin{bmatrix} A & B^T \\ B & A \end{bmatrix} \begin{bmatrix} x \\ y \end{bmatrix} = \begin{bmatrix} a \\ b \end{bmatrix} \quad \text{if } C^H = C$$

Furthermore, if C is Hermitian, the complex eigenvalue problem $Cw = \lambda w$ is equivalent to a partioned symmetric real eigenvalue problem:

$$\begin{bmatrix} A & B^T \\ B & A \end{bmatrix} \begin{bmatrix} u \\ v \end{bmatrix} = \lambda \begin{bmatrix} u \\ v \end{bmatrix} \quad \text{if } C^H = C \quad \text{and} \quad u + iv = w$$

Therefore, the methods developed for real matrices in Chapters 4 to 8 and 12 are applicable to complex matrix problems expressed in this manner.

14 Fourier Transforms

The discrete Fourier transform of a complex vector $\mathbf{z}$ of length n is a complex vector $\mathbf{t}$ defined by $t_i = (1/n)\sum_{j=0}^{n-1} z_j w^{ij}$, where $w = e^{-2\pi\sqrt{-1}/n}$. The exponent ij is an integer between 0 and $(n-1)^2$. The inverse DFT restores $\mathbf{z}$ and is defined $z_j = \sum_{i=0}^{n-1} t_i w^{-ij}$. I prefer to incorporate division by n in the forward transform because the components of $\mathbf{t}$ are then the same order of magnitude as the components of $\mathbf{z}$.

The DFT is tantamount to the multiplication of a complex vector $\mathbf{z}$ by a complex matrix $\mathbf{W}$ and a scalar $1/n$ [i.e., $\mathbf{t} = (1/n)\,\mathbf{W}\mathbf{z}$, where matrix element $w_{ij} = w^{ij}$]. The inverse DFT is equivalent to the multiplication of $\mathbf{t}$ by $\mathbf{W}^*$, the complex conjugate of $\mathbf{W}$: $\mathbf{z} = \mathbf{W}^*\mathbf{t}$. This implies that $\mathbf{W}^*\mathbf{W} = n\mathbf{I}$. In DFT applications we will number the rows and columns of matrices and the components of vectors from 0 to $n-1$. The C-style notation using brackets is ideal for this: `W[i][j]` and `z[j]`; `0≤ i,j < n`.

The fast Fourier transform algorithm is a way to apply a DFT with far fewer than the n^2 multiplications required for the product of a matrix and a vector. The FFT exploits certain regularities, such as $w^n = 1$, $w^{n/2} = -1$, and so on. To explain how the FFT algorithm reduces the computation required, I will follow the outline of Theilheimer [27], who describes the FFT in terms of matrix factorization.

Append a subscript n to $\mathbf{W}$, so that $\mathbf{W}_n$ is a DFT matrix with n rows and columns, and let n be a power of 2. Theilheimer's decomposition is $\mathbf{W}_n = \mathbf{V}_{n/2}\mathbf{R}_{n/2}$. $\mathbf{V}_{n/2}$ is a block matrix with two copies of $\mathbf{W}_{n/2}$ on its main diagonal. Each of these can in turn be factored as $\mathbf{W}_{n/2} = \mathbf{W}_{n/4}\mathbf{R}_{n/4}$, and therefore the process can be cascaded. It remains to define what the general form of $\mathbf{R}$ is.

Let us consider the specific case of $n = 8$. We have

$$\mathbf{W}_8\mathbf{z} = \begin{bmatrix} 1 & 1 & 1 & 1 & 1 & 1 & 1 & 1 \\ 1 & w & w^2 & w^3 & w^4 & w^5 & w^6 & w^7 \\ 1 & w^2 & w^4 & w^6 & w^8 & w^{10} & w^{12} & w^{14} \\ 1 & w^3 & w^6 & w^9 & w^{12} & w^{15} & w^{18} & w^{21} \\ 1 & w^4 & w^8 & w^{12} & w^{16} & w^{20} & w^{24} & w^{28} \\ 1 & w^5 & w^{10} & w^{15} & w^{20} & w^{25} & w^{30} & w^{35} \\ 1 & w^6 & w^{12} & w^{18} & w^{24} & w^{30} & w^{36} & w^{42} \\ 1 & w^7 & w^{14} & w^{21} & w^{28} & w^{35} & w^{42} & w^{49} \end{bmatrix} \begin{bmatrix} z_0 \\ z_1 \\ z_2 \\ z_3 \\ z_4 \\ z_5 \\ z_6 \\ z_7 \end{bmatrix}$$

We recognize that $w^8 = w^{16} = w^{24} = 1$, and so on, but we retain the explicit exponents.

For the case that n is a power of 2, Theilheimer's prescription for $\mathbf{R}_{n/2}$ is this: Take the top two rows of $\mathbf{W}_n$ and use those elements as the diagonal elements of (always) four block matrices, arranged as a 2×2 partitioned matrix. For the present example, that means

$$
\mathbf{R}_4 \mathbf{z} =
\left[
\begin{array}{cccc|cccc}
1 & & & & 1 & & & \\
& 1 & & & & 1 & & \\
& & 1 & & & & 1 & \\
& & & 1 & & & & 1 \\
\hline
1 & & & & w^4 & & & \\
& w & & & & w^5 & & \\
& & w^2 & & & & w^6 & \\
& & & w^3 & & & & w^7
\end{array}
\right]
\begin{bmatrix} z_0 \\ z_1 \\ z_2 \\ z_3 \\ z_4 \\ z_5 \\ z_6 \\ z_7 \end{bmatrix}
=
\begin{bmatrix}
z_0 + z_4 \\
z_1 + z_5 \\
z_2 + z_6 \\
z_3 + z_7 \\
z_0 + w^4 z_4 \\
w z_1 + w^5 z_5 \\
w^2 z_2 + w^6 z_6 \\
w^3 z_3 + w^7 z_7
\end{bmatrix}
$$

Together with this we will have

$$
\mathbf{V}_4 =
\begin{bmatrix}
\mathbf{W}_4 & \\
& \mathbf{W}_4
\end{bmatrix}
$$

The significance of the $\mathbf{V}_4$ structure is that $\mathbf{W}_4$ will multiply the first four rows of $\mathbf{R}_4 \mathbf{z}$, and then $\mathbf{W}_4$ will multiply the last four rows of $\mathbf{R}_4 \mathbf{z}$, without mixing top and bottom. For the top four rows,

$$
(\mathbf{V}_4 \mathbf{R}_4 \mathbf{z})_{\text{top}} =
\begin{bmatrix}
1 & 1 & 1 & 1 \\
1 & w^2 & w^4 & w^6 \\
1 & w^4 & w^8 & w^{12} \\
1 & w^6 & w^{12} & w^{18}
\end{bmatrix}
\begin{bmatrix} z_0 + z_4 \\ z_1 + z_5 \\ z_2 + z_6 \\ z_3 + z_7 \end{bmatrix}
$$

$$
=
\begin{bmatrix}
(z_0 + z_4) + (z_1 + z_5) + (z_2 + z_6) + (z_3 + z_7) \\
(z_0 + z_4) + w^2(z_1 + z_5) + w^4(z_2 + z_6) + w^6(z_3 + z_7) \\
(z_0 + z_4) + w^4(z_1 + z_5) + w^8(z_2 + z_6) + w^{12}(z_3 + z_7) \\
(z_0 + z_4) + w^6(z_1 + z_5) + w^{12}(z_2 + z_6) + w^{18}(z_3 + z_7)
\end{bmatrix}
= 8
\begin{bmatrix} t_0 \\ t_2 \\ t_4 \\ t_6 \end{bmatrix}
$$

These four sums are identified as the even-numbered components of the DFT, except for dividing by n. Clearly, $8t_0 = \sum w^0 z_j = z_0 + z_1 + z_2 + z_3 + z_4 + z_5 + z_6 + z_7$. More typical is the case

$$
8t_4 = \sum w^{4j} z_j = z_0 + w^4 z_1 + w^8 z_2 + w^{12} z_3 + w^{16} z_4 + w^{20} z_5 + w^{24} z_6 + w^{28} z_7
$$
$$
= (z_0 + z_4) + w^4(z_1 + z_5) + w^8(z_2 + z_6) + w^{12}(z_3 + z_7)
$$

This last line exploits the fact that $w^8 = w^{16} = 1$, and it is obviously identical to the t_4 row of the $\mathbf{V}_4 \mathbf{R}_4 \mathbf{z}$ product.

For the bottom four rows of the $\mathbf{V}_4\mathbf{R}_4\mathbf{z}$ product, we similarly find that

$$
(\mathbf{V}_4\mathbf{R}_4\mathbf{z})_{\text{bot}} =
\begin{bmatrix}
1 & 1 & 1 & 1 \\
1 & w^2 & w^4 & w^6 \\
1 & w^4 & w^8 & w^{12} \\
1 & w^6 & w^{12} & w^{18}
\end{bmatrix}
\begin{bmatrix}
z_0 + w^4 z_4 \\
w z_1 + w^5 z_5 \\
w^2 z_2 + w^6 z_6 \\
w^3 z_3 + w^7 z_7
\end{bmatrix}
$$

$$
=
\begin{bmatrix}
(z_0 + w^4 z_4) + (w z_1 + w^5 z_5) + (w^2 z_2 + w^6 z_6) + (w^3 z_3 + w^7 z_7) \\
(z_0 + w^4 z_4) + w^2(w z_1 + w^5 z_5) + w^4(w^2 z_2 + w^6 z_6) + w^6(w^3 z_3 + w^7 z_7) \\
(z_0 + w^4 z_4) + w^4(w z_1 + w^5 z_5) + w^8(w^2 z_2 + w^6 z_6) + w^{12}(w^3 z_3 + w^7 z_7) \\
(z_0 + w^4 z_4) + w^6(w z_1 + w^5 z_5) + w^{12}(w^2 z_2 + w^6 z_6) + w^{18}(w^3 z_3 + w^7 z_7)
\end{bmatrix}
$$

$$
= 8
\begin{bmatrix}
t_1 \\
t_3 \\
t_5 \\
t_7
\end{bmatrix}
$$

Here I claim we have the odd-numbered components of the DFT. For comparison, the definition of t_7 is

$$
8t_7 = \sum w^{7j} z_j = z_0 + w^7 z_1 + w^{14} z_2 + w^{21} z_3 + w^{28} z_4 + w^{35} z_5 + w^{42} z_6 + w^{49} z_7
$$
$$
= (z_0 + w^4 z_4) + w^6(w z_1 + w^5 z_5) + w^{12}(w^2 z_2 + w^6 z_6) + w^{18}(w^3 z_3 + w^7 z_7)
$$

This is quite obviously the same as the t_7 row of the $\mathbf{V}_4\mathbf{R}_4\mathbf{z}$ product.

We need to show that $\mathbf{W}_4$ is a proper DFT matrix:

$$
\mathbf{W}_4 =
\begin{bmatrix}
1 & 1 & 1 & 1 \\
1 & w^2 & w^4 & w^6 \\
1 & w^4 & w^8 & w^{12} \\
1 & w^6 & w^{12} & w^{18}
\end{bmatrix}
$$

$\mathbf{W}_4$ has matrix elements $w_{ij} = (w)^{2ij}$, whereas we expect that $w_{ij} = (w)^{ij}$ in a DFT matrix; the exponent appears to be twice too large. However, this w was generated for a DFT of length 8: $w = e^{-2\pi\sqrt{-1}/8}$. Doubling the exponent yields $e^{-2\pi\sqrt{-1}/4}$, the correct value for a DFT of length 4. Therefore, $\mathbf{W}_4$ is indeed a DFT matrix, and it can in turn be decomposed as $\mathbf{W}_4 = \mathbf{V}_2\mathbf{R}_2$, and so on.

Each $\mathbf{R}_k$ in the sequence has exactly two elements per row, and multiplying a vector of length n by $\mathbf{R}_k$ requires $2n$ complex multiplications. If $n = 2^M$, there will be M different $\mathbf{R}_k$ applied in succession. Therefore, the number of multiplications required to compute the DFT is $2nM$, rather than n^2. If n is 1024 (i.e., 2^{10}), this difference is a factor of 100.

Although $\mathbf{V}_{n/2}\mathbf{R}_{n/2}$ yields the same $\mathbf{t}$ components as $\mathbf{W}_n$, it produces them in a different order: all the even-numbered ones, then all the odd-numbered ones. To be completely correct, we should write $\mathbf{V}_{n/2}\mathbf{R}_{n/2} = \mathbf{PW}_n$, where $\mathbf{P}$ is a permutation matrix that reflects the rearrangement of rows.

The repeated application of the Householder transformation in Chapter 6 was symbolized as a straightforward product of matrices $\mathbf{Q}_1\mathbf{Q}_2 \cdots \mathbf{Q}_n$, and so on. In the FFT case, we speak instead of a cascade of factorization steps, because each step leads to *two* further factorizations of half the previous size. The FFT algorithm is implemented in the form of nested loops that break the problem into more and more subproblems of smaller and smaller size.

14.1 BIT REVERSAL

In summary, to apply DFT $\mathbf{W}_n$ to $\mathbf{z}$ in place, we first apply $\mathbf{R}_{n/2}$, which segregates the even-numbered components $(0, 2, 4, 6, \ldots)$ in the top half of $\mathbf{z}$, and the odd-numbered components $(1, 3, 5, 7, \ldots)$ in the bottom half. We apply $\mathbf{R}_{n/4}$ to each half in turn, which subdivides each half into top and bottom. We apply $\mathbf{R}_{n/8}$ to each quarter, which subdivides each quarter into top and bottom, and so on. Eventually, we get to

$$\mathbf{R}_1 = \begin{bmatrix} 1 & 1 \\ 1 & -1 \end{bmatrix}$$

which only mixes adjacent components, in place. The nested shuffling of the components within $\mathbf{z}$ is illustrated for the case $n = 16$:

$$
\begin{bmatrix} 0(0000) \\ 1(0001) \\ 2(0010) \\ 3(0011) \\ 4(0100) \\ 5(0101) \\ 6(0110) \\ 7(0111) \\ 8(1000) \\ 9(1001) \\ 10(1010) \\ 11(1011) \\ 12(1100) \\ 13(1101) \\ 14(1110) \\ 15(1111) \end{bmatrix}
\xrightarrow{\mathbf{R}_8}
\begin{bmatrix} 0 \\ 2 \\ 4 \\ 6 \\ 8 \\ 10 \\ 12 \\ 14 \\ 1 \\ 3 \\ 5 \\ 7 \\ 9 \\ 11 \\ 13 \\ 15 \end{bmatrix}
\xrightarrow{\mathbf{R}_4}
\begin{bmatrix} 0 \\ 4 \\ 8 \\ 12 \\ 2 \\ 6 \\ 10 \\ 14 \\ 1 \\ 5 \\ 9 \\ 13 \\ 3 \\ 7 \\ 11 \\ 15 \end{bmatrix}
\xrightarrow{\mathbf{R}_2}
\begin{bmatrix} 0(0000) \\ 8(1000) \\ 4(0100) \\ 12(1100) \\ 2(0010) \\ 10(1010) \\ 6(0110) \\ 14(1110) \\ 1(0001) \\ 9(1001) \\ 5(0101) \\ 13(1101) \\ 3(0011) \\ 11(1011) \\ 7(0111) \\ 15(1111) \end{bmatrix}
$$

In the first and last columns I have included the binary representation of the original index k of each z_k. The reader will note that the bit pattern for an entry in the last column is essentially the bit pattern for the first column *read backwards*. That is, 7 (0111) $\rightarrow$ 14 (1110), 14 (1110) $\rightarrow$ 7 (0111), 8 (1000) $\rightarrow$ 1 (0001), 1 (0001) $\rightarrow$ 8 (1000), 10 (1010) $\rightarrow$ 5 (0101), 5 (0101) $\rightarrow$ 10 (1010), and so on. When the binary representation is symmetric, the component remains in place: 0, 6, 9, 15. This is the phenomenon referred to as *bit reversal*, and it is intrinsic to performing an FFT in place. The overall result depends on the number of bits in the binary representation of n.

The following subroutine returns the result of reversing the bit pattern of the binary representation of index k, where $k < n$, and n is 2^M; log2_n equals M.

```
unsigned bitrev( const unsigned k, const unsigned log2_n)
{//VL92 [29] 1.5.1 p39
    unsigned s, m = k, j = 0;
    for(unsigned q=0; q<log2_n; q++){
        s = m/2; (j *= 2) += (m - 2*s); m = s; }
    return j;
}
```

Division of an unsigned integer by 2, shifts its bit pattern one to the right: (1011) $\rightarrow$ (0101). Multiplying that result by 2, shifts the pattern back to the left: (0101) $\rightarrow$ (1010). The round trip deletes the rightmost 1, if there was one. Therefore, the difference between before and after the opposite shifts, (m-2*s), is zero if m is even, one if m is odd. This process is repeated log2_n times. Result j accumulates the bit pattern of input k, in reverse order. The bitrev() function is its own inverse:

```
    unsigned k;
    for(k=0; k<32; k++) printf("%3u", k); printf("\n");
    for(k=0; k<32; k++) printf("%3u", bitrev(k,5));
        printf("\n");
    for(k=0; k<32; k++) printf("%3u", bitrev(bitrev
        (k,5),5));
```

This example yields

```
 0  1  2  3  4  5  6  7  8  9 10 11 12 13 14 15
16 17 18 19 20 21 22 23 24 25 26 27 28 29 30 31

 0 16  8 24  4 20 12 28  2 18 10 26  6 22 14 30
 1 17  9 25  5 21 13 29  3 19 11 27  7 23 15 31

 0  1  2  3  4  5  6  7  8  9 10 11 12 13 14 15
16 17 18 19 20 21 22 23 24 25 26 27 28 29 30 31
```

The FFT algorithm that accepts data in normal order and produces a DFT in bit-reverse order, by cascading a succession of $\mathbf{R}_k$ multiplications, is known as the

Cooley–Tukey algorithm. There is a complementary data flow that takes data in bit-reverse order and yields a DFT in normal order, and this is now called the *Gentleman–Sande algorithm* [29]. (I learned this as Sande–Tukey [1].) Numbers greater than 2 can be employed as the radix, or divisor d, of the $\mathbf{R}_{n/d}$ factorization [27].

14.2   FFT IMPLEMENTATIONS

When I wrote my first FFT routines 30-some years ago, speed was of the essence, and an entire program, including data, had to run in 204k bytes of memory. I used most of the "efficiency" tricks. The sine and cosine values were generated once, at the start of each run. The Cooley–Tukey algorithm applied the forward transform to the data and left the results in bit-reverse order. All frequency-domain operations (filters and correlations) were performed in bit-reverse order. The Sande–Tukey algorithm applied the inverse transform and produced the output in normal order. The loops were unrolled so that FFT stages of length 8 were coded inline. It was all accomplished in FORTRAN. The effort was justifiable, because an expensive IBM mainframe was spending a plurality of its CPU cycles on such computations.

I don't think we need to work that hard anymore. We are no longer so constrained by machine limitations and can give greater consideration to our own convenience. The old tricks are still available for use where they are justified. We should concentrate chiefly on the interesting details that arise in practical applications.

In Chapter 13 we demonstrated how pairs of real objects can be associated by means of a template `cplxfy<T>` to form complex vectors and matrices. The fundamental property of `cplxfy` objects is that they possess accessible `real` and `imag` parts. My intention is to emphasize real arithmetic when coding complex algorithms, although complex arithmetic can certainly be implemented.

The following is a concise and adaptable basic complex FFT. Its strategy is always to bit-reverse the input data and then employ the Gentleman–Sande data flow to produce output in normal order. The same code therefore performs both forward and inverse transforms. The argument `sign` controls whether the sign of the exponential $w = e^{\pm 2\pi \sqrt{-1}/n}$ is plus or minus. When `sign` is -1, the input is multiplied by $1/n$.

```
void cfft( cplxfy<matrix>& z, unsigned log2_n, int sign)
{
    unsigned n = pow( 2, log2_n); unsigned i, j, m, k=1;
    double c, s, arg, sc, pi = 4.0 * atan(1.0);
    unsigned N = real(z).N();   real_vector x(N), y(N);

    if(sign < 0){ sc = n; sc = 1.0/sc;
        for(i=0; i<n; i++){ real(z)[i] *= sc; imag(z)[i]
            *= sc; } }
```

```
//Bit-reverse preordering
   for(i=0; i<n; i++){
       j = bitrev( i, log2_n);
       if( j <= i ) continue;
       real(z).swaprows( i+1, j+1);
       imag(z).swaprows( i+1, j+1);
   }

//Gentleman-Sande algorithm [VL92 1.9.2 p67]
   while(k < n){
       for(m=0; m<k; m++){
           arg = pi * sign * m / k;
           c = cos(arg); s = sin(arg);
           for(i=m; i<n; i+=k*2){
               x                = real(z)[i+k]*c - imag(z)[i+k]*s;
               y                = real(z)[i+k]*s + imag(z)[i+k]*c;
               real(z)[i+k] = real(z)[i]      - x;
               imag(z)[i+k] = imag(z)[i]      - y;
               real(z)[i]   += x;
               imag(z)[i]   += y;   }
       }
       k = k * 2;
   }
   x.zap(); y.zap();
   return;
}
```

This is one-dimensional FFT that applies a DFT to all the columns of a complex matrix z *in parallel* by treating the rows of the matrix as the elements of the algorithm. It would serve as half of a two-dimensional transform. The number of rows can only be expressed as a power of 2 (log2_n), but the length of the rows is unconstrained.

This matrix FFT requires two temporary real_vectors x and y, of length N, the number of columns in z. The expression real(z)[i] denotes the ith row of the real part of z, and so on. In the bit-reversal loop, swaprows() expects row indices that range from 1 to n, rather than 0 to $n - 1$. Because each row of a matrix is a real_vector, the arithmetic within the Gentleman–Sande inner loop is carried out by real_vector member and friend functions.

The one-dimensional vector version of the same subroutine is

```
void cfft( cplxfy<real_vector>& z, unsigned log2_n,
   int sign)
{
   unsigned n = pow( 2, log2_n); unsigned i, j, m, k=1;
   dcuble c, s, x, y, arg, sc, pi = 4.0 * atan(1.0);

   if(sign < 0) { sc = n;   sc = 1.0/sc;   z *= sc;  }
```

```
//Bit-reverse preordering
   for(i=0; i<n; i++){
       j = bitrev( i, log2_n);
       if( j <= i ) continue;
       real(z).swapc( i, j);
       imag(z).swapc( i, j);
}
   (more...)
```

This excerpt illustrates the main differences. In this case, real(z)[i] denotes the ith component of the real part of cplxfy<real_vector> z. Temporaries x and y are merely scalars. Division by n is simply accomplished by z *= sc;. The swapping inside the bit-reversal loop is done by an inline member function swapc(). The code of the Gentleman–Sande loop, not shown here, appears identical to that of the matrix subroutine. This subroutine could be written as a template, were it not for the difference between scalar and vector temporaries.

The following is a second form of parallel FFT, in which the input is presented as a C-style array of cplxfy<real_vector> objects (i.e., complex vectors). This code provides an opportunity to exercise the cplxfy arithmetic functions defined in Chapter 13. The Gentleman–Sande loop is more compact and employs fewer hidden temporaries:

```
void cfft( cplxfy<real_vector> z[], unsigned log2_n,
    int sign)
{
    unsigned n = pow(2,log2_n); unsigned i, j, m, k=1;
    double c, s, arg, sc, pi = 4.0 * atan(1.0);
    cplxfy<double> cw( c, s);
    cplxfy<real_vector> ct( real(z[0]).N() );

    if(sign < 0){ sc = n; sc = 1.0/sc; for(i=0; i<n;
       i++) z[i] *= sc; }

//Bit-reverse preordering
   for(i=0; i<n; i++){
       j = bitrev( i, log2_n);
       if( j <= i ) continue;
       swap( z[i], z[j]);
   }

//Gentleman-Sande algorithm [VL92 1.9.2 p67]
   while(k<n){
       for(m=0; m<k; m++){
           arg = pi * sign * m / k;
           real(cw) = -(cos(arg)); imag(cw) = -(sin(arg));
               //now (-)
```

```
        for(i=m;  i<n;  i+=k*2){
            ct       = z[i];
            z[i+k]  *= cw;         //i.e.,  (-cw);
            z[i]    -= z[i+k];
            z[i+k]  += ct;         }
        }
    k = k * 2;
    }
    real(ct).zap();  imag(ct).zap();  return;
}
```

The reader will note that ct, a temporary cplxfy<real_vector>, must be deallocated before the subroutine returns.

The following code demonstrates the subroutine above in action:

```
void test(void)
{//2*pi/n is fundamental freq
    double pi = 4.*atan(1.0); double w, f = 2.* pi / 16.;
    cplxfy<real_vector> F[16];
    cplxfy<real_vector> G(9);
    real(G).init();  imag(G).init();
    (more...)
```

The array F of 16 cplxfy<real_vector> complex vectors is set up without allocating memory, through the specialized default constructor

```
cplxfy<real_vector>::cplxfy (){
    re = new real_vector();  im = new real_vector(); }
```

Memory is allocated to F[i] by the assignment operator (see Section 2.1.4):

```
    for(int i=0; i<16; i++){ w = f * (double)i;
        for(int j=0; j<9; j++) real(G)[j]
            = cos( w * (double)j );
        F[i] = G; }
    (more...)
```

Each column of the complex array F is thus defined as a cosine wave of relative frequency j, ranging from 0 to 8. Then F is submitted to cfft():

```
    cfft( F, 4, -1);
    for(int i=0; i<16; i++) real(F[i]).dumpall();
```

The output from `cfft` can be displayed as

```
f\ 0 1 2 3 4 5 6 7 8 <j
 0]|1|0  |0  |0  |0  |0  |0  |0  |0
 1]|0|0.5|0  |0  |0  |0  |0  |0  |0
 2]|0|0  |0.5|0  |0  |0  |0  |0  |0
 3]|0|0  |0  |0.5|0  |0  |0  |0  |0
 4]|0|0  |0  |0  |0.5|0  |0  |0  |0
 5]|0|0  |0  |0  |0  |0.5|0  |0  |0
 6]|0|0  |0  |0  |0  |0  |0.5|0  |0
 7]|0|0  |0  |0  |0  |0  |0  |0.5|0
 8]|0|0  |0  |0  |0  |0  |0  |0  |1
-7]|0|0  |0  |0  |0  |0  |0  |0.5|0
-6]|0|0  |0  |0  |0  |0  |0.5|0  |0
-5]|0|0  |0  |0  |0  |0.5|0  |0  |0
-4]|0|0  |0  |0  |0.5|0  |0  |0  |0
-3]|0|0  |0  |0.5|0  |0  |0  |0  |0
-2]|0|0  |0.5|0  |0  |0  |0  |0  |0
-1]|0|0.5|0  |0  |0  |0  |0  |0  |0
```

Here I have labeled each component (row) of the DFT with its frequency value, and each column with the value of j. The result is manifestly correct, because the Fourier transform of a cosine function of frequency $(2\pi j/n)$ should have nonzero amplitude 0.5 exactly at frequencies $\pm j$. Of course, frequencies 0 and $n/2$ combine the amplitudes for both positive and negative frequencies. Conversely,

```
cfft( F, 4, 1);
```

will restore F to the original array of cosine functions. At the conclusion of processing, the space assigned to F must be deallocated:

```
for(int i=0; i<16; i++){ real(F[i]).zap(); imag(F[i]).
   zap(); }
```

14.3 CONNECTING WITH THE REAL WORLD

In this book I define the discrete Fourier transform of a complex vector $\mathbf{z}$ of length n to be a complex vector $\mathbf{y}$ given by $y_i = (1/n)\sum_{j=0}^{n-1} z_j w^{ij}$, where $w = e^{-2\pi\sqrt{-1}/n}$. I define the inverse DFT as $z_j = \sum_{j=0}^{n-1} y_i w^{-ij}$. Other authors sometimes choose the opposite sign for the exponent in w and may postpone dividing by n until the inverse transform. Such divergence goes back to the original papers on the FFT [12]. I follow Cooley et al. [8]. Van Loan [29] concurs as to sign but postpones division by n. Press et al. [25] use definitions exactly the reverse of mine.

Engineers, on the one hand, and physicists and mathematicians, on the other, disagree as to whether j or i should represent the imaginary unit $\sqrt{-1}$. My preference is to reserve both i and j for subscripts, as much as possible, and to write $\sqrt{-1}$ explicitly. By my conventions, the expression for the sine function, $i \sin \omega t = (e^{i\omega t} - e^{-i\omega t})/2$, where $i = \sqrt{-1}$ (for the moment), *is* an inverse Fourier transform. Therefore, if I load a sine function into the imaginary part of a complex vector and execute a forward FFT, I expect to see real amplitudes $+0.5$ and -0.5 appear at plus and minus the frequency of that sine, respectively. This is useful in testing code.

Different authors seem to interpret positive and negative frequencies the same way. If $\mathbf{y}$ is a DFT of length n, then samples y_0 through $y_{n/2}$ correspond to nonnegative frequencies in increasing order, and samples y_{n-1} through $y_{n/2}$ correspond to negative frequencies in decreasing order. The (circular) frequency attributable to sample k is equivalently $2\pi k/n$ or $2\pi(k - n)/n$. For example the $(n - 1)$st (i.e., last) sample of $\mathbf{y}$ corresponds to frequency $2\pi(n - 1 - n)/n = 2\pi(-1)/n$.

When we rewrite the argument ωt suitably for sampled data, the chain of reasoning goes $\omega t = 2\pi f t = 2\pi (i \, \Delta f)(j \, \Delta t) = 2\pi i j/n$, because $\Delta f = 1/(n \, \Delta t)$. If the input vector $\mathbf{z}$ contains n uniformly spaced time samples, having sampling interval Δt, the entire time interval represented by $\mathbf{z}$ is $n \, \Delta t$. The basic frequency sampling interval for the DFT of $\mathbf{z}$ is the inverse of the time span, $\Delta f = 1/(n \, \Delta t)$. The maximum frequency that can be dealt with is $\frac{1}{2}(n \, \Delta f)$, the *Nyquist frequency*, which always works out to be half the sampling frequency. The sample $y_{n/2}$ is called the *Nyquist sample*.

The Dolby AC-3 audio compression scheme [21] samples a signal 48,000 times per second, so that $\Delta t = 20.833 \, \mu s$ (microseconds). The Nyquist frequency is half the sampling frequency, or 24 kHz. The system applies FFTs to the sampled signal in blocks of 512 samples, each of which spans 10.67 ms (milliseconds). The frequency sampling interval is thus $\Delta f = 93.75$ Hz. As a check, the Nyquist frequency $\frac{1}{2}(n \, \Delta f) = \frac{1}{2} \times 512 \times 93.75$ Hz $= 24,000$ Hz.

DFT methodology incorporates a subtle assumption, namely, that input $\mathbf{z}$ represents just one cycle of an infinitely long function that is periodic on the grand scale: $z_{j+nk} = z_j$, where k is any positive or negative integer. This constraint would have no practical consequences if we never modified the computed DFT $\mathbf{y}$, since the inverse DFT unconditionally restores $\mathbf{z}$. However, if we modify $\mathbf{y}$, *and* one end of $\mathbf{z}$ is not continuous with the other, artifacts are induced. A false image of each end of the data is overwritten onto the other end, in such a way that the phenomenon is called *wraparound*.

There are two accepted ways to mitigate wraparound. The simplest is to extend the length of the data by appending a large number of zeros. These induce no artifact at the other end, and the artifact that is overwritten onto the zeros can be ignored. The second method is to modify the data segment so that it tapers gradually to zero at both ends.

The AC-3 audio compression scheme chops its input stream into short blocks for FFT application, and it would suffer from wraparound (*blocking artifacts* in this context) were it not for the following solution: Each block of 512 samples includes 128 samples from the preceding block and 128 from the next block, with both ends tapering to zero. Each block of 512 samples therefore advances the signal by only 256 samples. This provides a very smooth transition from one block to the next. It is deemed adequate for all but the sharpest transients, to which the system adapts by halving the block length (to 5.33 ms and 256 samples) and using twice as many blocks. Temporal resolution is thus improved at the expense of frequency resolution.

The DFT transforms one complex vector **z** into another, **y**. However, real data (epistemologically speaking) are almost always real (mathematically speaking). The obvious thing to do is to regard real data as the real part of a complex vector whose imaginary part is zero. Here is a vector of eight random numbers loaded into the real part of a `cplxfy<real_vector>` z:

```
z:
Re:|0.0582345|0.533896|0.0854064|-0.828327
   |0.442375|-0.0356477|0.649489|0.0510901
Im:|0|0|0|0|0|0|0|0
```

Let us designate the DFT of z as y:

```
y:
Re:|0.119565|0.0800538|-0.0292858|-0.176089
   |0.189312|-0.176089|-0.0292858|0.0800538
Im:|0|0.0978996|-0.159436|-0.0431212|0|0.0431212|
      0.159436|-0.0978996
```

We note that y has nonzero real and imaginary parts and that certain symmetries are evident:

```
real(y)[i] =  real(y)[n-i],
imag(y)[i] = -imag(y)[n-i], 0 < i < n\2.
```

If we transform the same input as the imaginary part of a complex vector whose real part is zero, it is like multiplying both z and y by $\sqrt{-1}$:

```
z:
Re:|0|0|0|0|0|0|0|0
Im:|0.0582345|0.533896|0.0854064|-0.828327
   |0.442375|-0.0356477|0.649489|0.0510901
y:
Re:|0|-0.0978996|0.159436|0.0431212|0|-0.0431212|
      -0.159436|0.0978996
Im:|0.119565|0.0800538|-0.0292858|-0.176089
   |0.189312|-0.176089|-0.0292858|0.0800538
```

Here the imaginary part of y is symmetric and the real part is antisymmetric. These symmetries are general and follow directly from the definition of the DFT. The accepted terminology is that the DFT of a real vector is conjugate-even, and the DFT of an imaginary vector is conjugate-odd [29]. In particular, the zero and Nyquist samples of the DFT of a real vector must be purely real.

These properties are the basis of a trick that computes the DFTs of two real vectors for the price of one: Load vector 1 into `real(z)` and vector 2 into `imag(z)`. Execute `cfft( z, log2_n, -1);`. Then $(y_1)_i = \frac{1}{2}(y_i + y^*_{n-i})$ and $(y_2)_i = \frac{1}{2}(y_i - y^*_{n-i})$, where y represents z after FFT and y^* indicates its complex conjugate. The two DFTs can be separated by `twofer( z, log2_n, -1)` and recombined by `twofer( z, log2_n, 1)`. However, I recommend that this approach be limited to cases where the two DFTs don't need to be separated.

A more useful exploitation of the same symmetry properties is to compute the DFT of a single real vector for half price. Basically, the even- and odd-numbered samples of the vector are transformed as two vectors of half the length. Leaving aside the details of implementation, the pattern for using this capability is

```
    real_vector x(N);
    cplxfy<real_vector> z( sizeof_fft( x ));
    z.fft( x );
//    (freq-domain computation)
    x.ift( z );
```

14.4 FFT MEMBER FUNCTIONS

I find it convenient to implement the most commonly used FFTs and related functions as members of appropriate classes. The FFT that accepts a single real vector and produces a complex vector containing its DFT is declared as

```
cplxfy<real_vector>& cplxfy<real_vector>::fft( const
    real_vector& x);
```

There is no need for the length of x to be a power of 2. The subroutine is called as `z.fft(x)` after allocating `z( sizeof_fft(x))`. The dimension of z is determined by

```
unsigned sizeof_fft( const real_vector& x)
{
    unsigned N = next_pow_2( x.N() ) / 2;
    return N + 1;
}
```

This function computes a number that is one plus half the next power of 2. The next power of 2 is the least power of 2 greater than or equal to the length of x. Thus z contains results for frequencies 0 through the Nyquist frequency and omits the redundant negative frequencies. The inverse DFT is performed by

```
real_vector& real_vector::ift( cplxfy<real_vector>& z);
```

This is invoked as `x.ift(z);`. A complex inverse FFT is applied to `z` in place, and the result is sorted out and returned in `x`.

Among the useful tasks that can be carried out while in the frequency domain are various kinds of linear filtering. To delay a signal in the time domain by `tshift` samples, say, one can apply a *phase shift* in the frequency domain:

```
cplxfy<real_vector>&
cplxfy<real_vector>::phase_shift( int tshift, unsigned nyq);
```

This is invoked as `z.phase_shift( k, nyq);`, where `nyq` is the Nyquist sample number of the DFT stored in `z` and `k` is the number of samples by which the content of `x` is to be delayed. Negative `k` makes the signal appear earlier.

Another important frequency-domain operation is bandpass filtering [17]. This modifies a DFT to reject frequencies below a specified lower limit and above a specified upper limit. This rejection is a gradual attenuation rather than a sharp cutoff. One such filter is

```
cplxfy<real_vector>&
cplxfy<real_vector>::bandpass( double lo, double hi,
    unsigned nyq);
```

This is invoked as `z.bandpass( lo, hi, nyq);` where `nyq` is the Nyquist sample number of the DFT stored in `z`. Argument `lo` is the low-pass frequency, expressed as a decimal fraction of the Nyquist frequency. If `lo` is 0, the filter passes all low frequencies. Argument `hi` is the high-pass frequency, expressed as a decimal fraction of the Nyquist frequency. If `hi` is 1, the filter passes all high frequencies.

Linear filtering in the frequency domain is carried out as element-by-element multiplication of the DFT by a prescribed vector of complex numbers. That is what `phase_shift` and `bandpass` do internally. It is also possible to store the complex coefficients defining a filter externally in a separate vector. In that case, what is required to apply the filter is stand-alone element-by-element multiplication:

```
cplxfy<real_vector>&
cplxfy<real_vector>::operator*= (const cplxfy<real_
    vector>& f);
```

```
cplxfy<real_vector>&
cplxfy<real_vector>::operator*= (const real_vector& f);
```

If f is a vector of filter coefficients and z is a DFT, and if f and z have the same length and Nyquist frequency, z *= f; applies the filter. The compiler invokes the first operator if f is complex, and the second if f is real.

14.4.1 Example

The following code demonstrates several of the foregoing member functions. I have interjected the results *in italics*, and I have edited round-off error to zero.

```
{   real_vector x(16), y(16);   x.init();   y.init();
    cplxfy<real_vector> z( sizeof_fft( x ));

// 1.Delay by phase shift:
    x[5] = 1.;                  x.dumpall();
    z.fft( x );
    z.phase_shift( 3, 8);
       // delay by 3 samples
    x.ift( z );                 x.dumpall();
       |0|0|0|0|0|1|0|0|0|0|0|0|0|0|0|0
       |0|0|0|0|0|0|0|0|1|0|0|0|0|0|0|0

// 2.Bandpass filter impulse response:
    y[8] = 1.;                  y.dumpall();
    z.fft( y );
    z.bandpass( 0., .9, 8);
       // hi freq is 0.9 nyq
    y.ift( z );                 y.dumpall();
       |0|0|0|0|0|0|0|0|1|0|0|0|0|0|0|0

       |-0.0442205|0.0454055|-0.0488661|0.0543099
       |-0.0612231| 0.068832|-0.0760553|0.0814526
       | 0.916509|0.0814526|-0.0760553|0.068832
       |-0.0612231|0.0543099|-0.0488661|0.0454055

// 3.Coefficients of phase-shift filter:
    cplxfy<real_vector> f( 16 );
    real(f).init() +=1.;   imag(f).init();
    f.phase_shift( 6, 8);
       // delay is 6 samples
    real(f).dumpall();   imag(f).dumpall();
       |1|-0.707107|0|0.707107|-1|0.707107|0|-0.707107
       |1|-0.707107|0|0.707107|-1|0.707107|0|-0.707107

       |0|-0.707107|1|-0.707107|0|0.707107|-1|0.707107
       |0|-0.707107|1|-0.707107|0|0.707107|-1|0.707107
```

```
//4.Two for price of one:
   cplxfy<real_vector> q(x,y);
   x.init(); y.init(); x[2] = 1;  y[13] = 1;
   real(q).dumpall();  imag(q).dumpall();
   cfft( q, 4, -1);
   q *= f;
      // delay by 6 samples
   cfft( q, 4,  1);
   real(q).dumpall();  imag(q).dumpall();
      |0|0|1|0|0|0|0|0|0|0|0|0|0|0|0|0
      |0|0|0|0|0|0|0|0|0|0|0|0|0|1|0|0

      |0|0|0|0|0|0|0|0|1|0|0|0|0|0|0|0
      |0|0|0|1|0|0|0|0|0|0|0|0|0|0|0|0

   x.zap(); y.zap();
   real(z).zap(); imag(z).zap(); real(f).zap();
      imag(f).zap();
}
```

The first case takes a vector of length 16 containing a single nonzero in entry 5 and shifts that nonzero to entry 8 by frequency-domain manipulation. The length of z is 9, and the Nyquist frequency is 8.

The second case takes a vector of length 16 containing a single nonzero in entry 8 and applies a low-pass filter in the frequency domain. The inverse DFT of the result thus shows the effect of this filter upon a single pulse, called the *impulse response*. We see that the impulse response is symmetric, centered on entry 8, with a central spike and slowly diminishing ripples.

The third case stores the coefficients of a six-sample-delay phase-shift filter in the complex vector f. The Nyquist frequency is 8. By aligning the real and imaginary parts, the reader can verify that f contains $e^{6(-2\pi\sqrt{-1}/16)k} = \exp[-(3\pi/4)k\sqrt{-1}]$ in entry k. If we draw an analogy between the phase angle and the hourhand of a clock, each value f[k] is 4.5 hours later than the previous value.

The last case applies filter f simultaneously to two real vectors x and y of length 16. Their DFTs are computed simultaneously using the two-for-one approach. Linear filtering like this is an application in which it is not necessary to separate the two DFTs. The result shows that the single sample in vector x is shifted from entry 2 to entry 8 and that the single sample in vector y is shifted from entry 13 past the end, so that it wraps around to entry 3. This is because, modulo 16, $13 + 6 = 3$.

14.5   TIME AND SPACE

Up to this point, my presentation of FFT methods has presumed that the independent real variable represents time and that the transformed domain represents temporal frequency. No such specialization is intrinsic in the methods themselves. They are equally applicable to spatial variables and frequencies, which appear commonly in connection with wave phenomena.

If a sinusoidal wave of temporal frequency f is propagating with velocity c, it will be found to have a wavelength λ such that $\lambda f = c$. [If a 440-Hz sine wave (musical A) propagates in air at 345 m/s, its wavelength is 0.78 m.] Corresponding to the temporal (angular) frequency $\omega = 2\pi f$ is the spatial frequency or *wave number* $k = 2\pi/\lambda$. In three dimensions, solutions of the wave equation may be expressed in terms of superposed sinusoidal plane waves: $p(\mathbf{x},t) = \sum_{\mathbf{k}} P(\mathbf{k}) e^{\sqrt{-1}(\mathbf{k}^T\mathbf{x} \pm \omega t)}$, subject to the condition $k^2 - \omega^2/c^2 = 0$. If the initial condition $p(\mathbf{x},0)$ is given, the coefficients $P(\mathbf{k})$ are determined from its DFT: $P(\mathbf{k}) = (1/n_1 n_2 n_3) \sum_{\mathbf{x}} p(\mathbf{x},0) e^{-\sqrt{-1}(\mathbf{k}^T\mathbf{x})}$.

The strategy for applying FFT methods in the context of the wave equation is straightforward to implement [13]. Once the $P(\mathbf{k})$ have been computed by forward spatial FFT, the formula for $p(\mathbf{x},t)$ at time $t > 0$ is just the inverse spatial FFT of the modified function $P(\mathbf{k}) e^{\sqrt{-1}(\omega t)}$ [i.e., $P(\mathbf{k})$ with a phase shift applied]. The only subtlety is that ω must be computed from the *dispersion relation* $\omega = \pm c\sqrt{k_1^2 + k_2^2 + k_3^2}$.

Figure 14.1a displays a real matrix of dimensions 200 by 200 corresponding to the initial condition $p(\mathbf{x},0)$ for a two-dimensional wave-equation demonstration. The reader will observe a square, a segment of plane wave, and a polygon approximating a circle. Each of these objects serves as the source of propagating waves whose configuration at times $t > 0$ can be computed in the spatial frequency domain.

Figure 14.1b displays the same matrix corresponding to a time t, 50 time samples later. The square and circle have been turned into semicircular wavefronts, and the plane wave has advanced a certain distance. The direction of propagation is determined by the sign $(+)$ chosen for ω in the dispersion relation. For convenience, I have set the spatial sample interval $\Delta x = c\, \Delta t$, both horizontally and vertically.

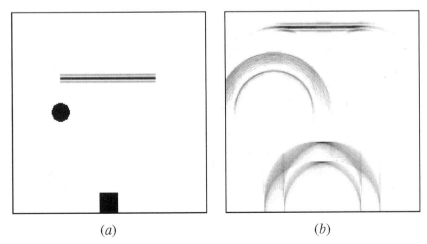

(a)   *(b)*

Fig. 14.1 Two-dimensional wave-equation demonstration: (a) input $p(\mathbf{x},0)$; (b) output $p(\mathbf{x},t)$ for $t = 50$.

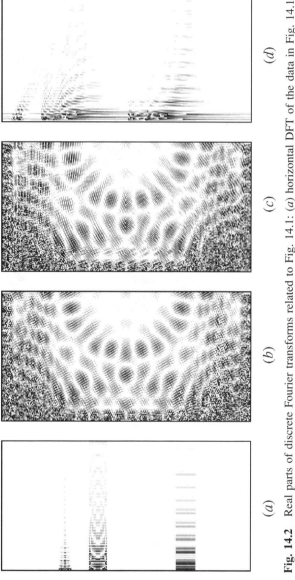

(a) (b) (c) (d)

Fig. 14.2 Real parts of discrete Fourier transforms related to Fig. 14.1: (a) horizontal DFT of the data in Fig. 14.1a; (b) vertical DFT of (a) (i.e., two-dimensional DFT of the data); (c) phase shift applied to (b); (d) inverse vertical DFT of (b) (Fig. 14.1b is the inverse horizontal DFT of this).

Therefore, the wavefronts in Fig. 14.1*b* will be seen to have advanced 50 space samples since time zero.

Figure 14.2 displays the real parts of the complex DFTs used in the computation of Fig. 14.1. The matrix in Fig. 14.2*a* has 129 columns and 256 rows. Each of the first 200 rows represents the one-dimensional DFT of the corresponding row of the matrix in Fig. 14.1*a*. The matrix in Fig. 14.2*b* results from applying cfft() to the matrix in Fig. 14.2*a*. The matrix in Fig. 14.2*c* results from applying phase_shift_2D() to the matrix in Fig. 14.2*b*. Figure 14.2*d* is the inverse DFT [via cfft()] of Fig. 14.2*c*. The inverse DFT of each of the first 200 rows of Fig. 14.2*d* finally yields Fig. 14.1*b*.

The required manner in which to calculate the two-dimensional phase shift is to retain the sign of the spatial frequency. For example, if k_i and k_j are the wave numbers corresponding to the row and column indices, respectively, use $\omega = ck_i\sqrt{1 + (k_j/k_i)^2}$. In other words, indices i greater than m/2 must be treated as negative frequency values (i-m), where m is the number of rows.

14.6 SUMMARY AND CONCLUSIONS

Discrete Fourier Transform. The standard form of the DFT of a complex vector **z** in this book is stated as $t_i = (1/n)\sum_{j=0}^{n-1} z_j w^{ij}$, where $w = e^{-2\pi\sqrt{-1}/n}$ and n is the length of **z**. The standard form of the inverse DFT that restores **z** is correspondingly stated as $z_j = \sum_{i=0}^{n-1} t_i w^{-ij}$.

Complex FFT. The subroutine cfft(z, log2_n, sign) performs one-dimensional in-place FFTs. The sense is forward when sign is -1 and inverse when sign is 1. The value of n is $2^{\log2\_n}$. Argument z can be one of three forms, but in all cases, z_j corresponds to z[j]:

```
cplxfy<real_vector>& z,  z[j] is a component of a complex vector.
cplxfy<matrix>& z,  z[j] is a row of a complex matrix.
cplxfy<real_vector>* z,  z[j] is a complex vector.
```

The latter two are parallel FFTs intended as second stages of two-dimensional FFTs.

Real-to-Complex FFT. If x is a real_vector, allocate cplxfy<real_vector> z(sizeof_fft(x));. Then z.fft(x); computes the complex FFT of x, and x.ift(z); computes the real inverse FFT of z. Result z represents only nonnegative frequencies 0 through Nyquist frequency (i.e., $0 \le i \le n/2$).

If x and y are real_vectors of length $2^{\log2\_n}$, define cplxfy<real_vector> z (x,y);. Then cfft(z, log2_n, sign) computes two FFTs for the price of one. The two complex FFTs can be separated and recombined in the frequency domain by twofer(z, log2_n, sign).

Linear Filters. Filters can be represented in the frequency domain as real or complex vectors. They are applied through element-by-element multiplication of the DFT of the signal. Two examples in this book are implemented as `cplxfy<real_ vector>` member functions: `z.phase_shift( k, nyq)` and `z.bandpass ( lo, hi, nyq)`.

References

1. G. D. Bergland, Fast Fourier transform hardware implementations—a survey, *IEEE Trans. Audio Electroacoust.* **AU-17** (1969), 109–119.

2. M. Berry, Large scale singular value computations, *Int. J. Supercomput. Appl.* **6** (1992), 13–49.
   `ftp://netlib2.cs.utk.edu/svdpack`

3. J. R. Berryhill, Diffraction response for nonzero separation of source and receiver, *Geophysics* **42** (1977), 1158–1176.

4. J. R. Berryhill, Seismic 3-D depth migration on the Cray-2, *Cray User Group Spring Proc.* (1988), 461–467.

5. Turbo C++ Version 3.0, *User's Guide*, Borland International, Scotts Valley, CA, 1992.

6. Borland C++ Version 5.0, *User's Guide*, Borland International, Scotts Valley, CA, 1996.

7. G. Buzzi-Ferraris, *Scientific C++: Building Numerical Libraries the Object-Oriented Way*, Addison-Wesley, Wokingham, Berkshire, England, 1993.

8. J. W. Cooley, P. A. W. Lewis, and P. D. Welch, The fast Fourier transform, *IEEE Trans. Audio Electroacoust.* **AU-17** (1969), 77–85.

9. I. S. Duff, A. M. Erisman, and J. K. Reid, *Direct Methods for Sparse Matrices*, Oxford University Press, New York, 1989.

10. B. Eckel, C++ programming style guides, *Unix Rev.* **13**, No. 3 (Mar. 1995), 43–54.

11. M. Metcalf and J. Reid, *Fortran 90/95 Explained*, Oxford University Press, New York, 1996.

12. G-AE Subcommittee on Measurement Concepts, What is the fast Fourier transform? *IEEE Trans. Audio Electroacoust.* **AU-15** (1967), 45–55.

13. J. Gazdag, Modeling of the acoustic wave equation with transform methods, *Geophysics* **46** (1981), 854–859.

14. G. H. Golub and C. F. Van Loan, *Matrix Computations*, 2nd ed., Johns Hopkins University Press, Baltimore, 1989.

15. A. Griewank, *Evaluating Derivatives: Principles and Techniques of Algorithmic Differentiation*, SIAM, Philadelphia, 2000.

16. J. C. Howard, *Mathematical Modeling of Diverse Phenomena*, NASA Scientific and Technical Information Branch, SP-437, U.S. Government Printing Office, Washington, DC, 1979.

17. E. R. Kanesewich, *Time Sequence Analysis in Geophysics*, University of Alberta Press, Edmonton, Alberta, Canada, 1973.

18. B. W. Kernighan and D. M. Ritchie, *The C Programming Language*, 2nd ed., Prentice Hall, Englewood Cliffs, NJ, 1988.

19. D. E. Knuth, *The Art of Computer Programming*, Vol. 1: *Fundamental Algorithms*, 3rd ed., Addison-Wesley, Reading, MA, 1997.

20. G. A. Korn and T. M. Korn, *Mathematical Handbook for Scientists and Engineers: Definitions, Theorems, and Formulas for Reference and Review*, 2nd ed., McGraw-Hill, New York, 1968.

21. G. J. McComis, Looking forward to DTV, *Poptronics* **1**, No. 9 (Sept. 2000), 43–50. http://www.poptronics.com

22. P. M. Morse and H. Feshbach, *Methods of Theoretical Physics*, McGraw-Hill, New York, 1953.

23. Netlib, Linear programming test problems. ftp://netlib2.cs.utk.edu/lp/data/adlittle

24. D. A. Pierre, *Optimization Theory with Applications*, Dover Publications, New York, 1986.

25. W. H. Press, S. A. Teukolsky, W. T. Vetterling, and B. P. Flannery, *Numerical Recipes in C: The Art of Scientific Computing*, 2nd ed., Cambridge University Press, Cambridge, 1992.

26. A. Ralston and H. S. Wilf, eds., *Mathematical Methods for Digital Computers*, Vol. 1, Wiley, New York, 1960.

27. F. Theilheimer, A matrix version of the fast Fourier transform, *IEEE Trans. Audio Electroacoust.* **Au-17** (1969), 158–161.

28. R. J. Vanderbei, *Linear Programming: Foundations and Extensions*, Kluwer Academic Publishers, Boston, 1998. http://www.princeton.edu/~rvdb/LPbook/.

29. C. Van Loan, *Computational Frameworks for the Fast Fourier Transform*, SIAM, Philadelphia, 1992.

30. J. L. Walsh, J. H. Ahlberg, and E. N. Nilson, Best approximation properties of the spline fit, *J. Math. Mech.* **11** (1962), 225–234.

INDEX